# MUSLIM WOMEN IN INDIA

# Muslim Women in India

*Political & Private Realities :*
*1890s - 1980s*

Shahida Lateef

**Zed Books Ltd**
London and New Jersey

*Muslim Women in India*
was originally published in India and S. Asia by

Kali for Women
A 36 Gulmohar Park
New Delhi   110 049,   India

and by Zed Books Ltd. 57, Caledonian Road, London N1 9BU, UK
and 171, First Avenue, Atlantic Highlands, New Jersey 07716, USA
in the rest of the world.

**British Library Cataloguing in Publication data**

Lateef, Shahida

Muslim Women in India : Political and Private Realities,
1890s-1980s

1.   India, Society, Role, History of Muslim women
1.   Title
305, 486971054

ISBN 0-86232 954 - X
ISBN 0-86232 955 - 8 pbk

Typeset by Wordtronic, 111/56 Nehru Place, New Delhi
and printed at Raj Press Pvt. Ltd., R-3, Inderpuri, New Delhi.

# Contents

# Acknowledgements

This project has taken so long from inception to final publication that some of the people who encouraged and helped me may well have forgotten their part in this endeavour. I owe a great debt to Dr. Vina Mazumdar who encouraged and supported my initial survey undertaken for the National Committee on the Status of Women in India. She was also responsible for my affiliation with the Indian Council for Social Science Research which helped me to complete the project with a field trip through the nine cities covered by my survey. I am greatly indebted to Minto Pande who was able to translate my survey questionnaire into computer language and helped with the initial survey returns. I would like to thank Dr Robin Luckham, my thesis advisor at the Institute of Development Studies at Sussex University, who allowed and encouraged me to weld two pieces of historical and sociological research, even when such an integration was without precedent and might not appeal to the purists. He persisted even when we found ourselves over the time limit and communicating across oceans and continents. I am also greatly in debt to Mr. Henry Lucas who goodnaturedly managed to deal with my computer ignorance, as we battled to process the computer data. I am very greatful to Dr. T.N. Srinivasan who suggested new approaches to analysing the data. I thank Ms. Patricia Lankester, who out of the goodness of her heart, took great pains to go through the thesis and edit it for publication. I would like to thank my parents, Najmul Hasan Naqvi and Khatoon Jannat Bibi, whose love and support have always strengthened me, for taking charge of my daughters, Asma and Zafira, while I did term at Sussex. My husband, Sarwar, who not only paid my "fees" but helped with the proof-reading and editing, when I was too jaded to be able to spot even the most obvious mistakes, and all of this cheerfully. I have to thank Asma who stopped me giving up the whole project, even though both she and Zafira were only too familiar with the many crises that dogged the last stages of thesis completion. I hope the memory of it will stand them in good stead. I would like to thank all the people I met in the course of the field trip who opened their hearts and homes and provided me with material and support, eager to find objective representation and sympathy for their "cause". Any shortcomings are, of course, entirely mine.

# 1

## Competing Realities

Minority communities that are not politically dominant have traditionally evolved a relationship with the majority community that has been based on social, political and economic dependency. In India, the introduction of economic and ideological changes in the 19th century dislodged this pattern and consensus; economic changes dismantled traditional hierarchies as industry and trade replaced land as the primary source of wealth and prestige; ideological changes, necessitated by the need to accommodate emerging changes in the political, economic and social structures, produced political changes which radically altered the established order between communities. However, the equality of citizenship which emerged at Independence did not necessarily lead to collaboration between different communities; often competition for economic and political power bases intensified. Minority communities, except for the Muslim community, were able for the first time to influence political and economic policies through concerted group action and therefore, could counteract the disadvantages of their minority position. Traditional groups based on caste, language and religion form multifaceted minority communities throughout India, all seeking to overcome, or in some cases to maintain, their traditional hierarchical positions.

All communities seek to impose ideological and organizational precepts on their members but these become particularly important for minority communities who wish to preserve and emphasize group differentiation for specifically political purposes. The preservation of group unity serves traditional religious purposes by reviving customs and traditions that are particular to the group, and also serves political purposes by unifying the community in support of its economic and political objectives. Such community objectives, never quite stated but implicitly understood, affect women of all communities, but for women in minority communities they fundamentally affect their ability to manipulate or alter their status and role. Muslim women in India present an interesting case study of women in a minority community which has been politically dominant and is adjusting to the limitations inherent in the position of minority communities. This study on Muslim women in contemporary India[1] evaluates their status and role in society in terms of current practices and attitudes and also examines the historical factors which have influenced it. It demonstrates the close correlation that exists between the political, economic and social position of the community in society and the status of women.

The study is based on a stratified survey of Muslim women in nine major Indian cities in different states. The survey intended to determine the impact of several decades of Indian independence and of planned economic development on Muslim women. The twin objectives of the questionnaire were to collect basic data and gauge attitudes to social, political and economic changes already initiated in the country in order to help in the formulation of social policy. The findings of the survey were supplemented by field trips to all nine cities, during which 50 female and male leaders drawn from different spheres were interviewed and several Muslim institutions were examined both for their effectiveness and the scope of their activities.[2]

The findings of the survey are set in the historical context of economic, political and social changes initiated in the 19th century. These changes led to structural changes within the community which in turn affected its relationship with other communities. Special attention has been paid in the review to Muslim women's education, Muslim attitudes to social legislation, the participation of Muslim women in the women's movement and the evolution of Muslim socio-political action.

The need for historical research arose because the survey tended to refute the conventional wisdom on Muslim social

[1]This survey was undertaken by me under the auspices of the National Committee on the Status of Women in India. It was completed in 1974 and a report presented to the Committee.

[2]From September 1976 to September 1978 I was a Fellow of the Indian Council of Social Science Research. This enabled me to undertake the field trip in August-September 1977 and to complete the historical research.

practices and attitudes but could not reveal the basis for the continuation of such beliefs. The use of historical material to explain the position of the community, in conjunction with a survey on current attitudes and practices, has provided a more rational explanation of both Muslim behaviour and attitudes and of the disparity between the Muslim female stereotype and the actuality. The approach has enabled a fuller explanation of the main hypothesis that the status and role of women in a minority community is as much affected by their perception of themselves as a minority within a minority, entrusted with the responsibility of preserving the community's identity in a society undergoing change, as it is affected by the strata and region to which they belong.

Regional differences can affect the Muslim community in two ways. Firstly, in regions with a history of communal tensions, the Muslim community's ability to create the institutional framework to assimilate and respond to changes can be adversely affected; secondly, the status and role of Muslim women is a reflection of regional practices and attitudes towards women. Strata are important, since in a developing country with limited opportunities, they constitute a critical factor in the allocation of resources which determine the range of an individual's development.

The study of the status and role of Muslim women, therefore, must take into account three key elements: (*i*) the extent to which they are affected by the economic, social and political conditions in India; (*ii*) the status and role of women in general in India; and (*iii*) the influence of Islam. In other words, the study examines the manner and extent to which the status of Muslim women is affected by being Indian, being Muslim and being women. These factors have a bearing on the attitudes, practices and capacity of Muslim women to assimilate and adapt to social changes in India. While all three factors are interdependent in the context in which they are being applied, it is useful to analyse them separately.

## The Indian factor

After Independence, wide-ranging political, economic and social changes were instituted in India. The restructuring of Indian society was undertaken by government, (Gough, 1973:9) introducing changes which would enable institutions to deal with and assimilate technical changes, to give impetus to economic progress and to counteract the inequalities of the traditional system of social stratification based on ascription. The establishment of democratic political institutions has resulted in a relative increase in the degree of politicization of the people. The conscious separation of the state and religion in the Indian constitution, it was hoped, would establish a secular tradition which would enable government to deal more effectively with a plural society. (Smith, 1963:102) To counteract the traditional system of social stratification the British in the 19th century, and later the Indian government, attempted to redefine status so that an individual's ascribed status, whether in terms of strata, birth, wealth or class is secondary to his or her achieved status. (Bopemange, 1967:3) Cultural stratification, which cuts across religious communities, is an important factor in India in undermining the strength of religious ties, and thus enabling movement towards a more integrated society. As social changes have taken effect, the traditional ascriptive social stratification is beginning to give way, particularly in urban areas, to new stratifications based on achievement as signified by education, occupation and income. (Smelser, 1966:12)

Thus constitutional rights apply to all Indian citizens. The Hindu Code Bill has cut across caste and class barriers; the Special Marriages Act has cut across community, caste and class; economic legislation has sought to reduce inequalities through land reforms and labour laws. These reforms have all had an integrative effect since they are no longer inevitably linked to traditional community affiliations (Bopemange, 1967:78). They have been further reinforced by market mechanisms and differentiated power bodies such as political parties, village councils and trade unions.

The introduction of such potentially far-reaching changes has produced disequilibrium (Geertz, 1963:4). Communities resisted assimilation as threatening to group differentiation as well as, increasingly, the possibility of domination by other well organized groups. Similar reactions and emphasis on group differentiation and organization have been observed in many contexts both in developing and developed countries (Glazer, 1975; Enloe, 1971; Cohen, 1969). It has been noted that these changes may have actually increased the salience of ascribed status.

Ethnicity is a new social category important for understanding the present day world since there has been, in recent times, a pronounced and sudden increase in tendencies by people in many different countries and circumstances to insist on the significance of their group distinctiveness and identity and on the new rights that derive from this group characteristic. Perhaps these are deeply felt human needs that have always been present, but only recently focused on by certain political and social developments. . .

Glazer, 1975: 2, 3.

While this hypothesis has not been examined in the Indian context generally, there are a number of regional studies which collectively confirm its relevance (Aggarwal, 1971; Mines, 1975; Brass, 1974; Beteille, 1965). While many of the 'new' groupings in India, vying for political and economic gain, are rooted in traditional garb and are dependent for cohesion on religious, caste or linguistic affinities, they are in fact a new phenomenon caused by inequalities between groups (Gough, 1973:9). In the case of the Muslim community in India such an explanation is both appealing and relevant. It also underlines the purely secular and often political, uses to which religion is being put. While religion serves as a useful adhesive for maintaining group cohesion, once established, it is used not to propagate religion but for political and economic gain.[3]

The Muslim community[4] should, therefore, be regarded as one of a number of communities seeking to increase its share of political and economic power by maintaining group cohesion to emphasize the numerical strength of the group and increase its credibility. The ability of each community to organize politically has been dependent on a number of factors such as traditional occupation, education, class and caste. These group organizations acquire special significance in societies moving to consolidate new economic and political structures (Geertz, 1963:4).

[3]The demand for Pakistan on religious grounds did not prevent its break-up later, when such diverse cultural groups as Punjabis and Bengalis were unable to share political power; similarly factionalism is causing divisions within the same religious community after a so-called religious revolution in Iran.

[4]The term Muslim community is used in the sense of an ethnic group whose members are distinct from members of other groups within the same society, in that they share compulsory institutions like kinship and religion with them. Abner Cohen, *Custom and Politics in Urban Africa: A Study of Hausa Migrants in Yoruba Towns*, University of California Press, 1969, p.5.

The use of religion and caste to promote community interests has evolved over the last hundred years in India. With the democratization of political structures, natural groups with established links quickly adapted to political representation. Over time a distinction was made between the political use of religious symbols and the private adaptation of group members to changing social needs and requirements. This dichotomy between public and private religion becomes clear as the reorganization of Muslim communities in the 19th century is considered in Chapter 2 and Muslim education and attitudes to social legislation are dicussed in Chapters 3 and 4. Many community leaders reflected this duality of exhorting members to assimilate changes necessary to maintain or improve the political and economic standing of the group, while reviving traditions and symbols which would increase group unity. Even among theocratic groups there was better understanding of the political role of group cohesiveness essential for secular gains. Group ideology came to represent an alternative both to western colonial ideology and to the ideology of other groups, and such Indian leaders as Swami Dayanand Saraswati, Syed Ahmad Khan, Bal Gangadhar Tilak, Mahatma Gandhi can be better appreciated in this light. All of them used religious symbolism to unite disparate groups into one large cohesive group to be more politically and therefore more economically effective; this constituted the politicization of religious ties.[5]

However, while the Muslim community in India was subject to pressures similar to those of other groups, their historically dominant role coupled with their minority position made their situation unique. Communal mobilization[6] (see Ch. 2) in the 19th century by all groups was complicated by traditional social struc-

[5]The term "political religion" is used here to mean the use of religion or religious differentiation in the pursuit of political or economic goals and not in the sense in which the term has been applied by David Apter, as the use of political ideology or secular social morality as a surrogate for religion; 'Political Religions in the New Nations' in Clifford Geertz (ed.) *Old Societies and New States; the Quest for Modernity in Asia and Africa*. Free Press, New York: 1963.

[6]Communalism is used in the sense of ethnicity which refers to strife among ethnic groups in which people stress their exclusiveness. Ethnicity awareness will produce homogenization of internal society and cultural values in order to increase interaction within the group while resisting homogenization with other groups. This requires creation and utilization of myths, beliefs, pressures and sanctions. Different elements are employed which become so interdependent that they seem an integrated ideological scheme (Abner Cohen *op. cit.*, p. 15).

tures, unable to differentiate between the secular aims of the group and the religious symbolism used to achieve it; the resultant tensions led to the partition of the country on the demands of the Muslim community[7]. This did not solve the basic problem which had been expressed by the Muslim League as the need for a 'homeland' for the Muslims. The two areas which went to form Pakistan were the two Muslim majority states, and seven million other Muslims migrated from the rest of the country, leaving some 40 million Muslims behind to continue the structural transformation already underway, but from a much weaker position. This made the community switch from seeking political solutions to their minority problems but it also intensified its concern for the preservation of group cohesion and identity.

The period after 1947 witnessed the rise of semi-political groups representing language, caste and regional interests,[8] reflecting both the communal mobilization of the 19th century, and the continuing relevance of groups, whether based on caste, religion, language or regional affiliation for the articulation of political and economic demands. Indian social scientists have shown that both religion and language are being used congruently for political purposes (see Ch. 2). This internal value creation and the emphasis on group traditions (Kothari, 1970: 333) has very specific connotations for women in society, particularly for women in minority communities.

## The woman factor

"The dilemmas and directions of women and society are not fortuitous. They are a result of multiple factors which determine the drift of the whole cultural complex considered as a part of the social realities of the period." (Reeves, 1971: 39) Most religious and cultural systems in the world endeavour to control men and women's lives and activities in order to ensure the continuity of society. This is not a system which can be linked to a specific religion or culture, because, while there are differences

[7]Louis Dumont has pointed out that communalism was not restricted to Muslims, nor was it due to Machiavellian British designs but, in fact, to a caste mentality which was responsible for the idea that national union could be affected by juxtaposing national and communal aims. *Contributions to Indian Sociology* Vol VII, March 1964, p. 41.

[8]Abner Cohen has shown that increasing interaction between groups as a result of social, political and economic changes increases intergroup competition. Each group uses and manipulates symbols from its organization which are used as weapons in the struggle with other groups (Cohen, *op. cit.* pp.1-3).

between cultures and religious systems on the extent of control exercised over women, nowhere are they wholly subjugated (Huston, 1979). It is clear that in older cultures, particularly in Asia, this ritualization of control has led to the greater subjugation of women. In India this control extended to all communities, as a result of which Indian women, like women in other societies, tended to become reified. The economic, demographic and social interplay (Aaby, 1977:39) in the case of Muslim women is rendered more complex by the minority status of their community and their historical background.

The conceptualization of what constitutes women's status has been undergoing changes as empirical studies further our understanding of the complexities involved in evaluating status. The discussion has centred around the causes of the universal subordination of women; the general/culturally specific attributes of status and the manner in which modern social, political and economic changes have affected it. Weber's attribution of women's subordination to the development of private property has been discredited by anthropologists on the grounds that even in societies without privately held property women are subordinate. (Sacks, 1975:20) According to Eleanor Leacock, the separation of the family from the clan privatized the socially necessary labour of women, (Webster, 1975:147) leading to their subordination. As the family became increasingly patriarchal (Gough, 1975:75) social organization confined women to domestic work for family use while men remained in social production for exchange. This enabled the latter to organize jointly, (1975:231). In this general debate, Irene Tinker, Paula Webster and others have pointed out that the concepts of subordination and concomitants of status lose some of their edge in cross-cultural references (Tinker, 1976:65-67); one woman's liberation may well represent another woman's subordination. The general definition of status advanced by Peggy Sanday, as the degree to which individuals have authority and/or power in the domestic or public domain, (Sanday, 1973:1695) can stand us in good stead, if "cross-culturally applicable definitions of power, authority, influence and status can be established" (Webster, 1975:154). Empirical studies on the status of women in different cultures have increasingly taken into account not only specific socio-religious customs and practices but also the effect of imposed social, political and economic changes which attempt to alter the basis of sexual segregation and division of labour. Such changes do not automatically benefit women, unless they are specifically designed to do so. While women's participation in production is important to status it is not sufficient to ensure social worth without economic control over production and without social support organizations (Sanday, 1973:1695).

Ester Boserup's inter-country study provided the evidence that economic changes based on development policies may affect women adversely, unless their specific problems as a group are given consideration. (Boserup, 1970) Even when women's participation in production and distribution has been ensured, their ability to exercise power and authority will depend on whether they are regarded as adults or dependents by society (Sacks, 1975:231). However, women's subtle exercise of power must not be overlooked; even in segregated societies where women appear to lack power and authority, segregation may be used by them to differentiate themselves as a group and thereby gain some advantages (Rosaldo, 1974:36-38). In this interplay the socio-economic stratum to which women belong becomes a vital factor; women in the lower socio- economic strata may be liberated to the extent that the family is able to segregate them, but they may suffer other disabilities related to their stratum. General aspects of status or the control women have over 'life options' such as choice in marriage, divorce, sexual freedom, freedom of movement, controlling reproduction, share of household power (Giele, 1975:4) can be usefully employed to evaluate the statu of women. This study uses a number of these indicators as well as socio- economic indicators, access to media, interaction with other communities, knowledge of legal rights, purdah and economic independence.

In dealing with women in a minority community (that is, not politically dominant) based on caste, colour, (Blood, 1972:84) religion or language, it is important to examine the social position of the community vis-a-vis other communities because in a threatening social environment, internal divisiveness may be suppressed in favour of group unity, (Denich, 1974:259) and the desire of women for change may be discouraged or may take place even as rhetorical support continues for traditional customs associated by the group. Here, the distinction between ascribed status referring to attributes individuals are born with in terms of community, religion, economic, political and legal rights, and achieved status which refers to changes made by individuals through education or other achievements, is useful. This distinction, along with the abovementioned indicators, brings out both the pressures which enforced differentiation can place on women in minority communities and the extent of change and adaptation taking place, which counteracts many aspects of traditional differentiation.

Historically the movement for the emancipation of Indian women in the 19th century was primarily directed at Hindu women due to the custom of widow immolation, the treatment of Hindu widows, the prejudice against the education of women, child marriage and the seclusion of women. The latter two customs were shared with Muslim women. However, most of these customs were regionally specific and did not affect all Indian women to the same extent. The general and more effective limitation was the attitude to women prevalent in Indian society as a whole, which assigned them certain roles, and all others were considered deviations from the 'ideal'. This 'ideal' glorified the lot of Indian women by making a virtue of their required patience, self-denial and chastity. When these customs came under attack from Christian missionaries and Indian reformers the focus was not on Muslim women, who had the right to divorce, inheritance, or remarriage when widowed or divorced, even though they seldom exercised their rights due to the prevailing ideal. The widespread custom of seclusion of women practised by all the communities particularly in the north, contributed to maintaining the 'ideal' and suppressing any rebellion which women may have harboured. Polygamy, too, was widespread among the communities, though its incidence had been declining.

The activities of reformers, the education of women and the formation of women's groups served to increase the need for legislative changes in the status of women. The anomalies in the status of Muslim women increasingly came in for attention, since their legal rights appeared to be eroded due to customary laws which many Muslim communities followed, and it seemed that a restoration of the Shariat or Muslim Personal Law would help Muslim women obtain their legal rights (see Ch. 4). The passage of legislation to restore Muslim women's rights was, therefore, welcomed both by women active in the social reform movement (see Chs. 4 and 5) and by Muslim political leaders. It coincided neatly with the desire of the community to find uniting symbols.

The initial phase of the women's movement in India created a platform for women leaders and provided them with enough to persuade political parties to adopt programmes favouring women. However, the leadership of the movement as well as the body of its supporters was to remain elitist, without the wider base of support enjoyed by political parties. Muslim women participated both in the women's movement and in the educational process, in keeping with the participation of women in similar socio-economic strata in other communities. Despite basic political differences between sections of Muslim leadership and the Congress, Muslim women supported the secular policies of the women's leadership (see Ch. 5). Due to the later beginnings of the women's movement and the many shared disabilities, the solidarity among women of different communities remained almost unimpaired. However, due to the much wider communal mobilization of the political movement and the narrow elitist base of the women's movement, this basic consensus is usually overlooked.

Muslim women found the situation substantially altered after 1947. Not only were they members of a minority community which faced considerable hostility, but after the passing of the Hindu Code Bill in 1956 giving Hindu women legal parity with Hindu men, their legal status became a matter of controversy, since they did not have legal parity with Muslim men. The rights to unilateral divorce and polygamy by Muslim men have been under attack in India for more than a century and are not in general use; Muslim resistance is not to a change in customs, but to formalizing such change through legislation. Muslim attitudes, based as they are on concerns of ethnic identity, have the support of large sections of Muslim women in resisting legislative changes. This has created the impression that real changes have not taken place in the community. In making an assessment of the importance of social law reform for the status of women, two considerations must be borne in mind. Firstly, legislative equality, if made use of, can lead to equality with men and is, therefore, desirable. Secondly, other factors such as education, economic independence and social strata remain equally important in status attainment, and without them legal equality lacks substance. The questions that need to be raised are: has social law reform significantly affected the achieved status of Hindu women? Has the lack of formal change in Muslim law meant that there has been no change in the achieved status of Muslim women? Do social strata and economic independence constitute the most important factors affecting the status of women in both communities?[9]

## The Islam factor

Islam defines religious beliefs and offers social prescriptions through which society can be regulated. The fulfillment of these social and religious prescriptions is left largely to the individual, there being no church to enforce their regulation. The underlying assumption is that the State is Islamic and will enforce legal aspects of social regulations, inheritance, dower, marriage, divorce, etc., as well as the upholding of certain values and religious identity through the educational system. In Sunni Islam, the courts are the interpreters of socio-legal regulations while religious duties can be performed by individuals themselves.

In many Muslim countries dominated by male politicians the State has been pragmatic on the side of conservatism as far as women's rights are concerned, rather than innovative. Politicians have been able to use religion as a political issue, and to capitalize on its ability to mobilise large numbers of people. This has meant that they cannot at the same time bring about radical changes. Individualism in Islam has meant that there has been no church at which a movement for reform can be directed; it has also meant that changes have been individualistic and have not followed any centralized guidelines. While the absence of a clear authority to sanction change has certain advantages, it also means that political expediency can cause the changes to be reversed.[10] As no rigidity was envisaged in Islamic law, the difficulty, therefore, has lain with the way different cultures have used Islam, and the twin formulae of consensus or *ijma* and

[9]J.S. Read in discussing "Women's Status and Law Reform" has pointed out the difficulties of assessing status thus: "Firstly, in considering the position of women in any society, it is seldom possible to collect and assess the relevant evidence from law, society and economic life, religion and ethics, and on that basis to award women of that society a definite rung on the fictitious ladder of women's status. This is essentially a subjective assessment of numerous complex factors.. Secondly, just as law is only one factor in the total position of women, although, of course, a highly significant one, so too reform of law is only one of the instruments by which that position can be altered." In J.N.D. Anderson (ed.), *Changing Law in Developing Countries*, Praeger, New York, 1963, pp. 214, 215.

[10]We have seen this happening in recent times in Iran, Pakistan and other Muslim countries. Till the feminist lobby in Muslim countries does not become powerful and demand and get popular ratification of these changes, Muslim women's status will remain tenuous.

individual reasoning or *ijtihad* were formulated to incorporate changes. Where Islam has been used as a uniting symbol in the struggle against colonialism, the dichotomy between political and private religion tended to become institutionalized and this has continued with the social, political and economic changes underway in all societies.

In India, the Islamic cultural and religious self-referencing of Muslims has interacted with other religious and cultural groups, and has undergone changes both subtle and overt. This self-referencing is particularly important since most Indian Muslims were Hindu converts, and reflect a certain orientation which was a part of their original social and cultural milieu (Aggarwal, 1971; Ahmad, 1973). Religious self-consciousness was induced by the imperatives of the 19th century, due to colonialism and social, economic and political changes. Islam, to the Indian Muslim, became a matter of group differentiation and group solidarity rather than a system of immutable customs. In this Muslims are not unlike other ethnic groupings in India. Due to the presence of a colonial power in India, Muslim thinkers in the 19th century were primarily concerned with explaining the loss of political power and in pursuing strategies to regain it. Their appeal was to tradition, to purer Islam, to create a semblance of unity and discipline. At a later stage this was abandoned for a policy which sought conciliation with the new power and success within the system, albeit necessarily in competition with other groups similarly engaged. Communal mobilisation meant using Islam as a political adhesive between Muslim communities which would otherwise have little in common.

During the 19th century Muslim intellectuals both in India and in other countries sought to bring about changes in traditional interpretations of Muslim Personal Law as well as in commercial practices. Between 1850 and 1883, an eclectic mix derived from different Muslim jurists was used to change family laws in Turkey and Egypt (Anderson, 1967:227-233); at the turn of the century in Egypt, Qasim Amin wrote *The Liberation of Women*. Similar concerns were voiced by reformers in India.

Attempts were made to resuscitate women's rights, which had been eroded, within the Islamic framework and it was hoped that this in itself would better the status of women. To this end, the Shariat Act was passed in 1937 ensuring women's right to property; and the Dissolution of Muslim Marriages Act, in 1939, which dealt with women's right to divorce. While the divorce law was liberal, culled from different schools of Islamic jurisprudence, women's right to property under the Shariat Act (1939) was amended to preserve landed property and prevent its division (see Ch. 4). The arguments advanced for the legislation by Muslim leaders focussed on the need to unite the community and to further the rights of women.

Since 1947, the Muslim community in India has been caught between the need to maintain its identity and the need to modernize its social structures. Legislative or community regulations of unilateral divorce and polygamy have been under discussion, however limited these practices actually are. One difficulty is the lack of uniformity in dealing with these problems in other Muslim countries. The Muslim community in India is, therefore, faced with the prospect of making such changes on its own, and while it has actually accepted a mass of secular legislation on economic matters and even on women before 1947, further changes are being resisted, not because the practices are widespread, but because the Shariat represents a widely accepted basis for Muslim differentiation which would otherwise be eroded. This view appears to have the support of both women and men.

The Indian government has consciously decided not to interfere with a matter so closely associated with Muslim sentiments. However, since the safeguards specified in the Shariat or Muslim Personal Law are not enforced in India, women have found it difficult to always get justice particularly in marital matters. Ad hoc solutions to these problems have been evolved in a few regions, but no formula has gained general acceptance in India. The lack of leadership due to the erosion of the Muslim middle class, particularly in north India after 1947 served to exacerbate the community's difficulties, leaving them fewer options for dealing with social issues. There is, however, evidence of a more robust approach to social and economic problems among some regional communities in the south.

Much of the existing literature on Muslim women in India is confined to a consideration of their status and role in the context of Islam and its tenets on women, which include customs and practices which differentiate between the status of men and women. In the Indian context, a prejudice against the assertiveness of women extends to all groups. This study, by differentiating between the Indian, Muslim and woman factors, is able to demonstrate that socio-economic circumstances and the pressures of a minority community are much more relevant determinants of status than religion or customs and practices. The survey, the field trip and historical research all indicate the extent to which social, political and economic developments affect communities and women in society, and show that such interaction becomes an important factor in the determination of the status and role of women, particularly those in minority communities.

# 2

## Setting the Pattern: Muslim Communities in the Nineteenth Century

### Introduction

This chapter evaluates the position of different Muslim communities in the 19th century, and the circumstances which led to the development of a consensus between them on broad political and social aims at the end of the century. This consensus, once arrived at, based on certain perceptions of the strategy necessary to deal with their minority political and economic position in Indian society, has tended to persist, particularly after Partition, as the community struggled to preserve its identity and survive. That process, in which women played almost no part, critically affects their present status and role. The pattern set in the 19th century needs to be understood not only for the political aims of the community, which have been exhaustively analyzed, but for the social repercussions of essentially political and economic objectives on Muslim women.

It is proposed to set political and social developments in the Muslim community in the context of developments in other regional communities to show the extent to which the actions and reactions of the Muslims were in consonance with developments elsewhere, and the extent to which they were reacting to their minority status after the loss of political power in the north.

In the 19th century, Muslim communities in India, like other caste or religious communities had little in common with each other; they were separated by language, cultural traditions and, sometimes, even religious practices. The occupational structure of communities, whether primarily engaged in agriculture, trade, professions or service industries determined certain cultural and religious practices. These differed between regional communities and affected their attitudes towards the role and status of women. Many socio-religious customs and beliefs pertaining to women and families tended to be localized.

Political changes instituted in the 19th century affected these disparate communities profoundly, by emphasizing numerical strength and cohesion to bring about greater political leverage with a foreign government. Communities were required to promote co-operation with counterpart groups in other regions. Improved communications hastened the formation of inter-group committees institutionalizing this solidarity. (Farquhar, 1967:346, 347; Seal, 173: 338; Hardy, 1972:126; Rudolph, 1969:32) Such co-operation encouraged the revival and maintenance of certain traditional customs and practices, many of which affected women, some adversely.

Social changes in the 19th century focused primarily on women, whose independence had been completely eroded by socio-religious customs which regulated the age of marriage, education, widow remarriage, inheritance, etc. By and large there was general acceptance of the need for change but, due to the politicization of group solidarity and the need to maintain identity, the debate on reform was between those who opted for covert change with no open rejection of past customs and practices which would make community solidarity in political and economic terms more difficult (see Ch.4) and those who felt social change to be a necessary prerequisite for the desired political and economic changes in the community. The reaction was fairly widespread as it was a response not to social reform, but to the all-pervasive political changes underway.

The response of different communities varied with regional practices, customs and their economic position; this pattern is particularly discernible in the case of the Muslim community. Its initial response on women's issues was positive (see Ch. 4) partly because Muslim practices, other than purdah, did not come under attack, polygamy being common to all communities at that time. The need to evolve a common political and economic strategy between different Muslim communities made it necessary to minimize differences between them; initially Muslim women gained from this process as Muslim communities sought to distance themselves from local communities and emphasize

Muslim women's rights in the Shariat.

This cooperation between communities led to the gradual emergence of a 'Muslim position' on many political, economic and social issues confronting them. The constraints imposed by the need for unity led to a reappraisal of the role of religion, and consequently to its politicization. Distinctions were increasingly drawn between the organization of family life or basic group identity through the restoration of the Shariat, and the compulsion to accept western education and employent imposed by economic necessities. It implied that changes could be contained in the political and economic sphere and would be unaffected by customs and traditions being used to unify the community. This attitude proved detrimental to the interests of Muslim women which were consciously subjugated to the perceived interests of the community.

The solutions proposed to the problems faced by Muslim communities in different regions varied between different Muslim leaders in the light of their local experience with and their perception of the nature of Muslim problems. But central to all the rhetoric, writings and debate of the time was the realization that Muslim communities in India were minorities and that the loss of traditional political power would mean their economic decline unless they could organize themselves better.

Partition on Muslim demand in 1947 proved most detrimental to Muslim interests since it further exacerbated political and economic problems and successfully stymied for the present, the fundamental rethinking necessary to resolve persistent social problems, particularly those pertaining to the status of Muslim women. Solutions to the legal status of Muslim women are not readily available since there is no church or central agency in Islam that can sanction such changes; nor has a unified formula been adopted by Muslim countries to effect such changes. No Muslim leadership exists in India which could delink the status of women from the present construct of Muslim identity, based as it is on Muslim Personal Law, and yet maintain the unity of the minority community.

The pattern of responses set in the 19th century continues to moderate thinking and rhetoric today. However, Muslim response and reaction in the 19th century can in no way be considered separate from the general Indian pattern, which it reflected.

## Muslim communities after 1857

In the hundred years preceding the Mutiny of 1857, Muslim communities all over India had been steadily losing political power and control to the British and to other Indian rulers. The process was particularly pronounced in Bengal, Maharashtra, Madras and Mysore. Real power in north India, both military and political, had already declined following successive raids by foreign and Hindu rulers; only the presence of the Mughal emperor at Delhi remained as a symbol of Muslim power. After the Mutiny, even this symbolic power was lost and the process of decline was complete. Those Muslim states that were not absorbed into British India retained only a partial semblance of autonomy.

Different Muslim communities faced the social, political and economic encroachments in different ways and at different times. Their response, as those of other affected communities was, at best, piecemeal and spontaneous, rather than premeditated or reasoned. Muslim communities had to deal with the reality of a new and powerful adversary who not only constantly and successively introduced changes which fundamentally affected their economic position, but also eroded the ascriptive rules by which success and status were determined. The attainment of new western learning became the basis of availing of economic and political opportunities. (Robinson, 1974:43, 44) As a dispossessed power group, the initial Muslim response was a rejection of those rules; however, the acceptance of the rules by other communities less directly dispossessed, meant that the Muslim rejection was both meaningless and harmful to their future economic, political and social interests.

The economic impact of the loss of power varied greatly in different regions. In Bengal, for instance, although Muslims were in the majority, they were mainly peasants; their ability to compete for employment and government patronage was, therefore, limited, and they could not easily gain the skills needed through education. In the Northwest Provinces and Oudh, the Muslim community was heavily dependent on government patronage for employment. To retain the dominant position they enjoyed here, they accepted the new ground rules and never lost their lead in acquiring western education, or in gaining government employment. In western India, where Muslims were mainly traders and less dependent on government patronage, they were able to collaborate with members of other communities and claim the attention of the government as a result of this cooperation. In the south except for Malabar, where they were mainly peasants, they were educationally and economically secure and able to withstand the competition for employment. Their concerns, however, in all regions were similar: the need to successfully compete for economic and political positions with other communities. The methods employed by different Muslim communities and the pressures to do so varied with their specific situation. By the end of the 19th century the economic position of different groups became increasingly dependent on their political ability to represent their particular problems and complaints to the government, and on their entrepreneurial skills; political and economic factors tended to reinforce each other, increasing the importance of group identification and ties. The Muslim and other communities felt the need to formulate and emphasize their group characteristics, and by the end of the 19th century, most communities had formed group associations and joined associations in cooperation with other communities.

The position of the north Indian Muslim community after the Mutiny, with which it was closely identified, had diminished politically and economically. This is reflected in the writings of the Urdu poet Ghalib, who lived through the Mutiny in Delhi. He wrote to his friend Ahram on June 12, 1859 (Russell, 1969:205): "The position here is that among Muslim nobles (who might have been able to subscribe to your publication) there are three: Nawab Hasan Ali Khan, Nawab Hamid Ali Khan and Hakim Ahsanullah Khan; but their position is such that if they feed themselves they cannot clothe themselves." Earlier he had written verses on the devastation of Delhi and the condition of the Muslim nobility. While this perhaps only reflected conditions in Delhi, there is little doubt that the emerging British power in India identified Muslims, whom they were displacing politically, as the group most hostile to them. Lord Ellenborough indicated as much in 1843 when he wrote, "I cannot close my eyes to the belief that the race (Mohammadans) is fundamentally hostile to us and our true policy is to reconciliate the Hindus." (Desai, 1966:393) Muslims had been forewarned of impending changes before the Indian Munity of 1857 which marked the death of the old order, and brought political, economic and cultural disaster to the Indian Muslims. (O'Malley, 1968:398)

Almost a century earlier, an intellectual framework for change was formulated by Shah Wali Ullah, (1703-1762) who taught at the Madrassah Rahmiyyah in Delhi. Commenting on the decline of Muslim power in the north, he wrote a monumental work, *Hijjat- ullah-il Belighah*, in which he outlined the reasons for the economic, political and social crisis faced by the Muslim community. (Nizami, 1969:19) He preached against the monarchy stressing the need for equity and justice in the life of an individual, and equilibrium in economic relationships. Pressure on the treasury, he wrote, was due to the demands of people who did not work but taxed people who did and were productive. In the religious sphere, he broke the monopoly of the ullema by translating the Quran from Arabic to Urdu. His efforts were directed at increasing the community's awareness of its economic and political decline, which he argued was due to eradicable social causes. He went back to the original sources of Islamic law, the Quran and the Hadith, and asked Muslims to free themselves from blind acceptance of the four schools of jurisprudence and to distinguish between pure, universal religions and local Arabic colouring. The Prophet, he argued, had kept in view cultural factors in formulating Shariat laws so as not to unduly constrain future generations or those living in other areas with different cultural, social and legal traditions; he did not intend that the Shariat be imposed rigidly. (Malik, 1963:128-132)

His son, Shah Abd Aziz (1746-1824), succeeded him at the Madrassah Rahmiyyah. He protested against the steady erosion of Muslim power in India and against the replacement of the Muslim penal code by new British legislation at the turn of the 18th century. He issued a *fatwa*, or ruling, that the territory under British rule was in a state of war but he urged Muslims to learn English and acquire technical skills from the British.

An active defence of Muslim rule came from Sayyid Ahmad of Rae Baraylly (1786-1831) in north India. In Bengal, Hajji Shariatullah (1871-1940) and his son Dudu Miyan (1819-1862) sought to organize Muslim peasants in a movement to change their economic and social conditions and fight the oppression of Hindu landlords. Titu Mir (1782-1831) led an agrarian revolt in western Bengal. These and other movements tossed the idea of what constituted Islam back and forth in an effort to find an ideological entity to replace the influence and control that had been lost. Ideas moved from using the Quran as the only true basis of Islam to purifying the customs which were not based on the Quran. These movements, combined with agrarian unrest, led to a series of Muslim uprisings in the 19th century which were finally crushed in Bengal and ended in the Wahabi trials in 1871. It was in response to the belief that the Muslims were dispossessed and rebellious that Lord Mayo commissioned a Bengal civil servant, W.W. Hunter, to write a book "on the burning question of the day: Are the Mussalmans bound by their religion to rebel against the Queen?" (Hardy, 1972:85) While not all Muslims could or did identify with the militant Muslim movements which were primarily lower class in origin, the debate on Islam and its meaning for Indian Muslims had raised the level of political and social consciousness, even as the "destruction of Delhi as the centre of Muslim culture" (Hardy, 1972:61) made them aware that there were limits to what they could now achieve.

The adoption of a new strategy was to take time and effort. It was complicated by the fact that the economic policies followed by the British were fundamentally changing the class structure in India as well as changing the modus of upward mobility from the traditional one of learning, inherited wealth or status to advancement through western education and economic achievement. The response of the Muslim communities of the north to political changes was specific. Other Muslim communities were not affected in the same way or to the same extent. The strategy adopted by Muslim leaders in different regions was more a reflection of their specific local political, social and economic problems and was heavily influenced by the reaction of other communities of the region to the pressures of British rule, rather than a "Muslim response". Over a period of time, however, a few areas emerged in which the actions of these diverse communities would synchronize to establish a basic Muslim "identity" to which they could all subscribe. That such an "identity" would be more or less on the pattern of the Muslims of Oudh and the United Provinces was due to the symbolic importance of northern politics under the Mughals and the surge of Muslim activity in the region, primarily due to the activities of Syed Ahmad Khan and his co-workers.

## Nature of changes

The British initiated a variety of changes which would help them in promoting and maintaining the commercial and industrial interests to which their rule in India was so closely linked. In the regions which they controlled, agriculture was reorganized for the purpose of easy revenue collection, by establishing individual ownership of land holdings. This had a profound socio-economic impact as owners of agricultural holdings who found it difficult to meet fixed revenue payments, were forced to sell. The new owners tended to be rich absentee merchant landlords from urban areas. (Hardy, 1972:34, 42, 44, 58) To establish a centralized administration capable of serving British interests at all times, western education was made an essential qualification for government employment and the traditional customary laws of each community were separately codified. These measures were designed to ensure the preservation and expansion of British interests by streamlining the administration and recasting it to the convenience of the new rulers. Indians took to the new education provided and accepted the changes introduced because between various Indian ". . . tongues, sects and communities there was intense competition . . . which under the circumstances of foreign rule mainly took the form of struggles for status". (Seal, 1971:11) Status could be attained politically and economically by government recognition that their group was important and represented powerful interests. Education was an important means of retaining or upgrading status, but belonging to a politically active group helped considerably when the benefits of education in the form of employment were to be reaped. Muslim political groupings, like those of other communities, were mainly busy tailoring their activities to those ends. To counteract the loss they had suffered politically, the emphasis among Muslim leaders was towards persuading Muslims to accept the change in political power and to adapt to the new rules. At the same time efforts were made to reaffirm the continuing validity of Islamic values in the changed context.[1]

Such movements took place among Hindu communities, who in the process of rejecting all external influences on Hinduism, rejected all accretions of Muslim culture and religion. Muslim reaction to the loss of political power was, therefore, also geared to internal consolidation to cope with and withstand physical, social and intellectual attacks. (Farquhar, 1967:347) British policies encouraged representation by organized groups; certain

[1]Sir Syed Ahmad Khan in his many speeches and articles tries to do this, as did Abdul Latif and Amir Ali who stated that 'In Islam is joined a lofty idealism with the most rationalistic practicality.' P. Hardy, *Muslims of British India*, Cambridge University Press, p.106; also see pp.94-106.

groups arose naturally out of ethnic or religious affiliations, others were born of a similarity of interests. The development of wider-based political associations was a response to social changes taking place through more widespread higher education and an increasing number of entrants into the professions. Better communications too created an awareness that went beyond caste, religion and locality. (Seal, 1973:202) Economic changes, however, were slow in coming and the newly created elite began looking for ways to increase their political leverage to gain from the limited opportunities available. These efforts tended to take on nationalist overtones. (Desai, 1966:74) While espousing policies of free trade and laissez faire the British government managed to systematize discrimination in favour of British goods and persons, barring the entry of Indians into important official positions or profitable enterprises. During 1870-1914 the pace of industrialization was extremely slow and the share of Indians in industry limited, increasing their dependence on agriculture. (Gough, 1973:52) This pattern of development effectively curtailed economic opportunities and increased the pressure on communities to pursue social policies which emphasized the distinction between them and other communities, so that their effectiveness as a pressure group could be maintained, and used to maximize economic advantage. (Gough, 1973:53)

In Bengal, where the vast majority were peasants, the small core of Muslim gentry organized two associations: the Mohammadan Literary and Scientific Society of Calcutta under Nawab Abd Al Latif in 1863 and later, National Central Mohammadan Association launched by Amir Ali in 1877 (Hardy, 1972:126) to promote Muslim interests by representations to government. Amir Ali effectively used Hunter's arguments from his report, *The Indian Mussalmans* to pressurize government into reserving jobs for Muslims and for providing special educational facilities for them. (Seal, 1973:312) By 1888 he had succeeded in extending the association's influence by opening 50 branches in Punjab, Bihar and even Madras. (Seal, 1973:313) The Ripon reforms of 1883 introduced the elective principle into rural and local government, and this affected the representation Muslims could muster in local bodies in Bengal. Muslim interests were, therefore, directed at maintaining their exclusiveness, stemming their economic decline and demanding concessions on that basis.

In the Northwest Provinces and Oudh the efforts of the Muslim community to maintain its position were supervised by

Syed Ahmad Khan (1817-1898). He had lived through the changes the community had undergone after the Mutiny, and was determined that it should function purely as a social and economic group so that it might be spared further political reprisals. He determined that the Muslim community would remain entirely loyal to the government. With this end in view, he spent his energies explaining the Muslims to the British and the British to the Muslims. In doing so he reformulated Islamic beliefs to bring them into line with modern western thinking. He also cooperated with elite members of other communities of the province to form The Scientific Society of Aligarh in July 1864 (Graham, 1909:49) and in 1867 to found a branch of the British Indian Association to promote co-operation between communities and the government. Education, he felt, was all that was needed for greater understanding, not only between the government and Muslims but between Muslims and other communities. "Educate, educate, educate, all the socio-political diseases of India may be curbed by this treatment, cure the root and the tree will flourish." (Graham, 1909:48) At the opening of Muhammadan Oriental College on January 18, 1877 he said, "Ever since I first began to think of the social question in British India, it struck me with peculiar force that there was a want between the two races whom Providence has placed in such close relation in this country. I often asked myself how it was that a century of English rule has not brought the natives of this country closer to those at whose hands Providence has placed the guidance of public affairs . . . It then appeared to me that nothing could remove these obstacles to progress but education." (Graham, 1909:188) He was against the use of Urdu as a medium of instruction and felt the future lay in English (Malik, 1963:213).

The Anglo-Mohammadan Oriental College was established through his endeavours in 1875 and was an effort to impart western education to Muslims. Religious education was an adjunct of the curriculum to maintain and strengthen community ties and reverse the irreligious effects of secular education. Leading Muslims like Altaf Husain Hali (1837-1914), the poet, were associated with the enterprise. Hali's major work, *Mussadas* created a stir by recalling the glories of the Muslim past and exhorting Muslims to greater effort in the present. He also wrote a poem on Muslim women, in favour of emancipation. The novelist, Nazir Ahmad of Bijnor (1836-1912), introduced a new form to the traditional Urdu novel, and through his novels indicated the changes taking place in the Muslim family and among Muslim women. Nawabs Viqar ul Mulk (1841-1917) and Mohsin ul Mulk (1837-1907) and Shibli Numani (1857-1914) each played a major role in guiding the Muslim community of the north and forging its links with other Muslim communities.

The movement to replace Urdu with Hindi in education as the medium of instruction created an awareness of the essential differences in group interests between the Hindu and Muslim communities. It also ended to some extent the co-operation between the elites of the two northern communities. (Robinson, 1974:74) Agitation for Hindi was part of the Hindu revivalism taking place in northern India under the leadership of Swami Dayanand Saraswati. In forming the Arya Samaj, his primary aim was to draw the different Hindu sects together; a cleaning of Hinduism internally and externally. A necessary part of the process was a rejection of western influence and elements of Islamic culture which had crept in over time. (Robinson, 1974:68) Opposition to the Muslims was clearly articulated and since it went along with the agitations against Urdu and for cow protection the movement took a decidedly anti-Muslim turn. (Robinson, 1974:77, 78) That this change in attitude was to have a long term effect is clear since, several decades later, Syed Nabi Ullah said in his Presidential address before the Nagpur session of the Muslim League,

> . . . I have no hestitation in asserting that unless Hindus and Mohammedans co-operate with each other in the general development of the country as a whole, and in all matters affecting their mutual interests, neither will develop to the full . . . I am grieved to say certain events and incidents have happened within recent years which have given offence to the Mohammedans and caused many searchings of heart among them . . . What is the inner meaning of these Shivaji celebrations? Do they not suggest the revolt of Hinduism against Islam? . . . these suggestively aggressive celebrations, however, to which I have just referred, went a long way to stealing our hearts against yielding on the question of separate electorates for Mohammadans . . .

Zaidi, 1976:280-281.

The formation of the Indian National Congress in 1885 led to opposition from the Central Mohammadan Association of Calcutta and from Syed Ahmed Khan in U.P. The Hindus in U.P. also opposed the Congress (Zakaria, 1970:64) which they felt constituted Bengali domination. The reasons for the two Muslim communities' opposition to the Congress were similar: to protect Muslim representation to government, and in government employment. Both felt that Muslims would lose out in open competition in U.P. because they already dominated the services, and in Calcutta because they were weak. In his speech at Lucknow (December 2, 1887) directed against the Congress, Syed Ahmad Khan's orientation is manifest. "... That is, on the supposition that all of us coming together, we could do something, what could it accomplish? ... If government entertains unfavourable sentiments towards our community, then I say with utmost force these sentiments are entirely wrong... If then Mohammadans also join in these monstrous schemes, which are impossible of fulfillment, and which are disastrous for the country, what will be the result? ... It will be necessary for government to pass a new law and to fill the jails." To the *Pioneer* newspaper he wrote on April 9, 1888,

> Those questions on which Hindus and Mohammadans can unite and on which they ought to unite and concerning which, it is my earnest desire, that they should unite, are social questions. We are both desirous that peace should reign in the country, that we two nations should live in a brotherly manner, that we should help and sympathise with one another, that we should bring pressure to bear on his own people, to prevent the arising of religious quarrels, that we should improve our social conditions, and that we should try to remove the animosity which is every day increasing between our two communities. The questions on which we can agree are purely social. If the Congress had been made for these objects, then I would myself have been its president ... but the Congress is a political congress, and there is no one of its fundamental principles and especially that one for which it was in reality founded, to which Mohammadans are not opposed.
>
> Zaidi, 1976:38-46.

Syed Ahmed Khan was so convinced of the need for Muslims to stay out of any political agitations that he would not even concede the need for a political agitation in support of the 1877-

78 Russo-Turkish war, and felt that Muslims should not consider the Sultan of Turkey as the Khalifa or head of Islam. (Robinson, 1974:112) The same war was used by Badruddin Tyabji to bring different Muslim sects in Bombay together in a meeting to form the Anjuman-i-Islam, a Muslim educational institution in which, for the first time, all Muslim sects collaborated. The war was also used to mobilize Muslim opinion in Madras.

In Bombay Presidency, the experience of Badruddin Tyabji was substantially different to that of Syed Ahmad Khan in U.P. Tyabji was younger and had been educated in England, where he had come into contact with people from Bombay with whom he was later to co-operate at many levels. His associates in Bombay were members of a powerful Hindu social reform movement. Names like Telang, Ranade, Sir Pherozeshah Mehta and Dadabhai Naoroji are associated with him, the very names that stood for social reform, particularly on the position of Hindu women and of Hindu practices. Co-operation and identification with the Hindu aim of social reform at a political level appeared logical and natural. The opposition to the reform movement came from Poona; it was led by Tilak, whose attempts at revivalism and unification of Hindus on a common platform under the symbol of Shivaji naturally contained anti-Muslim sentiments. Tilak also attacked members of the Social Reform Conference and opposed any legislation which affected Hindu identity, so it was easy for like-minded Hindus and Muslims of the region to collaborate on issues of mutual interest.

The concerns of Badruddin Tyabji were similar to those of Amir Ali in Calcutta (with whom he corresponded) and to those of Syed Ahmad Khan in U.P. His concern for Muslim education and employment and for Urdu as the medium of instruction in schools exhibited the same anxiety for the key constituents of Muslim identity. It also showed an acceptance of the concerns of north Indian Muslims, a pattern other Muslim communities were to follow. Badruddin Tyabji was able to advocate the emancipation of Muslim women and pronounce against the custom of purdah because he was in company with other reformers. Tyabji formed the Anjuman-i-Islam in 1876 to deal with social and economic questions before the community, and at the political level he realized that co-operation with other communities would benefit Muslims. This was stressed in his Presidential address to the Indian National Congress at Madras in 1887:

Gentlemen, it is undoubtedly true that each of our great Indian communities has its own peculiar social, moral, educational and even political difficulties to surmount, but so far as general political questions affecting the whole of India, such as those alone are discussed by this congress are concerned, I for one am utterly at a loss to understand why the Mussalmans should not work shoulder to shoulder. Gentlemen, this is the principle on which we in Bombay Presidency have always acted.

Zaidi, 1976:586.

He used the Russo-Turkish war of 1877 as a "Muslim Cause" to organize a common platform for different Muslim sects in Bombay within the Anjuman, an organization directed at co-ordinating the actions of different Muslim sects on social and economic matters. This effort at unity was a response to political changes already current. It was an important "first" in Bombay, in achieving a semblance of community unity. (Masselos, 1976:76)

That the sects were more than ready to find such a uniting platform is evident from the *Times of India* comment (Tyabji, 1952:80) on the first meeting of the Anjuman.

It was not a meeting composed of or organized by members of any particular section of the Mohammadan community, it was entirely representative of every class, section and creed into which the Mohammadan world is divided. A glance at the list of persons, many of which our reporter was able to ascertain on the spot, shows Shias, Sunnis, Arabs, Moghuls, Memons, Khojas, Bohras, Konkanis — all sent the leaders of their respective communities for the purpose of representing them and proving to the world how intense in the Muslim breast is the love of their religion . . . .

In the south, the Muslim elite was Urdu speaking, a device it had used traditionally in order to identify, and maintain contact with, the Muslim rulers of Delhi. (Ahmad, 1964:248) A distinction needs to be made between the elite and the Muslim masses who were in greater rapport with the local culture and language. At the turn of the century Muslim witnesses to various commissions appointed by the government were putting forward the same arguments as those used by north Indian Muslims. (see Chs. 3, 4) The British took Urdu-speaking Muslims of the south to be the leaders of the community under the leadership of the Nawab of Arcot. (*First Quinquennial Review of Education*, 1886:318) The Russo-Turkish war provided the Madras Muslims with an opportunity to mobilize support for a Muslim cause and *The Statesman (The Friend of India and Statesman*, May 11, 1877) reported that maulvis (clerics) in Madras were collecting money, house to house, for the Turkish cause.

An editorial in *The Statesman* on July 10, 1877 (*The Friend of India and Statesman*, 1877) commented on the extent to which Muslims all over the country had rallied:

> Indian Muslims have their local sects, their local shrines, and they have never been deposed to confess that these are insufficient for salvation ... the Indian Mussalmans cannot, save by a figure of speech, be called a single body moved by a common purpose. They differ from one another in race, in language, in customs, in dress, in local creed before they can combine with the subjects of the sultan ... they have first to learn how to come together with one another. Nor should we forget that the two great sects of Islam keep alive in India their traditional enmity ... What then is the origin and significance of the movement which has run through the Mohammadan population of India?

The editorial concluded that the western press' identification of Muslim interests with those of the Sultan of Turkey had roused Muslim consciousness. It added that this was far from "indicating a profound political movement swaying a united body of men towards definite purposes," but the success of some meetings in large towns led to the conclusion that "we have witnessed the growth of a new impulse, but henceforth we must reckon with its growth".

By the end of the 19th century there appeared to be some consensus among Muslim communities on issues of importance on which concerted action should be taken. That education and employment concerned all of them was evident from the hearings of the Education Commission of 1882. Badruddin Tyabji said in his evidence: "No system has been adopted with any reference to Muslim requirements" (Education Commission, 1884:498); and suggested that Muslim schools be established at centres of Mohammadan population with Hindustani and Persian to overcome their aversion to English education. He also stated that educated Mohammadans had the greatest possible difficulty in finding remunerative employment in or out of government. The community continued to be impoverished, due to the shift to English education and little value was placed on accomplishments in Persian and Arabic, due to political prejudice. He added, "I know several Mohammadan graduates belonging to the most respectable families who are unable to get employment although most strenuous efforts were made on their behalf by men of position and influence. And, further, I am convinced that Mohammadans in the Bombay Presidency do require exceptional treatment in the matter of English education . . ." It was pointed out to him by Mr Lee Warner that Mohammadans on Bombay island had a larger percentage of children in schools than Hindus, but he retorted that they did not appear at higher educational levels (Education Commission Report, 1884:507).

In the report of the Education Commission in U.P., Sir Syed Ahmad Khan (now knighted) stated that the lower and middle classes availed themselves of education provided by the government. (A distinction must be drawn between the education provided by government and the unrecognised Muslim schools to which Muslim children might be sent. All statistics on Muslim enrolment are for recognised schools and do not represent total Muslim school attendance.) He pointed out that according to the Census for 1871-72, two-fifths of the population was Muslim but there were only 57 graduates compared to 3,155 Hindu graduates. He cautioned that "Mohammadans themselves must change, government can't because of the nature of the problem". (Education Commission Report, 1884:286-292) This was contrary to the evidence that Muslims were well ahead of other communities in the region both in education and in employment.

In Madras (Madras Provincial Report) Mir Ansuruddin Sahib, Presidency Magistrate at Madras said in his evidence,

> To go a great distance is no obstacle to the rich but the poor, which is generally the condition of the Mohammadan community, will find it difficult to raise the wherewithal. Mohammadans furthermore, in pursuance of their studies, would have to go to some Hindu school, where they would be deprived of their own vernaculars, Persian and Hindustani . . . Upper classes are against European education because of the danger of it undermining the religious sentiments of their youth. They have grotesque confidence in their wealth; middle classes are

more receptive and lower classes need government help to reap the benefits of English education. (Education Commission, 1884:17)

From Syed Ahmad Khan's evidence in U.P. and from the evidence in Madras it is clear that the less well-off sections among Muslims were not abstaining from western education, for they had already realized its importance for their future economic welfare.[2]

From Calcutta, the National Mohammadan Association in a memorial to the government had stated that, "It is only by frankly placing themselves in line with Hindus and taking full advantage of the government system of high, and especially of English education, that the Mohammadans can hope fairly to hold their own in respect of the better description of state appointments.' (*First Quinquennial Review*, 1886:314) The case of Bengal was special. Hunter's report had carefully documented the declining economic status of the community, and the reasons for this were attributed to government prejudice and Muslim reluctance to educate their children at government schools, which would enable them to get government employment, adding, "Had the Mussalmans been wise, they would have perceived the change and accepted their fate, but an ancient and conquering race cannot easily divest itself of the traditions of its nobler days." The report also pointed out the repercussions of such policies on the community in Bengal: "During the last forty years they have separated themselves from the Hindus by differences of dress, of salutations and other exterior distinctions such as they never deemed necessary in their days of supremacy." (Hunter, 1964:112, 132, 133)

The 1881 Census indicated that similar movements were discernible among other Muslim communities as well; it attributed the general awakening of Muslim consciousness to the "savage British suppression of the Mutiny and rising" (Hardy, 1972:61). The movements were also a result of discrimination in employment, which gradually impoverished Muslims. Aspects of Hindu

---

[2]Anil Seal has calculated that in 1867 Muslims held 11. 7 per cent of government jobs in Bengal. In 1871 this dropped to 8 per cent, and in 1886-87 there were only 53 Muslim officials in the uncovenanted judicial and executive service of Bengal. In the legal profession there had been more Muslim pleaders in Calcutta than other communities combined; between 1852-1869 there were no Muslim pleaders. This, according to Seal, was due to poor Muslim showing at the higher levels of education in Bengal. Anil Seal, *The Emergence of Indian Nationalism*, Cambridge University Press, 1971, p.302.

revivalism were pointedly anti-Muslim[3] (Morrison, 1906:41). Moreover, the attacks on Islam by Christian missionaries led both Syed Ahmad Khan and Amir Ali to rewrite Islamic teachings as close to the Christian image as possible.

All communities felt the pressures of change and were impelled to react similarly to the government which, while professing indifference to an individual's communal origins in matters of employment and education, nevertheless required them to identify themselves according to caste, creed and religion for political group representation, if they wanted to influence legislation or policy. It became important for communities to identify themselves by defining their group characteristics.[4] In order to increase cohesiveness as a group, differences were more sharply defined, and conversely, certain sectarian differences were subsumed in the process and absorbed into the group; an "ethnogenesis by census". (Geertz, 1963:109) What draws particular attention to the manner in which the Muslim community dealt with the new situation is not their strategy, which was similar to those of other communities, but their historical position in India, and the resulting partition.

The gradual acceptance of the north Indian Muslim model by all other Muslim communities is evident from their identification with Urdu as the language of the Muslims, as per the evidence before the Education Commision of 1882. The use of certain symbols with natural Muslim associations, like the Turkish Khalif during the Russo-Turkish war, helped to unite Muslims inter-regionally and to increase co-operation between them. Anxieties with regard to Muslim education and employment helped to cement this definition of what was to constitute Muslim interests and identity, despite the fact that the basis for such anxieties differed greatly between regions. The implications of this for Muslim women were twofold. A reiteration of the need

[3]A pamphlet published in 1903 drew the distinction sharply between communities when it spoke of the relationship of Indians (Hindu) to other races such as Mohammadans, Parsis, Sikhs. J. Rev. Morrison, *New Ideas in India*, 1903, p.41.

[4]Charles Heimsath has shown that Indian nationalism was not a unified movement and that there were many nationalisms of a regional character. While mass education, economic advancement and social reform produced a semblance of unity, Bankim Chandra Chatterjee argued that genuine unity meant stimulating cultural and religious loyalties at the provincial level; a grander coalescence required a revival of Hinduism. Extremist Hindu leaders emphasized this. Bankim Chandra Chatterjee, *Indian Nationalism and Hindu Social Reform*, New Jersey, Princeton University Press, 1964, pp.133, 139.

for a Muslim community identified by Muslim Personal Law would benefit Muslim women by enabling them to inherit and by increasing widow remarriage. But the move by other Muslim communities to emulate the north Indian Muslim community meant reinforcing their seclusion and increasing conservatism in the domestic realm, a characteristic which the Muslim community shares with other communities of the north.

Historically, therefore, the economic and social changes of the 19th century were a result of wide-ranging political changes. This historical perspective in the context of Indian Muslim women suggests that initiatives taken to liberalize women's role were not initially motivated by a desire to promote women's interests but to improve the image of the community and further its objectives. This is particularly true of minority communities whose concerns were more related to their perception of their self-interest. This survey of Muslim communities confirms that their attitudes and strategies were both a reflection of other communities but also dependent on the political, economic and social situation of the community.

# 3

# Education and the Question of Urdu

## Introduction

The introduction of new political and economic institutions under British rule in India made traditional education and learning redundant since it was no longer a useful prerequisite for employment or other economic opportunities. The new western education, limited though it was, offered potential employment and vicarious association with power by permitting access to the new rulers. Education represented a means of economic advancement "more subscriptions, more candidates for government employment, more lawyers to fill seats in councils and more political power generally", (Rudolph, 1972:200) This change of attitude towards education from learning and scholarship to its ability to provide cash returns — "it remained virtually the only way by which individuals could partially dissociate themselves from traditional society and enter the small but relatively lucrative number of posts open to natives" (Foster, 1968:64,65) — was reflected in many colonial societies.

This chapter discusses the changes in attitude to education and the consequent politicization of the issue. (Brass, 1974; Bahadur, 1954; Thorpe, 1965) For women at the end of the 19th century, professional or government employment was not an option, and the progress of education for women of all communities was quite slow and dependent on regional norms. Since formal women's education came in the late 19th century, general Muslim acceptance of western education had already paved the way for it. Considerable regional differentiation characterized Muslim educational levels for men and women. This differentiation was a result of regional development and variations in the occupational patterns of different Muslim communities. In regions other than Punjab, Kashmir and Bengal they were not represented evenly throughout the socio-economic stratum and were, therefore, not always logical participants in western education. In the Muslim majority states of Kashmir and Bengal they were mainly agriculturists, and it is therefore difficult to form an accurate picture of Muslim education as a whole. For our purposes however, the debates, the emphasis on Urdu as a mode of differentiation, and the extent of Muslim women's participation in western education despite purdah, is of interest.

The issue of education came to be used by all communities and caste groupings to identify and differentiate themselves from others in the eyes of government. The opportunity was used to establish sectarian educational institutions with the twin objectives of encouraging community members to enter such institutions and to maintain group distinctions. (Rudolph, 1972:21) Within the Hindu spectrum, various caste communities found that separate educational institutions improved their social status, economic opportunities and group solidarities. In the north, Vaishya, Kayasths, Rajputs, Nairs, Sats and Ahirs founded their own community organizations and educational institutions; in the south and west, Ezhavas, Nadars, Mahars and Lingayats did the same. (Rudolph, 1972:21) Education was also the means by which the newly formed Arya Samaj tried to unify different castes and to promote pride in the new Hindu identity (Rudolph, 1972:21). In keeping with these trends the Muslim community in U.P. began to establish its own educational institutions to provide western education, while maintaining religious and cultural continuity. (Rudolph, 1972:183)

## Education as distributor of life chances

Before the introduction of western education in India, the criteria for achievement and success were dependent not so much upon individual ability or educational achievement, but on ascriptive factors such as caste, socio-economic strata and community. The introduction of the achievement criterion brought about a profound change in the path to upward mobility. After 1835, a deliberate attempt was made to introduce western education, with the twin objectives of creating a strata of people through whom India could be governed, (Bottomore, 1972:265) and for the propagation of Christian values. (Rudolph, 1972:16) Although this motivation led to some mistrust of the educational system, the acceptance of the system by the Brahmo Samaj in Bengal and its increasing linkage to employment helped to overcome most of the resistance.

Education had always been important to the Muslim community, not as a distributor of life chances, but for the propagation of Islamic values[1]. In the absence of a church in Islam these values were traditionally transmitted through the school system. With the introduction of western education, the traditional schools lost much of their educational significance, while the new schools provided pertinent education for employment, but did not fulfill the theological requirements of the community.[2] The initial response of the northern community to western education was hesitant, but the setting up of the Muslim Anglo- Oriental College at Aligarh combined modern education with religious instruction, and provided the required synthesis between tradition and modernity. The retention of Urdu was important, since it provided a link between different Muslim communities, and its similarity to the Arabic script gave Muslims access to scriptures. Urdu was also the lingua franca in U.P. at that time and gave the community an advantage in employment.

The transition to the new western learning was uneven among the different Muslim communities and depended on their specific resources and requirements. The concern for Muslim education was initially voiced by the British government in Bengal in the 1870s, which was seeking ways of neutralizing Muslim opposition to their rule. The government emphasized that this opposition was due to the declining economic circumstances of the community, caused by its resistance to the new western education required for employment. (Robinson, 1974:103) This focus on the participation of Bengali Muslims, primarily peasants, in western education was used by the Muslim community in Bengal (Brass, 1974:150) and elsewhere to get Muslims

[1]Clifford Geertz has noted that the Muslim educational system was important in the propagation of Muslim values; for example Indonesia, without it, would not even nominally have been a Muslim society. Clifford Geertz, *Modernization in a Muslim Society: The Indonesian Case*. R.N. Bellah, in *Religion and Progress in Modern Asia*, Free Press, New York, p. 96.

[2] The First Quinquennial Review of Education, 1881-1886, noted that ". . . Mohammadans are not so much averse to the subjects which the English government has decided to teach as to the modes and machinery . . . and the absence of instruction in tenets of their faith . . ." Superintendent of Government Printing, Calcutta, 1887, p. 312.

special consideration by establishment of special schools and curricula for them. Debates on Muslim education tended to over-look regional and occupational differences between communities and the politicization of the educational issue helped to keep alive Muslim demands for better employment opportunities. A number of historians have attributed Muslim separatism to their resistance to new education in the 19th century, arguing that it was responsible for their exclusion from employment, leading to their economic decline and, consequently to their separatist politics. (Bahadur, 1954:12) However, the minority character of the Muslim community in most regions should be given due consideration in any analysis of education. Their participation would reflect the distribution of Muslims in different socio-economic strata.

## Muslim education becomes an issue

Muslim education in India was raised to the level of an issue by the publication in 1871 of W.W. Hunter's report, *The Indian Mussalmans: Are they Bound in Conscience to Rebel against the Queen?* Since the report was written after the Revolt of 1857 in which the Muslims had been actively involved, and in the light of the Wahabi trials in Calcutta[3], the concerns voiced by the report reflected the desire of governments to neutralize Muslim opposition to British rule. One of the reasons for Muslim opposi-tion to British rule advanced by Mr. C.S. O'Kinealy, officer in charge of the Wahabi prosecution, was "the great hold which the Wahabi doctrines have on the mass of Mohammadans to the neglect of their education." (Hunter, 1964:111) Mr. E.C. Bayley CSI, Secretary to the Government, wrote: "Is it any subject for wonder that they (Muslims) have held aloof from a system (of education) which however good in itself, made no concessions to their prejudices, made, in fact, no provision for what they esteemed their necessities and which, in nature, was unavoidably antagonistic to their interests and at variance with their social traditions?" (Hunter, 1964:111) The report added that public instruction ignored the fact that education in the vernacular was despised by educated Mohammadans, taught as it was by Hindu

[3]The Wahabis were Indian followers of an Arab preacher, Ibn Wahab. They felt duty-bound to resist British encroachments on what used to be Muslim lands. They, therefore, indulged in guerilla type warfare and many Muslim preachers joined their ranks. P. Hardy, *The Muslims of British India*, Cambridge University Press, 1972, pp. 80, 83.

teachers. Moreover, the absence of instruction in Persian or Arabic was an important impediment since every Muslim was his family's priest. Private education among Muslims had declined due to the impoverishment of the elite after the Permanent Settlement and the 1828 Resumption Act and as a result of misappropriation of Muslim educational endowments by the government. The publication of this report on the Bengal Muslims, with its focus on their educational and economic decline led, in 1871, to a government resolution on Mohammadan education in which the "inability and unwillingness" of the community to take advantage of education was singled out as the chief cause of their backwardness. The Earl of Mayo regretted that "so large and important a class should anywhere stand aloof from cooperation with the educational system and thus lose the advantages, both material and social, which other subjects of the empire enjoyed . . . (*Fifth Quinquennial*, 1902-07:368).

The impression created by highlighting the problems of Bengali Muslims was that all Muslim communities were affected in the same way. This was despite repeated regional reviews of education which refuted such generalizations. As early as 1869, when the educational requirements of the Muslim community were beginning to attract attention, Mr. Peiles reported:

> I do not find reason to concur in the common opinion that Mohammadans repudiate education and avoid government schemes . . . they were suppressed . . . and practice the reserve of a people fallen from power, but the returns of various races of scholars will show that if, as is commonly held, Mohammadans nowhere exceed 10 per cent of the population of a district, then the proportion of them under instruction is not below that of other races, and it is worthy of note that they are found in greater numbers in government than in private schools. A distinction must be made between the Mohammadan cultivator who generally speaks vernacular and the town Mohammadan who preserves Urdu and therefore requires special education.

Education Commission, 1882:38.

Sir E. Gait pointed out that "the low position of Mohammadans is due largely to the fact that they are found chiefly in north-west India, where all classes are backward in respect of education, and in East Bengal where they consist mostly of local converts from a depressed class. In U.P., Madras and Central Provinces and Berar, they stand above or on equality with Hindus and the same is the case with Bombay, including Sind." (*Seventh Quinquennial,* 1912-17:198) Muslim educational statistics tended to include Bengal and Punjab, where there was a Muslim majority, but where Muslims were primarily agriculturists, which lowered their participation rates. (Rizvi, 1969:27) The Hunter report and the interest it generated was used by leaders of different Muslim communities as a rallying point for organizing the community to take advantage of the government's attention, and to press for inclusion of Urdu in the curriculum. The 1881 Quinquennial Review of Education noted that in those areas where Muslims had no special language requirements and the vernacular, or the Urdu script was widely used, they had no problems. It was only where special arrangements for instruction in Urdu were needed that difficulties arose. (*First Quinquennial,* (1881- 86:318) While Muslim participation in government run education varied greatly in each region, there was a general consensus on the economic decline of the community in most regions. Kingsley Davis, in analysing the 1931 census, noted that the Hindu-Muslim differential in literacy ratios (illiteracy was 93.6 per cent for Muslims and 91.6 per cent for Hindus) could be due to the lower average socio-economic status and their later start (Davis, 1957:153-154) in western education. In analysing the causes of Muslim separatism, historians have tended to cite Muslim resistance to western education as a contributory factor to their relatively poor socio-economic position. This had led to debates between those who regarded discrimination against Muslims in government employment as the primary cause of their poverty, and those who cite their inherent social backwardness and the machinations of British policy (Bahadur, 1954:8; Chugtai, 1974:245, 246).

A shift from education for the simple pursuit of knowledge of Persian or Urdu literature and religious purposes to education solely for employment required some adjustment. It was easier for those communities to whom it merely represented a change of language and did not symbolize loss of political and economic power, as it did for the Muslim community. The change in government had impoverished Muslim families and discrimination in employment contributed to reducing the value of employment incentives built into the participation in western education. "The impression that in the face of official preference for Hindus and others it is useless to prepare themselves for the service of government," (Chugtai, 1974:245-246) was noted by Lord Hobart as a major factor in the relatively lower participation of Muslims in education. The divergence in participation between the Muslim and other communities in education, therefore, reflects not so much a difference in achievement motivation but a logical response to the complex historical circumstances facing the community.

## The Urdu issue

No discussion of Muslim education can be complete without reference to the question of Urdu. The replacement of traditional Muslim schools with new western education meant that religious links were weakened, as were the links with Muslim communities in other regions. Urdu represented this link. In the north, it was the language of government and, as such, meant that Muslims enjoyed an advantage in employment opportunities. When the British replaced Persian with the vernacular language in Bengal in 1835, the Muslim elite was adversely affected; their training and skills were made redundant. (Robinson, 1974:36) However, in the United Provinces and Oudh, where Urdu was considered the vernacular language, Muslims continued to be in a strong position, both in employment and education. It was, therefore, with some concern that Muslims viewed the agitation for the replacement of Urdu with Hindi as the language of government, business and instruction in schools. (Brass, 1974:129) Urdu had been the vernacular from 1837; in 1900 Hindi was given equal status with Urdu by Sir A.P. Macdonnell, Lieutenant-Governor, who had earlier replaced Urdu with Hindi in Bihar. (Brass, 1974:156)

In the late 1890s, Sir Antony Macdonnell was in favour of bureaucratic reforms in U.P.; he was convinced that Muslims were disloyal to government and, therefore, of the need to limit their numbers in it. To do this he fixed quotas for Muslims by passing a resolution which made the knowledge of both Nagri and Persian characters essential for government employment. (Robinson, 1974:44) Hindu revivalism stimulated the demand for the introduction of Hindi and, increasingly, the Urdu and Persian script became identified with Muslim power and influence. Economic rivalry spilled over to community rivalry. (Robinson, 1974:69) "If Urdu ceases to be a court language," Harish Chandra prophesied, "the Muslims will not easily secure the offices of government such as peshkarships, sarishtadar ships, muhariships, etc., in which at present they have a predominance." (Robinson, 1974:75) It was the agitation against Urdu that specifically brought about a split between the Hindu and Muslim elites in U.P. (Robinson, 1974:83) They had so far collaborated on issues of mutual interest (Seal, 1971:308); the Aligarh Scientific Society formed by Syed Ahmad Khan had included among others, his good friend Jain Kishan Das who was secretary to the society. When Jain Kishan Das began to press for the establishment of Hindi as vernacular of the province,the co- operation on other counts suffered. In his evidence before the Education Commission of 1882, Das declared: ". . . It is impossible to make education general through Urdu . . . Urdu makes Hindu boys indolent and unthrifty . . . Nagri produces no such results." (Education Commission, 1884:229) In a memorial meeting members of the Satya Dharmolambini Sabha at Aligarh pleaded in favour of Hindi. An address from the representatives of the Mohammadan community in the districts of Aligarh and Bulandshahr and the Mohammadan Association of Rurk and Mizat stated that they were in favour of higher education, religious neutrality and the Urdu language as vernacular medium of instruction. ". . . Urdu is not our religious or national tongue, nor is it introduced here from a foreign country. It is a produce of India itself. It owes its origin to the joint action of both Hindus and Mohammadans." (Education Commission, 1884:421) As the movement for Hindi progressed it became increasingly identified with Hindu interests and tended to become a "communal crusade against Urdu language and Muslims in government". (Robinson, 1974:75) As this was combined with the cow protection movement it further strengthened the anti-Muslim stance. (Robinson, 1974:77)

In education, the increasing identification with Urdu was to make things more difficult for the Muslim community. The earlier Quinquennial Review of Education had pointed out that "wherever it appeared the ordinary vernacular of the country was Hindustani or Urdu written in the Persian character, or again, whether Mohammadans used a form of country dialect, there the Mohammadans occupied their proper position in the primary and secondary schools founded or aided by the state. But where, on the other hand, they spoke a language different from that of the majority population, or expressed in a different character, there the special arrangements necessary to meet the

circumstance have not always been organized, with the inevitable results that claims of the Muslims . . . were disregarded."
(*First Quinquennial*, 1881-16:311)

Evidence to the Education Commission clearly indicated the extent to which Urdu or Hindustani was being identified with the Muslim community, and its increasing acceptance by the community that this was indeed their language, even in those regions where they in fact used and spoke the local vernacular. While witnesses to the Commission had stated that Urdu was necessary for Muslims, in different parts of the country reports on education pointed out that:

> Mohammadans avail themselves freely of the advantage of the existing system . . . while the recommendations as to the peculiar linguistic conditions of the south ignore the extent to which Mohammadans use its vernacular language. Mohammadan schools have a special curriculum in Hindustani though the experiment of separate schools has not been successful and is not in fact necessary except, to some extent, in Madras and one or two large Mohammadan centres.
>
> *First Quinquennial*, 1881-16:318.

Mir Ansuruddin Sahib had said in his evidence before the Commission that Mohammadans did not go to schools because their own vernacular, Persian and Hindustani, were not taught. This ignored the fact that Muslims in Madras, as shown in the Commission's report were, if anything, ahead of other communities in both male and female education (Education Commission, 1884:316).

Similarly, the Bombay report of the Commission noted that while Muslims attended vernacular schools in areas of high concentration of Muslim population they preferred Hindustani schools (Education Commission, 1884:109). During this period there was a shift towards Urdu by Muslims in Bombay (Tyabji, 1952:72) and witnesses complained to the Commission that Muslim boys in the Presidency were not receiving instruction in Urdu. (Education Commission, 1884:109) In his evidence before the Commission, Badruddin Tyabji emphasized that schools must teach Hindustani for Mohammadans, and that Gujarati and Marathi were not suitable for them (Education Commission, 1884:505).

The report on the problem of Urdu teaching in Bombay

Presidency stated:

> ... sentiment may be guided, but it cannot be easily forced, and perhaps the national sentiment of a minority needs the most delicate handling of any. An interesting instance of this has recently been seen in the Presidency of Bombay in the shape of Mohammadan thought, that the children of the community must be taught from primary school upwards through the medium of Urdu rather than in the official vernacular of the part of the Presidency in which they may happen to live. The Mohammadan contention in its most extreme form is that Urdu is the mother tongue of all Mohammadans, wherever they may reside. But the fact remains, even if this contention is granted, it is absolutely essential for Mohammadan residents of this Presidency to be thoroughly conversant with the language of their Hindu neighbours.

The Anjuman-i-Islam founded in 1875 by Badruddin Tyabji, and the largest Muslim educational institution in Bombay acknowledged this in an 1885 memorial to government stating that two languages must be learnt ". . . if this were not done Mohammadans would be learning an ornamental language at the expense of a useful one. What should be aimed at really is to combine a knowledge of both, if possible, so that a Mohammadan youth should not merely be an accomplished member of his own community, but a useful citizen as well" (*Problem of Urdu*, 1914:1-2).

The report of the Committee appointed by the Bengal government to consider questions relating to Mohammadan education in 1915 pointed out that Urdu was needed by Muslims because access to knowledge from religious books was necessary for proper Muslim gentlemen (*Report on Mohammadan Education*, 1915:8). The introduction of Urdu would popularise education among Muslim boys and enable them to come to school at an earlier age since they felt it necessary to go to other schools to learn Urdu before entering government schools. The report was based on a conference on Muslim education held at Barisal in 1905. The conference also suggested the need for a special Urdu syllabus for Muslim girls (*Report on Mohammadan Education*, 1915:15).

In the Deccan region, the use of Urdu as the link with the

Delhi empire had been traditional but confined to the elite. In 1908 the Central Committee of the Deccan Provincial Muslim League presented an address to H.E. Sir George Clarke, Governor, stating

> Urdu is the mother tongue to the majority of Mohammadan boys attending elementary school . . . In all Urdu schools, the medium of instruction is Marathi or the language of the district. Urdu is being taught as a second language for a few minutes; this is an unnatural arrangement which compels a Mohammadan boy not only to begin his education in a language not his own, but also to learn two languages together at a tender age and this seriously handicaps him in his competition with non-Mohammadan boys later in his high school and college

Problem of Urdu, 1914:3.

The government report pointed out that many Mohammadans in the Presidency did not know Urdu, and those who used the vernacular complained that their children were being driven to Urdu schools. There was thus a difference between the use of Urdu by Muslims as a means of political differentiation from other communities, and practical considerations, i.e., the use of the vernacular at home and, therefore, finding this the most convenient medium of instruction. The report adds that the need to know the script in order to be able to read the Quran seemed to be the primary reason for this emphasis on Urdu (*Problem of Urdu*, 1914:3).

The Mohammadan Educational Conference, founded by Sir Syed Ahmad Khan in 1886, held conferences in different parts of the country every year, which increased the interest and the desire of the Muslim community for higher education. It also led local Muslim leaders to persuade provincial governments to take a greater interest in the education of Muslims (*Second Quinquennial*, 1887-1892:381-382). The Mohammadan Educational Conference espoused the cause of Urdu, and helped to serve the economic interests as well as the sentiments of the Muslim elites, since a defence of Urdu in the north helped to retain their dominance in government education and employment and maintain cultural cohesiveness (Brass, 1974:179). It also helped the Muslim community of the north to maintain its domination and leadership of the Muslim communities of all regions. It proved, as the Hindi agitation had already done for the Hindus, to be a useful platform for mobilising the community.

That this mobilisation appeared to carry all the Muslim communities is evident from the comments of a deputy inspector in Burma who commented that the future of Urdu is "... not all dark; symptoms of its progress seem to be looming on the horizon. Urdu, which was quite Greek to the people some five years ago, has now become a lingua franca in the Mandalay bazaar. It is hoped that in a very short time, it will be a home language among Mohammadans here." (*Eighth Quinquennial*, 1917-22:201)

With the advent of secular education the transmission of religious beliefs and culture became increasingly difficult. The desire for Urdu education was twofold: firstly, Muslims did not wish to lose touch with the script of the Quran; secondly since Urdu was identified with Muslims by proponents of Hindi, Muslim support for Urdu became increasingly identified as part of their traditional cultural heritage and, therefore, indispensable to their cultural baggage. That Muslims of different communities continued to use their regional languages and even educated their children in local vernacular schools despite their professed necessity for Urdu, and that Urdu continues to be important to the community was clearly stated by respondents during my field trips, the only exception being Trivandrum in Kerala.

## Women's education

The question of women's education in India in the 19th century was beset with difficulties. In the words of the Education Commission of 1880

> ... there is no demand in the case of girls and women for education as a means of livelihood and thus the most effective stimulus to the spread of education is removed. The system of child marriage necessitates the seclusion of girls at an age when their education has scarcely begun. The supply of teachers for girls' schools is both insufficient in quantity and inferior in quality. The school system of instruction needs modification to meet the needs of girls.
>
> *First Quinquennial*, 1881-86:278.

William Adam wrote in his report on education:

> ... a feeling is alleged to exist in the majority of Hindu females, principally cherished by the women, and not discouraged by the men, that a girl taught to read and

write will soon after marriage be a widow, and the belief is also entertained that intrigue is facilitated by a knowledge of letters on the part of females. The Mohammadans participate in all the prejudices of the Hindus against the education of their female offspring.

As one deputy inspector of education put it, "girls' education in India is carried out in response to a demand that does not exist". (*Eighth Quinquennial*, 1917-22:128)

Despite such unpromising beginnings, Christian missionaries and Indian reformers, concerned with the plight of child widows and child brides, began to strongly advocate the education of girls, with a view to raising the age at marriage and to enable young widows to earn a living. Initial attempts at establishing schools for girls were made by Christian missionaries in 1819 in Bengal (Edwardes, 1967:254) and the setting up of the Brahmo Samaj movement by Raja Ram Mohun Roy gave it intellectual impetus and credibility. The Bengal movement was followed by the Presidencies of Bombay and Madras, although in north India progress was much slower. In 1858, Sir Syed Ahmad Khan in his book, *Causes of the Indian Revolt* (Khan, 1970:24) listed one of the causes of the Mutiny as missionary schools, where no Sanskrit or Arabic was taught: ". . . it makes villagers fear the reasons for the school. Also, all the talk of female education is annoying to natives since pupils go about unveiled; such schools have actually been established in Bengal." However, in his evidence before the Education Commission of 1882 (Education Commission, 1884:286) he stated that, "In India, women are almost entirely excluded from education . . ." He urged that English and not vernacular be used as the medium for education and went on to say:

> I beg to say that the general idea that Mohammadan ladies of respectable families are quite ignorant is an entire mistake. A sort of indigenous education of a moderate degree prevails among them . . . the poverty of Mohammadans is the chief cause of the decline of female education among them . . . I admit, however that the general state of female education among Mohammadans is far from satisfactory, but at the same time, I am of the opinion that government cannot adopt any practical measure by which respectable Mohammadans may be induced to send their daughters to a government school for education . . . in fact, no satis-

factory education can be provided for Mohammadan females until a large number of Mohammadan males receive a sound education. The present state of education in my opinion is enough for domestic happiness, considering the present social and economic conditions of life of Mohammadans in India ... when the present generation of Mohammadan men is well educated and enlightened, the circumstances will necessarily have a powerful, though indirect effect on the enlightenment of Mohammadan women, for enlightened Mohammadan fathers, brothers and husbands will naturally be most anxious to educate their female relatives. There are even at this time, significant indications of this desire on the part of educated men ... Any endeavour on the part of government to introduce female education among Mohammadans will, under present circumstances prove a complete failure as far as respectable families are concerned.

Other evidence from U.P. echoed this. Raja Jai Kishan Das, CSI, said in his evidence, "Female education is for name's sake, nor can it be improved unless the education of men is placed on a better footing. It is on them that the education of women depends. The peculiar circumstances in which women of this country are placed will not allow them to benefit from girls' schools or other public institutions; neither is such a thing likely or advisable." (Education Commission, 1884:286)

In Bombay, Haji Ghulam Mohammad Munshi, Hon. Secretary, Anjuman- i-Islam, claimed that there were indigenous Quran schools for Muslim girls on every street corner and Muslim teachers could be found to teach Urdu and the Quran, but no Muslim girls' school was provided by government (Education Commission, 1884:319). Muslim female education differed from region to region. The *First Quinquennial Review of Education* (1881- 1886) pointed out that in fact the people of India at large encourage or tolerate the education of their girls only up to an age and in standards at which it can do little good or, according to their point of view, little harm. There appear, however, to be varieties of provincial feelings; in Madras and Bombay the desire for female education, however limited, appears to be steady and genuine; in Bengal a different view is expressed," *(First Quinquennial*, 1881- 86:279). According to the same review only 0.97 per cent of Hindu girls and 0.86 per cent of Muslim girls were attending recognized schools, and in both Bombay and Madras no Hindu or Muslim girl had so far passed the matriculation examination (*First Quinquennial* 1881-86:282, 284).

The Fourth Review of Education (1897-1902) continued to cite the resistance to women's education by all communities. It was noted that the education of females was attended by peculiar difficulties. Strict seclusion was practised both by Hindus and Muslims and formed an obstacle to the instruction of girls at school beyond a very elementary level. The strong incentive of material gain which had furthered the education of boys did not exist for girls (*Fourth Quinquennial*, 1897-1902:300). In 1901-02 there were only 44,695 female secondary students in British India which, broken down by community, represented 27 out of 100,000 Hindu girls and only four out of 100,000 Muslim girls. In the United Provinces, however, there were only four Hindu girls attending secondary public schools, compared to 28 Muslim girls. The overall enrolment figure for Muslim girls, including primary schools, compared favourably with other communities, in some regions indicating that the drop-out rate was quite high. The Review noted that two per cent of Hindu girls of school-going age were pupils in public primary or secondary schools, while 1.2% per cent of Muslim girls of school-going age attended such institutions. The proportion of girls under instruction varied from province to province.

According to Table 1, Muslim girls were, therefore, in advance of Hindu girls in Madras, Bombay, the United Provinces and Central Provinces and greatly behind them in Bengal and Punjab.

### Table I

Hindu and Muslim girls attending public schools as a percentage of the total number of girls of school-going age in their respective communities

| Province | Hindus | Muslims |
|---|---|---|
| Bombay | 3.7 | 4.0 |
| Madras | 3.1 | 5.9 |
| Bengal | 2.0 | 0.8 |
| Punjab | 1.6 | 0.5 |
| Central Provinces | 1.0 | 2.3 |
| United Provinces | 0.3 | 0.7 |

*Source: Fourth Quinquennial Review of Education, India, 1897- 1902,* Supdt. of Government Printing, Calcutta 1904, p 308.

Since the latter two provinces were the most populous Muslim states, and Muslims here were mainly cultivators, their interest in education was limited. (*Fourth Quinquennial* 1897-1902:308).

Early in this century the Muslim community as a whole, and women in particular appeared to be progressing somewhat. This was a result of greater government interest and the promotion of education in the community, as well as due to the activities of the Muslim Educational Conference (Mirza, 1969:8). The Memorandum of the Progress of Education in British India 1916-1926 (Memorandum on Education, 1916-26:55) pointed out that Muslims formed 24 per cent of the population of British India and though they were regarded as educationally backward, Muslim pupils were seldom under-represented. In Madras and U.P. Muslim participation was higher even at the secondary and collegiate levels; for both boys and girls in other areas Muslim participation was primarily confined to the primary levels of education (Memorandum on Education 1916-26:47-59).

Table 2 shows that for both Muslim males and females the percentage of pupils to population in the relevant age group had risen between 1916 and 1926, in all regions, the highest rise being in Madras, both for males and females. Noting the increase, the Memorandum commented that "in both periods, therefore, the percentages for the Mohammadan community were more favourable than the percentages for all communities together,

**Table 2**

Comparison of education of Muslims and non-Muslims
(percentage of Muslim and non-Muslim population with education)

| Province | Year | % of Muslim male pupils to population | % other males | % of Muslim female pupils to population | % other females |
|---|---|---|---|---|---|
| Madras | 1916 | 4.9 | 3.6 | 1.8 | 1.4 |
|  | 1926 | 7.9 | 4.1 | 3.1 | 2.3 |
| Bombay | 1916 | 3.1 | 3.8 | — | — |
|  | 1926 | 4.5 | 5.4 | 1.4 | 2.1 |
| Bengal | 1916 | 3.2 | 3.9 | 1.3 | 1.3 |
|  | 1926 | 3.8 | 4.6 | 1.4 | 1.6 |
| U.P. | 1916 | 1.7 | 1.6 | — | — |
|  | 1926 | 3.1 | 2.5 | — | — |

Source: *Memorandum on Progress of Education in British India, 1916-1926*, Calcutta, 1927, pp. 47-59.

and even figures for Mohammadan girls alone did not fall below the figures for all classes for female pupils. Even at the collegiate and secondary stages, the proportion of Mohammadans has been well maintained." (Memorandum on Education, 1916-26:59).

These increased figures were generally in keeping with the surge of women's education as the issue was taken up by the emergent women's movement. The women's movement which had so far made only tentative beginnings, organized the first All India Women's Educational Reform Conference (later called the All India Women's Conference) at Poona. In a speech the Rani Saheb Sangli declared:

> There was a time when the education of girls had not only no supporters but open enemies in India. Female education has now gone through all the stages of total apathy and indifference, ridicule, criticism, and acceptance. It may now be safely stated that everywhere in India, the need of education for girls, as much as for boys is recognised as a cardinal need of progress, a sin qua non of national advancement.

*Ninth Quinquennial*, 1922-27:171.

The *Ninth Quinquennial Review of Education* noted that the Muslim population of British India was 59.5 million, or 24 per cent of the total population, and on the whole Muslim pupils under instruction were also 24 per cent (*Ninth Quinquennial*, 1922-27:148).

Table 3 shows that although Muslim participation was lower than the average for all communities in all regions other than the Central Provinces, there was a steady rise of Muslim scholars, in proportion to the Muslim population, over the five year period. Muslim girl scholars shared this increase in Bihar and Orissa and the Central Provinces; the participation rate was higher than the average at the end of the period for all communities. Whereas in Punjab the increase has been a particularly dramatic rise in other regions, the rise over the period had mainly offset the initial backwardness. The all-India average for Muslim girls had surpassed the national average, and Muslim women could be considered within the mainstream of women's education of the time.

This trend continued in the period 1932-1937. The Education Review noted that it was able to report several positive trends; "the prejudice which has hindered its (education) progress in the past appears to be dying away" (*Eleventh Quinquennial*, 1939:148).

In 1937, as in other years, (Table 4) the proportion of Muslim pupils to the Muslim population increased steadily for both males and females, and exceeded their share, proportionately, of the total population, except in Bengal and Delhi. In Bombay, although the share of Muslim female pupils in the total female population declined, it increased as a proportion of Muslim female population, reflecting a large overall increase in the number of females under instruction. On an all-India basis, Muslims broadly retained their share in education. The review went on to note that Muslim participation increased in secondary schools and in colleges (*Tenth Quinquennial*, 1932-37:242,243).

**Table 3**

Percentage of Mohammadan scholars
(in recognised institutions only)

| Province | Year | % of all Mohammadan scholars to Mohammadan population | % of all scholars to total population, 1926-1927 | % of Mohammadan girl scholars to Mohammadan female population | % of all girls scholars to total female population 1926-1927 |
|---|---|---|---|---|---|
| Madras | 1921 | 5.5 | — | 2.3 | — |
|  | 1926 | 8.5 | 5.8 | 3.8 | 2.5 |
| Bombay | 1921 | 4.1 | — | 2.0 | — |
|  | 1926 | 5.0 | 5.8 | 2.3 | 2.4 |
| Bengal | 1921 | 3.4 | — | 1.4 | — |
|  | 1926 | 4.4 | 4.9 | 1.8 | 1.8 |
| U.P. | 1921 | 2.3 | — | 0.4 | — |
|  | 1926 | 3.3 | 2.8 | 0.5 | 0.6 |
| Punjab | 1921 | 2.0 | — | 0.3 | — |
|  | 1926 | 4.6 | 5.3 | 2.2 | 0.8 |
| Bihar and | 1921 | 2.4 | — | 0.9 | — |
| Orissa | 1926 | 3.7 | 3.1 | 1.2 | 0.7 |
| Central | 1921 | 5.2 | — | 1.4 | — |
| Provinces | 1926 | 6.4 | 2.8 | 1.5 | 0.6 |
| Assam | 1921 | 2.0 | — | 0.3 | — |
|  | 1926 | 2.9 | 3.5 | 0.4 | 1.0 |
| India | 1921 | 3.0 | — | 1.1 | — |
|  | 1926 | 4.4 | 4.3 | 1.4 | 1.0 |

Source: *Ninth Quinquennial Review of Education, Education Classes and Communities*, Calcutta, 1928, p 237.

**Table 4**

Progress of education for Muslim and non-Muslim males and females, 1932–1937

| Province | Year | MALES | | | FEMALES | | |
|---|---|---|---|---|---|---|---|
| | | % Muslim population to total population | % Muslim pupils to Muslim population | % Muslim pupils to total pupils | % Muslim population to total population | % Muslim pupils to Muslim population | % Muslim pupils to total pupils |
| Madras | 1932 | 7.5 | 9.7 | 10.9 | 7.5 | 5.1 | 11.5 |
| | 1937 | — | 10.8 | 11.2 | — | 6.3 | 11.4 |
| Bombay | 1932 | 8.8 | 5.8 | 19.4 | 8.4 | 2.9 | 19.8 |
| | 1937 | — | 11.6 | 13.7 | — | 6.9 | 12.4 |
| Bengal | 1932 | 54.9 | 5.4 | 51.7 | 55.2 | 2.3 | 55.5 |
| | 1937 | — | 6.0 | 51.7 | — | 3.0 | 55.2 |
| U.P. | 1932 | 14.8 | 3.9 | 18.6 | 14.9 | 0.8 | 15.7 |
| | 1937 | — | 4.2 | 18.3 | — | 1.0 | 15.5 |
| Delhi | 1932 | 32.5 | 6.4 | 30.0 | 32.2 | 2.6 | 23.3 |
| | 1937 | — | 7.7 | 31.0 | — | 3.8 | 25.5 |
| British India | 1932 | 24.7 | 5.2 | 26.7 | 24.1 | 2.0 | 26.0 |
| | 1937 | — | 5.5 | 26.1 | — | 2.5 | 25.6 |

*Source:* This Table is derived from Tables CXXIII and CXXIV of the *1932–1937 Review of Education* Vol. 1, pp. 242, 243, Calcutta 1939.

From this brief review of Muslim women's education it is possible to conclude that, while the community initially reacted adversely to its political, economic and social disadvantages arising from its political displacement, the need for expanding economic opportunities and employment helped overcome this hesitation in most regions. The push for male education meant that female education was able to respond almost in step with the education of women in other communities.

## Conclusion

The minority nature of different Muslim communities becomes apparent when considering Muslim participation in education. The appeal of education, less universal in the 19th century, was related to occupation and tradition, and could, therefore, only appeal to a small section of the community. Differences between Muslim communities engaged primarily in agricultural pursuits and those dependent on government or other employment are immediately apparent in their participation in education. Initial resistance to western education was natural for the section of the community most directly affected by the loss of political power and unwilling to give up both political power and cultural moorings. However, economic necessity carried its own logic. Kingsley Davis has related the educational differential between Muslim and other communities to urbanization and socio-economic status, noting that since the turn of the century Muslims had improved their relative position, and that between 1891-1931 theirs was the largest percentage gain in literacy among the various religious communities (Davis, 1957:154).

The issue of women's education at the end of the century was related more to regional norms and responses, and less to the needs of specific communities, unlinked as it was to the widening of economic opportunities. Muslim women's participation tended to follow this pattern while also reflecting the community's minority and socio-economic position.

# 4

## Attitudes Towards
## Social Legislation

### Introduction

One important issue before the Muslim community in India today is the legal rights of Muslim women. The reform of Muslim law as it pertains to women has been the subject of debate both within and outside the community. This debate has greatly intensified in the post-Independence period, especially after the passage of the Hindu Code Bill in 1956 which gave Hindu women legal parity with Hindu men. The Muslim community has so far resisted any changes in Muslim Personal Law through legislation, insisting that it forms an integral part of the Muslim socio-religious identity and is, therefore, unalterable.

The status of women in India was a major social issue during the 19th century. Governments, both British and Indian, were increasingly pressured by Indian reformers and Christian missionaries into introducing legislation which would strengthen the forces of social change. The legislation pertaining to women was not a result of popular demand, but it sought to create public awareness of women's limited roles and status. New legislation was seen as a means of educating public opinion and providing women with the facility to take their grievances to court, if they wished. Due to lack of education and economic independence, Indian women in the 19th century were scarcely in a position to take advantage of the new laws, primarily because social attitudes upheld by family structures did not encourage them to seek independent action. However, once the issues had been raised, Indian reformers continued to press their case and both upgraded existing legislation and introduced new legislation in areas needing change.

This task was complicated by the competition for education and employment at the end of the 19th century, and different communities evolved varying strategies to deal with it. A show of numerical strength designed to emphasize the importance of the community and stake its claims to education and employment was a common strategy. This process emphasized group differentiation by recalling past history, customs and traditions which revolved around the status and role of women in the community.

There were divergent views on the manner in which social change should be implemented. Community leaders, conscious of the importance of group cohesion, sought to make changes within established structures, while social reformers fought for legislatively enforced secular changes. The attitudes of communities to proposed legislation pertaining to women was that it constituted undue interference in the internal structure of the community and in religion, which was the sole concern of the community and outside the realm of government. Most reformers focussed on the status of Hindu women who lacked legal rights to inheritance and divorce and were subject to social customs which made them entirely dependent on family and male support. While differences existed between religious communities on women's rights, and Muslim women already enjoyed inheritance, divorce, and other rights, regional customs subjugating women were shared by all communities. The passage of 19th century legislation helped to pave the way for legislation in the 20th century. Reformers were helped in their efforts by the growth in the education of women and the emergence of women's groups and institutions. After Independence, the Hindu Code Bill was enacted, bringing a kind of pressure to bear on other communities to change their personal laws. The Muslim community has not done so because the unity of different Muslim communities under one personal law has come to represent a fundamental basis of their identity.

Initially, therefore, while Muslim communities supported legislation changing customs prejudicial to women, they soon came around to the view that Muslim women's interests would be best served with the restoration of rights under the Shariat or Muslim Personal Law, which had over time been superceded by custom and tradition. Muslim women's rights, under Sunni law are derived from four schools of jurisprudence: Hanafi, Hambali,

Shafi and Maliki (Levy, 1930:236-258). Shias follow a different set of laws, as do the many sects who follow separate practices, (Rothermund, 1975:7) depending on their regional environment in India. Despite the many centuries of Muslim rule, the community did not adopt the Shariat as a basis of law; women's rights in the Shariat were almost never complied with or enforced, and even their right to divorce and widow remarriage suffered (Andrews, 1939:103). Therefore, it was not till the turn of the century, when concerns for ethnic differentiation and identity had become important, that the Shariat was evoked. Women's groups, both Muslim and other, pointed out that Muslim women did have rights under the Shariat and urged the community to support the application of those laws to improve the status of women. Consequently, they supported the passage of the Shariat Act in 1937 and the Dissolution of Muslim Marriages Act in 1939. The enactment of both legislations was endorsed by women's groups as having furthered the cause of women. The basis for these enactments was derived from the eclectic approach adopted in Egypt and Turkey, which amalgamated the different schools of jurisprudence to favour women (Anderson, 1959:22,26). Muslim activists in India were influenced by Indian reformers and by social change in Muslim countries. Even as Muslim reformers in other countries were pleading for change, in India, Hali in his poem *Chup ki Dad* or Ode to the Silent, and Maulvi Nazir Ahmad through his novels, were stimulating the process of change (Nehru, ND: 23). The Muslim Educational Conference, in recognition of the importance of women's education had established a special section for women at the turn of the century (Mirza, 1969:8).

However, with Independence and the passage of the Hindu Code Bill, Muslim women's rights and status became an issue both within the community and with other communities, who now regarded it as an indication of Muslim backwardness and intolerable differentiation (*Towards Equality*, 1974·142). These sentiments have been effectively expressed by J. Duncan Derrett (Derrett, 1968:322):

> Muslims in India have as much need from an academic and a practical point of view, to have their personal law (or rather laws) reformed and perhaps codified, but the movement towards that end, skilfully led by able people, cannot get off the ground ... Even the excellent attempts

at reform of Islamic law in Pakistan have not evoked a response in India, and various excuses are given why the matter cannot be tackled. The reasons for this have to be conjectured for they cannot be determined by the simple process of listening to what people say.

Since the question of legal changes is central to the issue of the status of Muslim women, this chapter examines the attitudes of different Muslim communities to various social legislations enacted by government, by using their written representations to government as an indication of their motivations and of the concerns of other communities on the same issues. The similarity in views expressed by Muslim and other communities in the same region suggests that attitudes towards women's roles and rights were less affected by religious considerations than by regional ones, and even where religious reasons were advanced there was little dissension from other communities. The maintenance of identity was considered of primary importance by all communities; this was embodied in religious customs and practices which were maintained through supporting the traditional ideal of Indian women. Such concerns were expressed by all communities and were not special to the Muslims.

## Nineteenth century legislation

Historical evidence on the Kazi Act discussed in this chapter suggests that the process of disintegration of the organized Muslim system of law created a situation which was particularly detrimental to Muslim women. Though Muslim women had certain rights of inheritance, marriage repudiation, divorce maintenance etc., within religious laws, cultural factors evolved to make such rights ephemeral. This is particularly apparent when we consider the response of the Muslim community to social legislation, and the manner in which even when the Shariat Act of 1937 was enacted supposedly for the protection of women, their inheritance rights were curtailed in the interests of men and the family. This should be viewed within the parameters of the rigidly organized social structures in nineteenth century India which subsumed individual interests to those of the family and the community. Women bore an inordinate responsibility in the maintenance of the system as the controls on them maintained through early marriage, lack of education and inheritance rights were particularly inflexible. It was the plight of Hindu widows who lacked education or inheritance rights that hastened the need for change. The situation of Muslim women though not as difficult, had long been affected by regional customs and traditions (Rathbone, 1934: 23) and with the dismemberment of Muslim legal institutions their legal rights were further eroded.

Both Indian social reformers and government sought to induce change through legislation. Communities already grappling with political and economic changes tended to resist social legislation. They felt that they could do so without political or economic loss and that the community could only profit from political and economic changes through a display of numerical strength and organization which required ethnic differentiation and solidarity, based on traditions and customs antithetical to the exercise of women's rights. A brief review of social legislation and the response to it from different regional communities illustrates the above argument.

In 1869, a Bill was proposed to legalize marriage between members of certain natives of India not professing the Christian religion, and the opinion of different groups was solicited. The content of the bill brought protest from the Principal Sadr Amin of Calicut (19 June 1869) (Legislation, 1872:3).

> The Act of the Indian legislature in passing this bill into law in the present form would, therefore, violate the solemn promise by Her Majesty in her gracious proclamation issued at the time of the transfer of Indian government to the Crown of England. In the words of Section 2 of the bill, "Natives objecting to be married according to Hindu and Mohammadan or other religions." The legislation is not compulsory; but there can be no doubt it encourages natives to dissent from the established religions of India. Such legislation is quite incompatible with the avowed objectives of the British government in India. (signed J.K. Raman Nayar)

The Diwan of Cochin, Shungoony Menon, wrote on the same bill: "All orthodox Hindus believe their laws to be of divine origin and will consequently view with disfavour and suspicion any legislative enactment, altering or superceding, under any circumstances, the marriage rituals prescribed by laws." (Legislation 1872:3).

In reaction to the same bill, the late Principal Sadr Amin of Vishakhapatnam wrote on 29 May 1868:

The existence of the law of civil marriage in Europe can afford no justification for its introduction in India. There people are of one common religion, so that an intermarriage between different classes would in no way affect their religion. But here in India, where people are of different religions, marriages such as those between Hindu men and Mohammadan women would leave a man without any religion at all — he forfeits one and does not embrace the other. The extent of evil arising from such irreligious people being spread over the country cannot easily be estimated and such a mixture of castes cannot but affect Indian nature and society in a great measure, for nature and society in India depend much upon castes in the same way as European society is regulated by classes of people" (signed P. Srinivasa Row) (Legislation 1872:12).

The conduct of Muslim law during Muslim rule in India had been mediated through the appointment of a Kazi. The British government, having abolished the post of Kazi in 1864 (Kazi Act, 1880:2) left the organization of Muslim personal law, and the restrictions within it, to individuals. In 1880 Syed Ahmad Khan proposed that government appoint a Kazi, but on an honorary basis, so that the duties and ceremonies enjoined upon Muslims could, once more, be performed on a regulated basis rather than by self-appointed Kazis. The evidence collected for this bill throughout the country, quite clearly demonstrated the dilemmas of the Muslim situation.

While many Muslims expressed such sentiments they are best summed up by the editor and proprietor of the newspaper, *Khasim ul Akhbar*, when he wrote to the Chief Commissioner, Coorg:

There are now Kazis who receive certain stipends and emoluments from government for the exercise of their functions, but they have no power to enforce their decisions in certain religious matters, for instance in the case of divorce, maintenance, etc., since their office holds no good (i.e., is not upheld legally). Besides, as there are no restrictions placed from government, that only a Kazi properly so called, and none else perform the religious ceremonies and rites of the Mussalman population of any local area, there is no bound now to persons who have made it their business to encroach upon the prescribed duties of these Kazis; hence a great shameful irregularity has been in force, to remove which was the constant prayer of the Mohammadans (Kazi Act, 1880:2).

In a similar vein, a letter from Abdul Khader, Deputy Commissioner from Chitaldrug, dated 20 February 1880, pointed out that the Kazi must have official status otherwise "fail to see the name of a kazi being given to an individual unless it is just a personal title" — a strong plea that the office of the Kazi should carry some weight and not be merely titular. The duties of the Kazi were described by Syed Mustapha Sahib, district Munsiff of Dindigul on 3 March 1880 to include "performing marriages, deciding disputes arising between husband and wife regarding mehr or dower and divorce, performing various funeral rites for four days from the date of death and slaughtering sheep." (Kazi Act, 1880:3)

Another letter from Mohiuddin Sheriff Khan Bahadur, Honorary Surgeon, Triplicane Dispensary, dated 5 March 1880, pointed out the deficiencies of the proposed legislation:

> The bill prepared by Hon. Syed Ahmad Khan is extremely short and vague. . . . The Mohammadans at Madras are very anxious to make registration of their marriages, divorce and wills compulsory and have been trying to do this for the last several years. They have forwarded a petition for the same purpose to government three years ago (April 11, 1877) with more than 2,000 signatures . . . A dishonest and incompetent Kazi is a serious evil to the community for whose benefit he is intended. (Kazi Act, 1880:1)

A memorial from Maulvi Syed Habibulla Mufti and 122 others, in the district court at Ratnagiri, dated 31 July 1876, declared:

> Several husbands do not behave with their wives as the law requires of them. Several wives are shy to lay their grievances before government (public authorities) with a view to obtaining redress; they have, therefore, to continue their misery. It would be convenient to have a Kazi who may hear their grievances and grant redress. Some husbands are away from home and there are no Kazis to grant their wives to remarry. . . . It is further stated that while the office had been discontinued, the need for a Kazi

continued, particularly where women's rights were concerned. Other opinions pointed out that no qualified person could be got gratuitously. (Kazi Act, 1880:4)

The Kazi-i-Islam of Lahore pointed out "... certain evils in connection with marriage ceremonies, divorce and other matters are being constantly introduced in our (Mohammadan) religious transactions ..." in the absence of an official Kazi. Among the areas neglected were marriage of divorced women, where the necessary period of waiting was not enforced; marriage of minor females without permission of the guardian; writers of *talaqnama* or divorce were frequently not acquainted with the law. This was signed by 246 people and dated Lahore, 16 July 1874 (Kazi Act, 1880:4). It was clear that while the Shariat was not fully in force the official Kazis, paid for from government coffers, did dispense legal absolution in cases of marriage, divorce, dower, etc. Once the post of official Kazi was abolished, the community was left to having to make do with Kazis who had no official authority and who were perhaps less well trained and therefore carried less clout with the community to enforce compliance with some of the injunctions. This must have caused much hardship to women and left them vulnerable to the whims of men in the family.

Due to changes in legal procedure the implementation of women's rights had undergone changes and had become the subject of many irregularities, a situation acknowledged by community leaders. Concern for such erosions was felt by Muslim communities all over the country. A number of other sources have pointed out the lack of Muslim women's rights due to social conditions in India. Eleanor Rathbone wrote, "It is probable that through close association with Hindu neighbours they (Muslims) are gradually assimilating more and more social customs of the majority community. Muslims have abandoned women's inheritance rights in favour of Hindu customary law in Punjab" (Rathbone, 1934:61). The Census of India, 1872, pointed out

> ... the same may be said of Mohammadans whose long residence among the Hindus, and there being a considerable number of converts from Hinduism, keeps up among them most of the Hindu habits and customs with trifling variations. Indeed, except for the rules of inheritance, in her occupation and mode of life the Mohammadan female does not differ much from the Hindu, although among

Mohammadans marriage takes place at a little more advanced age, but the proportion in the age of the wife and husband is not materially different. According to Mohammadan law, a girl should be married at puberty; as far as I can ascertain Mohammadan girls are generally married between 13-15 years, the husband between 16-18 years. (Census of India, 1872:44-45).

The Census of India, 1901, declared

... Divorce among Mohammadans is, of course, permitted with the usual formalities and restrictions of Mohammadan law; but whatever the practice in other Mohammadan countries, it is most exceptional in these provinces. In practice it is made impossible by the enormous dowers promised at marriage which have to be paid if a woman is divorced, and in consequence of a law suit in which this appeared to be a hardship, opinions were collected as to the advisability of allowing courts to reduce a promised dower when it was excessive. The unanimity with which the proposal was condemned by all classes of Mohammadans showed that the restrictions on dower were recognized as beneficial. The feeling among Muslim communities was, therefore, that due to the accretion of customary laws the rights of Muslim women had been eroded. However, there was no clear consensus within the community on how this could be redressed — it appeared to be just one of the many problems in which the community found itself. However, they have formed associations which were alert to the possibilities of moderating government's legislative moves by representing Muslim interest; their objective appeared to be to represent ideal Islamic rules and create an awareness among Muslims and government of those rules. (Census of India, 1901:120)

This concern was demonstrated by two letters, one from the Mohammadan Literary Society in Calcutta and the other from the Central National Mohammadan Association on the contents of the Guardian and Wards Act of 1890. These stated that while there was nothing intrinsically objectionable about the bill, Muslim law had already prescribed the rule of guardianship and any interference or reference of Muslim cases to government judges would be regarded as a departure from the principle of non-interference in religious laws recognized by the British government (Guardians Act, 1890). The bill was seeking to regulate the relationship between guardians and wards and has since been used in India. At that time the Muslim community did not object to the law being uniformly applied to all communities, a stand they were to take later.

When Act X of 1891 was proposed to amend the Indian Penal Code and the code of criminal procedure of 1882 in order to raise the age at cohabitation from 10 to 12 years, even for husbands, there were objections from other communities on grounds of custom and lack of usage, but Muslims in the main supported the bill. Maulvi Abdul Jabbar, Deputy Magistrate and Deputy Collector, Alipore, wrote to the Chief Secretary, Government of Bengal, "The existing law has already introduced a change in the penal system of Mohammadans . . . age of consent provided in section 375 of Indian Penal Code raised the limit to 10 years. The Mohammadans will, therefore, not regard the amendment as a novelty" (Act X, 1891:16). The bill was supported by Nawab Abdul Latif, Secretary to the Muhammadan Literary Society and by Syed Ahmad Khan, member, Legislative Council (Act X, 1891:16).

The bill was a result of the efforts of Hindu reformers in Bombay, and particularly of Bahramji Malabari, a Parsi gentleman (1853-1912) who wrote a pamphlet entitled, *Notes on Infant Marriages and Enforced Widowhood*, and took his campaign for a legislative change to London, finally persuading government to introduce the bill (Underwood, 1930:112). There were two petitions from women's groups in favour of the bill. One was from the Aryan Ladies' Association of Poona which was signed by 65 Hindu ladies and 23 Bene Israel. It stated ". . . We the women of India who number over 125,000,000, being immersed in ignorance, and kept almost all places in subjection by men are unable to open our lips and acquaint the government with our grievances. We, therefore, pray government will have mercy on us and pass a law whereby our little immature girls will be protected till at least 12 years from a horrible outrage" (Act X, 1891:32). There was also a petition from Parsi and native Christian ladies of Poona on 23 February 1891. In a memorial addressed to Her Gracious Majesty, Queen Victoria, Empress of India, they demanded the age of consent be raised to at least 14 years ". . . several doctors and Hindu and Mohammadan scholars have shown that their religious works do not countenance any such pernicious practice. The last social conference held in Bombay also passed a resolution against the present law" (Act X, 1891:33).

Opposition to the law came from Poona, where those opposing Hindu reforms had organized themselves. In their letter to government authorities opposing the passage of any legislation, they stated:

> ... however, Mr. Malabari who, being an outsider, does not fully understand Hindu Shastras and customs and has carried to England his groundless agitation against the social customs of the Hindus ... that the number of those who call themselves reformers is infinitesimally small, while that of the people who are proud of their religion and time-honoured customs (is) exceedingly large, it is the prayer of all such people who respect their religions that government should not pass any law interfering with their social or religious customs in any way.

It was signed by Ramashastri Apte Mhahmopadhaya, President, and Balgangadahr Tilak, Secretary and 2,700 other Hindu gentlemen (Act X, 1891:10).

Rao Sahib Rao Patwardhan, Officiating Small Causes Court, Nagpur, in a letter dated February 9, 1891, informed the Deputy Commissioner, Nagpur, of Tilak's campaign against the bill. In an article written in his own paper, *Kesari*, on 3 February 1891, and also in the *Bombay Gazette* of 31 January, 1891, he was critical of the efforts of reformers such as Mr. Justice Telang (Act X, 1891:15). His objection to the bill was supported by others, and Pandit Ishwar Chandra Sagar wrote, "I am not able to give (unequivocal) support to the bill; if passed into law it will prevent the performance of ceremony of *garpharhana* (Act X, 1891:37)." These objections arose out of a desire to prevent changes which would erode the traditional customs of the group and thereby affect their identity. Lord Landsdowne, Viceroy, indicated his sympathy for their aims when he noted "... with sympathy your endeavours to cling and preserve, amid rapid changes, moral and material, through which India is passing all that is noblest and best in Hindu character and traditions ..." (Ryder, 1903:36).

Thus, concerns for the preservation of identity through customs and traditions was displayed by all communities in India, including the Muslim communities, even when the customs in question such as age at marriage, legalizing intercaste marriages, etc., were already altering as a result of social and economic changes in the country.

## Legislation before 1947

In February 1922 the question of raising the age of consent came up again. The government asked state governments to solicit public opinion on the desirability of new legislation. The governments of Bihar and Orissa noted that such legislation would lead to public agitation and that this reform would be well ahead of public opinion. A similar response came from the governments of the Central Provinces, Berar and Bengal. Madras declined to hazard an opinion and Punjab felt it should be left to public demand. Only Bombay, U.P. and Assam supported the move. Early attempts to introduce the bill proved abortive until women's groups began to organize public opinion and lobby for its passage. Since they had been newly enfranchised in some provinces, they were better able to mount an effective campaign. The report prepared on the feasibility of the measure by government noted that the age of consent had indeed been rising not because of any law, but because of the difficulty of finding suitable marriage partners, dowry, changing economic conditions, the movement for the education of girls and boys, and the activities of the social reform movements (Age of Consent, 1928-29:11-12).

The bill was finally introduced by Sir Hari Gour in 1927. It proposed increasing the age of consent to fourteen years for married girls and eighteen years for others. A Committee was appointed under the chairmanship of Rai Sahib Harbilas Sarda to enquire into the acceptability of legislation. The Committee included two women, Mrs. M. O'Brian Beadon, an MBBS from London and Superintendent at the Victoria Government Hospital in Madras, and Mrs. Brijlal Nehru. It also included three Muslim men. One of them was Shahnawaz, whose wife was an active member of the All India Women's Conference and other women's groups. He had supported the bill when it was first introduced in the Assembly (Shahnawaz, 1971:97). The Committee travelled to Lahore, Peshawar, Bombay, Delhi, Calicut, Madras, Patna, Banaras, Allahabad, Lucknow, Karachi, Ahmedabad, Ootacumund, Madurai, Vishakhapatnam, Dacca, Shillong and Nagpur (Age of Consent, 1928- 29:17). A questionnaire was published in newspapers and the public were invited to respond. The social reform movement had had such an impact that, despite the feeling that religious sentiments were going to be violated, one member stated during the Assembly debate that ". . . if the Shastras and later marriage are incompatible, Shastras must go" (Gray, 1944:31). In commenting on the findings of the Committee, one member said, "Things are far worse than they are described in the report because we did not wish to excite or provoke unnecessarily the feelings of orthodox people." (Rathbone, 1934:23)

The committee's report noted that Hindu opinion was either progressive or conservative, and the latter would be against the legislation because of the injunction in the Shastras (Age of Consent, 1928-29:5). Muslim evidence was in three parts: (*i*) those who held that early marriage was no evil and that it was sanctioned by Islam, and any legislation to the contrary would interfere with their religions; (*ii*) those who felt that the spread of education and progress of social reform would automatically raise the age at marriage and that, therefore, no government action was needed, and (*iii*) those who were for the legislation (Age of Consent, 1928-29:5). It was the first indication of the present attitude of the Muslim community to legislative changes which were designed to cut across religious or communal lines. Few objections were raised on real religious grounds by the Muslims in their evidence, and it became clear from the Committee's report that Muslims shared many of the customs of the regional communities to which they belonged. In Madras, neither the Hindu nor the Muslim community practised early marriage; in Bengal both communities followed the custom; in Bombay there was early marriage for most classes except upper caste Hindus and upper class Muslims; in U.P., early marriage was confined to lower caste Hindus and lower class Muslims; and in Gujarat too, the lower age at marriage was confined to lower class Muslims (Age of Consent, 1928-29:53,65,36,80).

One of the primary objections to the law was on the grounds that it would interfere with the religious laws of the Hindus and Muslims; the Jains too objected to interference in their laws. It was argued, for instance, that among Brahmins and certain other castes post-puberty marriage was a sin and that the government was not justified in putting people of these castes in a position where they might have to transgress either the religious custom or the laws of consent and marriage (Age of Consent, 1928-29:33). The report noted that Muslim opinion had stated that the spirit of Islamic law is to let women have a voice in the choice of husband and that minor girls given in marriage had the right of repudiating the marriage on attaining puberty. Therefore, the law should apply to Muslims, since it did not breach any religious sentiments (Age of Consent, 1928-29:178,179).

The Muslim evidence, given by Khan Bahadur Wali Muhammad Hasan, Special Magistrate at Karachi, noted that since Muslims ordinarily married their daughters after fourteen years anyway, the community would be indifferent to the law, though orthodox opinion might raise objections (Age of Consent, 1928-29:39). Mrs. Tyabji in her evidence said she had not come across any Muslims objecting to raising the age at marriage (Age of Consent, 1928- 29:167). Yet Muslim leaders objected to the bill, while ordinary Muslim opinion was for it, though even the leaders did not pretend that there was a religious basis for their objection (Age of Consent, 1928-29:219-220)

Muslim leaders displayed the dilemmas that face a group using symbolic differentiation to promote cohesion, because such symbolism becomes not ". . . anymore the essence of the community, but the essence of distinction." (Dumont, 1964:45). The dichotomy between political religion and private religion is clear in reactions to this bill, because despite considerable testimony to the contrary, and despite the leadership's own support for the rights of women, (Age of Consent, 1928-29:102) and the active involvement of Muslim women in the Indian women's movement, the opposition continued largely because the bill would apply uniformly to all communities and Muslim symbolic differentiation would be wiped out. (Karandikar, 1969:184) Sayad Nawab Ali summed up the Muslim dilemma: he noted that government could make changes in consultation with religious experts, i.e., the ullema, and this would not constitute interference with Islamic law. However, he pointed out that changes could be brought about by consensus or *ijma*, which is allowed in Islam, but this was difficult due to the lack of scholarship and knowledge of the people (Age of Consent, 1928- 29:259).

The 1937 Shariat Act was passed to enable Muslim women to regain their rights of inheritance, dower and divorce under Muslim Personal Law. The object of the Shariat Act was defined as clarifying

> questions regarding succession, special property of females, betrothal, adoption, marriage, divorce, maintenance, dower, guardianship, minority, bastardy, family

relations, legacies, gifts, partition, etc. The rule of decisions, in cases where the parties are Muslims, shall be Muslim Personal Law, although there may be custom or usage to the contrary. . . . The bill aims at uniformity of law among Muslims throughout British India in all their social and personal relations. By doing so it also recognises and does justice to the claims of women for inheriting family property who, under customary law, are debarred from succeeding to the same. This bill in this respect does the same thing for Muslim women as my honourable friends Messrs. Deshmukh, Hosmani and Gupta's bill wants to do for Hindu women. (Legislative Assembly Debates, 1939:2528)

The bill, debated during the heyday of the Indian women's movement, aroused considerable public interest. By urging support for the bill the Muslim community could claim to have both furthered the interests of women and unified the community. The bill was endorsed by Muslim women's groups and this was noted by Sir Muhammad Yasmin Khan in the course of the Assembly debate, when he said

. . . The point pressed by Muslim women of Punjab is that being Muslim why should they not get the benefit of Islamic law. . . . In Islam a woman is fully entitled to share, she becomes the full owner of the property. . . . I hope that this legislation will come in her way simply because a particular custom prevailed which was made by men and not by women . . . no . . . person who wants that human society must live on the right principles of equity should accept those principles is so against the very root of the principle which gave the weaker sex a genuine and specific. . . . It would have been different if Muhammadan women were not wanting to have any change. (Legislative Assembly Debates, 1939:2530)

In a similar vein, Fazl-i-Haq Pracha, member from north-west Punjab declared: "Educated woman is coming into her own. The growing majority of educated Mohammadan men are supporting, directly or indirectly, her claims to more humane and rational treatment." (Legislative Assembly Debates, 1939:2539). But an equally important part of this process was the consolidation of Muslim identity, admirably articulated in the course of the Assembly debates on the bill, when one member stated ". . . this law is perfect . . . this is a sort of domestic law for us and unless we come under this law there is great danger of the Muslims losing their solidarity and national unity." (Legislative Assembly Debates, 1939:1823)

Members of other communities were too conscious of the significance of the bill. Dr. G.V. Deshmukh said ". . . this bill, which in principle gives economical status to one half of the society, has my wholehearted support . . . if today Mohammadan society progresses, in the future every society in India will follow the same example, not that in Hinduism the principle does not exist . . . the chilling hand of custom has barred all progress from society of womenfolk as far as India is concerned." (Legislative Assembly Debates, 1939:1826). The bill was edorsed by all shades of Muslim political opinion. Muhammad Ali Jinnah, then a prominent Muslim legislator, put it thus, "I entirely agree that these customs which exclude female heirs are to my mind unjust and not only unjust but they are keeping down the economic position of women which is the foundation of their development and rise, and their proper and equal share along with men in all walks of life." (Legislative Assembly Debates, 1939:1832)

However, while paying lip service to the cause of women's economic rights, Jinnah proposed an amendment to one clause in the bill under which the Shariat alone would apply to men and women "notwithstanding custom, usage and law". He wanted to change the wording to "custom and usage" only, implying that prior legislation would be upheld, even when it clashed with the rights of women. It was an important amendment because a number of Muslim trading communities had already legislated away the inheritance rights of women, (i.e., the U.P. Land Holders Act, the Cutchi Memon Act 1920) and without this amendment the Cutchi Memons, the Khojas, the Moplahs and the Baluchis would have to divide their financial holdings. The realization that the amendment would restrict women's rights of inheritance under the Shariat led to an outcry among some Muslim legislators and the President of the Legislative Assembly, Sir Abdur Rahim, declared,

> The object of this amendment is quite clear. In the provinces of Bihar, Orissa and Bengal, there is no custom or law standing in the way of Muslims regarding the application of their personal law . . . if you look at the opinions received on the bill. . . . Sir, I fail to understand what

remains after various amendments of my learned friend, Mr. Jinnah: the words or law? Wills, legacies, adoption have already been taken away from the bill to suit the purposes of a few people. The Select Committee exempted agricultural lands from the operation of this bill. In Bihar, Bengal, Orissa and also parts of other provinces, women are enjoying advantages of Muslim personal law and getting their full shares according to Shariat laws in all their ancestral property. . . . I say, Sir, the mover of the bill as well as a few of my Muslim friends . . . will have the only consolation that they have got the Shariat Bill passed by this house. . . . I don't like to be party to such a crippled measure which gives nothing but name. . . . I know the amended bill restricts the rights of Muslims in provinces where they are already enjoying full advantages of Muslim Personal Law. (Legislative Assembly Debates, 1939:1854).

The ullema, too, chided Mr. Jinnah for not supporting the bill initially and then amending it, but the amendment stood and the rights of women were made subservient to the rights of men (Mujeeb, 1972:95).

The Dissolution of Muslim Marriages Bill was debated and enacted in 1939. It was specifically directed to benefit Muslim women, and was compiled as an amalgam of the four schools of jurisprudence, picking the most liberal features from each of them. In proposing the bill, Qazi Ahmad Kazmi said:

The other reason for proceeding with the bill is the great trouble in which I find women in India today. Their condition is really heartrending, and to stay any longer without the provisions of the bill and allow the males to continue to exercise their rights and to deprive women of their rights given to them by their religion would not be justifiable . . . the rights of women should not be jeopardized simply because they are not represented in this house. I am sure if we had a single properly educated Muslim woman here in this house, then absolutely different ideas would have been expressed on the floor of this house. I know, Sir, that the demand from educated Muslim women is becoming more and more insistent, that their rights be conceded to them according to Islamic law . . . I think a Muslim woman must be given full liberty, full right to exercise her choice in matrimonial matters. (Legislative Assembly Debates, 1939:616)

During the course of the debate, Mr. M.S. Aney, a member from Berar, pointed out that by using the legislature to reform Muslim law, the law was being secularised and government courts should, therefore, be allowed to judge cases; there was thus no need for a special Kazi, as had been proposed (Legislative Assembly Debates, 1939:868).

Mrs. K. Radhabai Subaroyan, the only woman member of the Assembly, expressed her support of the bill:

> Mr. Deputy President, I rise with pleasure to support the motion moved by my honourable friend, Mr. Kazmi. I feel this bill recognizes the principles of inequality between men and women. It has been stated here and outside that though Islamic law lays down this principle, in actual practice in several parts of our country, it is ignored to the disadvantage of women. It is heartening ... to hear my Muslim colleagues condemn this state of affairs and advocate that justice shoud be done to women and that women should have the rights to claim divorce on the same terms as men ... it definitely raises the status of women and recognizes their individuality and ... human personality. (Legislative Assembly Debates, 1939:881).

However, opponents of women's rights put in a word of caution, indicating that there should be no clubbing together of Indian women as far as such rights were concerned. Bhai Parmanand states, "I hold it is the business of the Mussalmans themselves to make any changes in their religion they like. We do not want to oppose them and in the same way I expect the Muslims to remain neutral when purely Hindu questions are discussed." (Legislative Assembly Debates, 1939:885) This was said apropos the bill on Hindu women's rights to divorce, since he had declared on the bill's debate that "My real objection is that in Hindu society there is no room for divorce ... this custom has no place in Indian society. In spite of our advance, Hindu widows of respectable families are not allowed to get married again...women too have to live according to certain social standards. We cannot allow our women to go about and do what they like." (Legislative Assembly Debates, 1939:175)

During the same debate, Babu Baijnath Baijoria, another member declared, "In these days of so-called female emancipation, divorce has become a craze among certain sections of educated ladies." (Legislative Assembly Debates, 1939:182) Muslim leadership during the period of these two Acts regarded the Shariat as a goal realized, that it could not prevent the legislature from acting in a sovereign manner. It appeared that the Muslim community was willing and able to utilize the legislature for bringing about more changes in their laws which affected the status of Muslim women. (Brass, 1974:165) In pointing this out, Mr. Justice Ranade, one of the important advocates of change in Hindu society, had declared ". . . if we abjure government help under all circumstances, we must perforce fall back, behind Parsees, Mohammadans and Christians, who have freely availed themselves of such help in recasting their social arrangements." (Fuller, 1900:187) Since the Muslim desire to unite the community under a uniform law could so successfully be combined with improving the status of women, particularly at a time when women's groups were clamouring for change, the legislation was welcomed by all groups interested in the progress of women. It was not till the passing o f the Hindu Code Bill in 1956 that the question of the status of Muslim women was to come up again.

# 5

## Growth of the Indian Women's Movement and the Attack on Purdah

### Introduction

What may be called the first phase of the women's movement emerged in India in the 1920s; it had the effect of consolidating changes which had been initiated in the 19th century through social reforms, and of instituting further and more radical changes in the range and variety of roles women could play in society. It also provided Indian women with a platform from which they could function as a pressure group and influence political parties and government to support their causes. Their role was greatly limited by the social structure that enforced the seclusion of women, early marriage, and reduced access to education. The political and economic changes of the 19th century had induced a societal reassessment as Indian reformers and Christian missionaries combined to press for changes in the status of women, beginning with education and raising the age of marriage. These goals were to be greatly expanded in the decades before Independence to include political participation, and the fight for expanded social and economic roles. While the movement's leadership remained the preserve of a few political families, it nevertheless provided opportunities to a variety of emerging leaders to express their views and disseminate the message of the movement to women's groups. By concentrating on legislative equality it enabled the post-Independence movement to focus on economic and implementation of rights issues that were to animate the discussions of the 1970s and 80s.

This chapter uses the inter-relatedness of attitudes to purdah and the growth of the Indian women's movement to assess the manner and pace of change. Purdah is regarded as Islamic and seen as historically responsible for the limited participation of women in activities outside the domestic sphere. We will examine the religious basis for purdah and the involvement of Muslim women in the women's movement to establish the extent to which purdah may have impinged on women's activities outside the community. We also examine the extent to which the universality of problems faced by Indian women, irrespective of community, caste or class, made it possible for the women's movement to establish cooperation and consensus between women of different communities despite political currents to the contrary.

The status and role of Muslim women in India before Independence could not be significantly differentiated from the status and role of women in other communities; the difference was a matter of region, class and caste, more than of religion. Purdah, or the practice of the seclusion of women, varied in form between regions and communities; in general, it was more formal and restricted the freedom of women more severely in the north than in the south. Other customs which circumscribed the role of women were child marriage, enforced widowhood (which in an earlier period had even led to widow immolation), female infanticide and polygamy, but these were specific to castes, classes or regions, and not necessarily common to all Indian women. There was, however, a general attitude towards women which assigned them certain domestic roles and confined them within its parameters. Without education or rights of inheritance, customs effectively restricted their activities, and these elaborate devices for control reinforced those social norms which linked the honour of the family and community to the behaviour of women. Such norms were not confined to any religion, caste or class, and regional practices may be considered variations on the same theme. While Muslim women were clearly also affected, they continued to retain in theory, if not exercise in practice, their rights to property, divorce, widow remarriage, dower and the ability to repudiate a marriage on attaining puberty. (Census NWP 1982,93:44).

The initial attempts to bring about a change in the status of women came in response to the strictures of Christian missionaries. (Lateef, 1977:1949) Missionaries attempted to reach

Indian women through the school system, which they tried to set up as early as 1819. (Edwardes, 1967:254) However, since their primary aim remained proselytisation, their attempt to persuade parents to send their daughters to school met with limited success. The aims were discussed openly and the general Decennial Conference on Women went so far as to pose the question, "Are we to evangelise first and educate afterwards, or to educate first?" The conference also discussed the best way of converting Muslims to Christianity. (*The Friend of India and the Statesman*, 1883:59) Not surprisingly this approach created some resistance to western education, which was gradually overcome when early Hindu reformers in Bengal espoused the education of women as a means of preventing early marriage and widow dependency. (Heimsath, 1964:12).

It is interesting to note the reaction of different communities to the criticisms levelled by Christian missionaries against what were regarded as universal Indian customs and practices. Since much of this criticism exposed inadequacies in the status of Hindu women, most Hindu reform movements were directed at improving status through education, example and exhortation. Most Muslim attempts were directed at reinterpreting general Islamic tenets to show that Islam was not antithetical to minority status or western education. The attempts of Nawab Abd Al Latif and Syed Amir Ali in Calcutta, and Syed Ahmad Khan in north India were directed to this end. Communities also differed in their approach to the onslaught of Christianity and to the stabilisation of British rule in India. This naturally affected the way they later approached problems related to the status of women and foreign rule.

## Purdah

There has been and continues to be considerable discussion on the origins of the custom of seclusion of women in India. This discussion has varied from those who ascribe it entirely to the advent of Muslim rule in India, (Menon, 1944:4; Ward, 1963:478; Abhenanda, 1901:20; Mujeeb, 1972:XI) to conceding that some form of seclusion existed before Muslim rule, (Altekar, 1956:169,169,171,173,175) to attributing it to social structures which have reinforced the system. (Sorabjee, 1908:84; Fuller, 1900:36; Shridevi, 1965:33; Gray, ND:17; Nehru, ND:X) There has also been discussion and debate between those who argue that Islam propagated the seclusion of women, (Field, 1929:291) and those who contend that this was not the intention of the Quran, but developed after the Arab conquest of Persia where the practice was widely prevalent.

The sanction for purdah or the seclusion of women is supposed to lie in the verse from the Quran enjoining modesty: "Say to the believers, that they cast down their eyes ... And say to believing women, that they cast down their eyes ... and reveal not their adornment save such as is outward; and let them cast their veils over their bosoms." (Arberry, 1973:49) Maulvi Mohammad Ali interpreted this as an injunction against illicit relationships and not as requiring purdah, arguing that were purdah customary, and women "totally forbidden to go out of their houses" the above injunction would be superfluous. "Adornment" could refer to the body or to jewellery and "save such as is outward" to what is "customary and natural to uncover", implying that total covering of the body was not intended. Cloaks for women were to be worn, leaving the faces open so that they would be recognized and not teased or annoyed. (Ali, 1917:701) Tabari, the famous commentator on the Quran, described the conflicting viewpoints in the debate on the seclusion of women; should women be fully veiled or merely modestly dressed? During the pilgrimage to Mecca, women's faces and hands remain exposed throughout the rituals which, it is argued, reflects the intention. (Lokhandwala, ND:20) The intention of the Quran is perhaps better illustrated by the injunction that prospective marriage partners meet before the marriage consent is given, and the requirement that women share in property and manage it themselves. Both injunctions would require women to make decisions and control their lives, a function not associated with women in complete seclusion. However, since the interpretation of the Quran remained a male preserve, many theologians supported purdah. (Lokhandwala, ND:21; Maududi, 1972) As a result, restrictive social structures led to a complete erosion of the rights of Muslim women in the 19th century (Loania, 1934:34), greatly reduced their access to education, deprived them of control of their property, and ruled out divorce or remarriage, thus effectively undermining their economic independence.

The attempts by Christian and Indian reformers to raise the age of marriage through education reduced the inflexibility of seclusion in all communities. Different communities approached these attempts by realistic reappraisals of the effects of purdah and the need for internal change. In an article on purdah, K. Kalina Swami stated that the practice had been institutionalized into the Indian social structure long before the advent of Islam, and that there was ample evidence in the Ramayana, Puranas and Mahabharata to support this. Therefore, changes in this custom would have to be the outcome of internal structural change. (de Stuers, 1968:79; Lokhandwala, ND:; Gordon, 1968:7)

Muslim leaders too gradually developed the theme that purdah did in fact interfere with the development of women and that there was no religious basis for it. The Begum of Bhopal was in the forefront of the movement to educate girls; the prevalence of purdah prevented her from supporting co-educational institutions initially, but she was later to publicly repudiate the custom and deny its religious basis for Muslim women. In 1922 she reportedly wrote against co-education: ". . . to expect Muslim girls to go to schools and colleges with open faces or with veils on and with boys and obtain instruction . . . is tantamount to the death of their finer sentiments, morality and religion" (*Roshini,* 1946:11,92). Several years later, in a report of the All India Women's Conference, she is quoted as having said: "The present strictness of purdah system among Muslims does not form part of their religious obligations. The Mussalmans should coolly and calmly decide whether by respecting a mere custom they should keep their women in a state of suspended animation." (Kaur, 1968:26) Finally in 1929, when she presided over the AIWC session, she publicly and symbolically removed her veil, and a resolution against purdah was passed at the meeting. (Caton, 1930:123)

The emergence of the women's movement in the 1920s strengthened the movement against purdah and prepared society and women for greater participation in social activity. Anti-purdah meetings were held in many parts of the country after 1900 and women at last had a forum to express their dissatisfaction with the custom. (*Roshini,* 1946:28) These meetings were the outcome of groups already organized by women to lobby government on education and other social issues. In 1888, 800 ladies presented an address to Lady Dufferin, regretting her departure from India, which represented a departure from traditional seclusion and caste exclusiveness. (Cousins, 1922:53) In 1891, when evidence was being gathered for raising the age of consent for girls to 10 years, there were three memorials presented to the committee considering the legislation by women's groups, and some women also gave evidence before the 1882 Educational Commission. Education was seen as an alternative to child marriage and as a means of providing employment opportunities for widows who could not remarry due to prevailing social norms.

The earliest effort at organizing educational opportunities for widows was made by Pandita Ramabai, whose entire life was an example of the travails of Indian womanhood. Her parents were ostracized by their village when her father decided to teach his wife and daughter the Vedas, since women were not allowed to study the scriptures. Her father's training made Ramabai an authority on Hindu scriptures and later in life she could lecture and hold her own in any debate on the subject. From this unusual and controversial beginning, she proceeded to marry outside her Brahmin caste and, when she was widowed shortly afterwards, to devote herself to alleviating the difficulties of Hindu widows. She set up a home for them and provided opportunities for them to learn to be self-supporting. When she was examined by the Education Commission of 1882, she declared that the education of girls should be in the hands of female teachers and that " . . . in 99 cases out of a hundred, men of this country are opposed to female education and the proper position of women" (Chapman, 1891:19). After spending some time in England and America learning how to set up a women's home, she returned to Bombay in 1889 and immediately set about establishing the Sharada Sadan or widows' home. Her conversion to Christianity however, detracted from the tremendous success her work would otherwise have had, because it implied a rejection of religious institutions rather than their reform through internal change. Other reformers found it possible to work within the system and so retained their credibility.

One of the widows trained at Ramabai's home married D.K. Karve, himself a widower, teacher and reformer. Their marriage drew attention to the cause of widow remarriage and helped fight the prejudice against it although the couple were ostracized by their village. Karve was instrumental in establishing a Hindu Widow Remarriage Association to encourage remarriage. (Education Commission Report, 1882:438) He also founded a home and educational centre for widows in Poona in 1896, and in 1916 he established the only Women's University in India. His efforts, unlike those of Pandita Ramabai, were to prove that Indian society could be reformed from within. In this he was part of a wide circle of reformers working through the Indian Social Reform Conference. These included Ranade, Telang and Sankaran Nair. In the Muslim community, there were similar movements aimed at liberalising the role of women and decrying the custom of purdah. Purdah, it was noted, was not a religious requirement but "largely a custom, a fashion, a standard of respectability" (Karve, 1936:53) and was observed only by certain sections of north Indian society, although it affected all communities by its pervasive social effect. However, it was breaking down in the urban areas particularly among the educated in northern cities, while elsewhere it was no longer rigidly adhered to. (Fuller, 1900:83) The changes were confirmed by the Muslim Educational Conference which noted in 1930 that economic forces were working against purdah. (Caton, 1930:115)

While this process of emancipation continued, similar progress was being made in unifying the position of the community on social issues as a means of increasing political power which, in turn, could be translated into economic patronage for the community. The dual pressures on Muslim women were immediately apparent, for while the message to educate and participate in public affairs had been delivered, the appeal to tradition was being made to maintain community cohesion. The dilemma this posed for the community and women is evident from the conflicting stand on purdah. When Rajagopalachari addressed the Mohammadan Education Association of South India and stressed the need for women to come out of purdah, there was a storm of protest (*The Modern Review*, 1931:13) by the Muslims of south India to whom purdah had never been particularly important. They further regretted that at the Muslim Ladies Conference, Muslim women had allowed their pictures to be taken, and urged the Mohammadan Educational Association to give scholarships only to those ladies who would not overstep the mark. At the Mohammadan co-educational college in Madras, girls were required to wear their burqas and at Aligarh, male teachers sat behind a curtain. However, not all Muslim leaders found it necessary to support community cohesiveness at the expense of women. The Nizam of Hyderabad spoke out strongly against the custom as did M.A. Jinnah when he addressed Aligarh students. (*Roshini*, 1946:97) The desire for symbolic forms of exclusiveness continued because the need for such forms was based on modern social, political and economic changes and pressures rather than on simple traditionality. This was imperfectly understood both by the participants in the process and by the observers.

Attia Habibullah, writing in *Our Cause* noted that political rights could not be meaningfully exercised if women were in purdah and further that the extent to which women were in purdah depended upon their economic position, i.e., only the rich could afford to do so. (*Roshini*, 1946:99) Other communities had adopted education as a means of improving the status of women; the Muslim community followed suit: in Bengal, through the activities of the Central Mohammadan Association, in Bombay, through the Anjuman-i-Islam, in Lahore, through the Himayat-i-Islam, and in U.P. through the activities of Syed Ahmad Khan and the Mohammadan Educational Conference. Their activities focused on education and did not include women's rights because Muslim women already had legal rights which other Indian women did not.

However, by the turn of the century, the writings of Hali and Maulvi Nazir Ahmad showed a recognition of the fact that Muslim women had no power to exercise any of their rights, due to purdah and lack of education. The Mohammadan Educational Conference, established in 1886, passed its first resolution urging the eduation of women in 1888. It was not till 1896, however, that a separate section devoted to women's education was established to monitor the progress of their education, and only in 1903 did women participate in the activities of the conference. The Urdu publication for women was founded in 1904 by Sheikh Abdullah, secretary to the women's wing of the Educational Conference. The magazine propagated women's education, urged the removal of purdah and generally espoused feminist causes. These themes were taken up by Urdu journals all over the country. (Nehru, ND:23)

### Muslim women organize

By 1900 purdah clubs were being set up throughout India to cater to the new needs of Muslim women. They provided a forum for Muslim women to meet and discuss common issues — for the first time women were brought together who were otherwise confined to their own families. This led to an exchange of ideas, cooperation with similar groups and, eventually, a resolve to widen the base of their organizations and encourage each other to greater participation in social and educational issues. However, these women were generally members of families already involved in western education and in the emerging national movement, and thus had the support and encouragement of their families in undertaking these activities. In 1905, a Muslim Ladies Conference was organized by Attiya Begum in Aligarh, (Mirza, 1969:13) and in 1907 the Anjuman-i-Khawateen-Islam was set up in Lahore by Begum Muhammad Shafi. She also presided over the Muslim Ladies Conference in 1909. (Shahnawaz, 1971:25)

The activities of the Muslim Educational Conference, which met every year, had expanded to include Muslim women and expressly to encourage the education of girls. The Begum of Bhopal, who was involved with the activities of the Conference, made funds available in 1907 for the establishment of a girls' school at Aligarh. In 1914 she convened a Muslim women's meeting at Aligarh which met every two years as the All India Muslim Ladies Conference. (*Women in India*, 1935) At the 1914 meeting, the Begum of Bhopal was elected President, and Nafis Begum was secretary of the Conference. Its meetings were held in different parts of the country and managed to attract delegates from Muslim women's groups from other provinces. Mrs. Muhammad Shafi organized the Conference meeting held in Lahore in 1917; Masuma Begum, one of the Muslim women leaders interviewed in Hyderabad (August 17, 1977) had attended the conference held in Patna in 1918 at which her mother had presided. At these meetings resolutions on education and purdah used to be passed routinely. Her mother and Lady Afsar ul Mulk had organized the Anjuman- Khawateen in Hyderabad as early as 1901. (Zaidi, 1937:107) At the session in Lahore presided over by Abru Begum (Abul Kalam Azad's sister) a resolution against polygamy was proposed by Begum Shahnawaz, and passed. (Shahnawaz, 1971:42) The activities of this conference at Lahore were reported on by Margaret Cousins, who noted that at the Fifth Annual Conference of Indian Muslim women held on March 3-5, four hundred attended and Jahanara Begum made two speeches against polygamy. (Shahnawaz, 1971:50) The 1921 session met at Agra and Lady Shafi presided (Zwemmer, 1926:78); the 1921 session again condemned polygamy. (Shahnawaz, 1971:71) Apart from this inter-regional conference, many local Muslim women's organizations were formed from which delegates to the inter-regional conference were drawn. Among the many such organizations were the Anjuman-i-Khawateen-Deccan formed in 1919 (Cousins, 1922:6,103,105), and the Lucknow Women's Organization to which Muslim women activists such as Begum Habibullah, Begum Waseem, Begum Aijaz Rasul and Lady Wazir Hasan belonged. The Imperial Ladies Club of Allahabad was formed by Lady Sulaiman who was also President of the Hamidia Girls School established in 1925. (*Modern Review*, 1924:242) These activities, particularly those of the All India Muslim Ladies Conference, declined with the establishment of the All India Women's Conference in 1926 (Zaidi, 1937:118) which most of the Muslim women leaders joined.

The activities of Muslim women leaders reflected their concern for education, polygamy and even economic independence. In Calcutta Suhrawardiya Begum opened the Purdahnashin Madrassah (a high school for girls in seclusion) in 1913. A Ladies Health and Recreation Club followed, organized by Nawabzadi, Sarah Banu Begum, wife of a prominent Bengali politician, Hasan Suhrawardy (Shahnawaz, 1971:94). The leadership of the Muslim women's movement, as with the movement in other communities, tended to become identified with particular families; in Bombay for example, their activities were closely connected with the activities of the women from the Tyabji, Rahimtoola and Chinoy families, in Punjab with those of Muhammad Shafi and Abdul Qadir (Zaidi, 1937:107) and in U.P. with the leaders mentioned earlier. This list is by no means exhaustive, merely illustrative. Muslim women leaders were articulating their concern that women should exercise control over their own condition. Princess Durreshahvar of Hyderabad advised Muslim women to "... let your ambitions strive to remove the legal and social disabilities that stand in your way. Let your ability prove the supreme justification of that removal." (Zaidi, 1937:118)

In 1917 the Women's Indian Association had been formed in Madras, and drawn many women of ability into its fold. Sarojini Naidu was one of them, and in 1917 she led a delegation of its members to wait upon Lord Montague to ask for the enfranchisement of Indian women. Among the delegates was Bibi Amman, who had just attended the Calcutta session of the Indian National Congress at which Annie Besant had presided. (Zaidi, 1937:122) She was the mother of Muhammad and Shaukat Ali, both representative of the new generation of Muslim leaders who were moving away from conciliation with to criticism of the British government. Their attacks were launched through the publication of two weeklies, *The Comrade* in English, started in 1911 and *Hamdard* in Urdu started in 1912. (Zaidi, 1937:120) Their mother in turn had organized women's protest meetings criticising the government, particularly in its policy towards Turkey. She was joined in these efforts by her daughter-in-law, and the wives of other Muslim leaders. (Zaidi, 1937:109) She had also addressed the Muslim League on behalf of her jailed son when he was elected President of the 1917 session. Thereafter, she fully participated in the joint Muslim League and Congress non-cooperation movement. This was an agitation against British policies in Turkey which Muslims used to unite the community, just as they had done during the Russo-Turkish war earlier. It also provided a temporary alliance between the conflicting political and economic aims of the Congress and the League. (Mina ult, 1973:10)

## Indian women make gains

The disabilities of Indian women were listed by *Stridharma*, (*Stridharma*, 1935:305) the publication of the Women's Indian Association, and used to indicate the minimum change acceptable to women. Foremost among the disabilities was the lack of choice in marriage partners, the need to obtain guardian's consent to marry and husband's complete control over the wife, who could neither leave him nor dissolve the marriage. Lack of divorce rights, polygamy, and no rights to property were seen as structural limitations. As mentioned earlier many of these rights existed for Muslim women, but often women were powerless to exercise them. These issues were voiced on many occasions by Hindu and Muslim women leaders (Shahnawaz, 1971:50; *Stridharma*, 1935:184), particularly in cases of unilateral divorce, and polygamy which was prevalent in all communities. All women leaders realized that purdah was the instrument through which women were denied their rights and it was uniformly and routinely denounced. In her Presidential address to the AIWC, Her Highness the Maharani of Travancore, reiterated, "Under Mohammadan law the property and marital relations are safeguarded, yet seclusion of women (has) led to serious difficulties. Indeed in many regions the strictness of purdah is regarded proportionate to the status of the family, and much patient work needs to be done to eradicate such ideas." (Shahnawaz, 1971:184)

In commenting on a bill before the Legislative Assembly to enable Hindu women to inherit property, *Stridharma* noted that the princely states of Baroda, Mysore and Travancore had already enacted such legislation, while British India lagged behind and that Christian and Muslim women had better rights and status than other women. Hindu daughters were never welcome and the Hindu widow was always considered inauspicious and a burden. D. Bhagwandas's bill to validate marriages between castes, it noted, should be amended to make polygamy among Hindus and other communities impossible. (*Stridharma* 1935:3) The British government was extremely circumspect about passing any legislation which might impinge upon the religious sensitivities of any community and it was only when Indian reformers demanded any changes that some progressive legislation was enacted. This attitude was a result of the Revolt of 1857 which had been attributed to social changes brought about by the British, particularly with regard to women. This pragmatism on the part of government was condemned by the leaders of the women's movement. *Stridharma* noted that a British civil servant had had the maxim, "Keep your hands off religion and women" impressed on him by his superiors and that this accounted in part for the difficulties the women's movement experienced in having any social legislation passed. (*Stridharma*, 1936:173-176)

The link between social reform, the status of women and the national movement proved a source of numerical strength for the national movement and of political support for the women's movement. This mutually beneficial relationship led to considerable co-operation between leaders of the national movement and the women's movement. The fact was frequently commented on by women leaders to boost its acceptability among women, while maintaining the support of men for its increasingly radical demands. The Maharani of Baroda said ". . . a noteworthy feature of this achievement, to contrast with the experience of other countries, has been the sincere co-operation of men and the absence of serious opposition from the sterner sex." (*Stridharma*, 1933:12) Dr Muthulakshmi Reddi, founder of the Women's Indian Association, and sometime Vice-President of Madras Legislative Assembly, too, felt that

> There was no sex rivalry, no sex antagonism. The public, the press and the platform all co-operated with me and advocated women's cause and women's reform. Not only did Indian men themselves initiate the many reforms of women's uplift in their country, but also at every new step we took in public life, they continued to give their full

support, sympathy and co-operation. Indian women are
very fortunate in this respect.

*Stridharma*, 1934:102

This co-operation hastened the enfranchisement of Indian
women, because the support for each issue, either women's or
national, was seen to further the struggle against colonialism.
Sarojini Naidu's delegation of women requesting enfranchisement met Lord Montague, the leader of the 1917 Southborough
Franchise Committee. The committee, however, left the extension of the franchise to women to the Indian state legislatures
and Lord Montague commented ". . . the social conditions of
India make it premature to extend the franchise to Indian women
at this juncture . . . until the custom of seclusion of women
followed by many classes and communities is relaxed, female
suffrage would hardly be a reality" (*Stridharma* 1934:102). The
political parties, the Congress and the League immediately endorsed the decision. (Nehru, ND:353) The states in the north
where the seclusion of women was considered important, were
among the last to do so. (Gedge, 1929:8) Madras was the first
state to give women the vote in 1921; Bombay and U.P. voted
unanimously for it in 1923; Bengal initially defeated the vote in
1922, finally passing it in 1929. Also in 1921, sex disqualification
was removed and women were admitted to the central and
provincial legislatures. Travancore was the first princely state to
grant women the vote in 1920 and its example was followed by
Mysore, Jhalawar and Cochin.

Having won the right to vote, the women's movement next
turned its attention to the linkage of women's status as voters to
their husbands through property. Protesting against this, they
stated they were "against the elementary rights of women being
contingent upon her relationship to man". Indian women
pressed for universal adult franchise and at the Round Table
Conference in London in 1931 their stand was that "every man
or woman of the age 21 should be entitled to vote and to offer
himself or herself as a candidate at any election to an administrative or legislative institution". (*Stridharma*, 1932:413; Hauswirth,
1932:27).

The Simon Commission reported that

The Franchise Committee which visited India . . . in 1919
expressed the view . . . that the social conditions of India
made it premature to extend the franchise to Indian

# DATE DUE

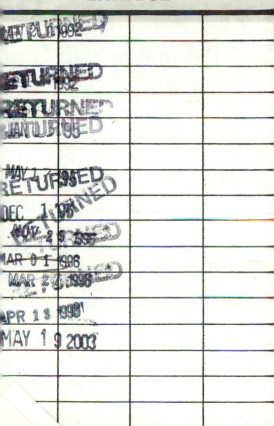

women at this juncture . . . If this advice had been followed a beginning could not have been made until now, and the request that Indian women should have some direct opportunity of influencing the course of politics in the land to which they belong would have remained wholly unsatisfied. But the claim was pressed by the Women's Indian Association and its allies and the electoral rules made under the Act were so drawn and a resolution was passed in favour of removing the sex disqualification; this should become an operative decision and a corresponding facility was conferred on both houses of the Indian legislature.

Hauswirth, 1932:27

The Indian women's movement was also seen by the Commission as the possible "key of progress" for an India free of communalism. (Women's Indian Association Report, 1933-34:2) The Commission stated in its report,

Except for a mention of the obstacles which social customs set up in the way of female education, there is hardly any reference in the Montague-Chelmsford report to the women of India. It is a striking proof of the change which has come over the Indian scene in the last twelve years that no document discussing India's constitutional development and directions, which can be developed and improved, could omit the women of India today.

Rathbone, 1934:85

British women members of Parliament supported the efforts of Indian women—they demanded that they be allowed into the Indian provincial upper chambers, that the franchise be extended to all adults in urban areas and, in the meantime, that the wives of all male voters be given the vote. *Stridharma*, commenting on this support, thanked Miss Rathbone, Lady Hartog, Mrs. Lankester, Miss Agatha Harrison and Miss Ward for their efforts on behalf of Indian women, despite the fact that these did not quite match the demands made. (Report of the Indian Statutory Commission:49) These demands had been outlined at the Ninth Annual Conference of the All India Women's Conference (*Stridharma*,1935:371), and had unequivocally stated that any declaration of rights should remove sex disability. Women should be admitted to the upper chamber of provincial councils and the literacy qualification for voting should be universal, not just applicable to women. They also rejected, in principle, the reservation of seats but, if that were the expedient adopted for the allocation of seats, it should be extended to the Assembly. These demands were endorsed by the Women's Indian Association and the National Council of Women.

One of the noteworthy features of the Indian women's movement was the co-operation and unity which existed between women of different communities on issues specific to women despite the unbridgeable political differences which separated the men of their communities. Margaret Cousins' Presidential address at the Mysore State Women's Conference, listing women leaders, mentioned the Begum of Bhopal, Mrs. Annie Besant, Mrs. Sarojini Naidu, Lady Mirza Ismail, Dr. Muthulakshmi Reddi, and Kamaladevi Chattopadhyaya, a mixture of many communities. (*Stridharma*, 1935:128-132) Lady Lytton noted that there was great cooperation between all Indian women, whether Hindu, Muslim, Parsi or Christian. (*Stridharma*, 1935:104,129) Begum Shahnawaz believed that Indian unity was only possible through its women, and in a message to south Indian women said ". . . let us join together to work for the uplift of Indian women." (Edib, 1937:47). The All India Women's Conference, the Women's Indian Association and the National Council of Women presented a joint memorandum to the Indian Franchise Committee and sent their representatives to give evidence before the Committee. These included Dr Reddi, Mrs. Hamid Ali, Begum Habibullah, Rajkumari Amrit Kaur and Lakshmi Menon. They spoke in support of joint electorates for women and when, despite their united stand, the White Paper on the Indian Constitution proposed to divide women into communal constituencies, the three women's organizations met in Bombay and sent a telegram to the British Prime Minister deploring separate electorates. The telegram was signed by Sarojini Naidu and Begum Shahnawaz (*Stridharma*, 1934:379), and the Indian Franchise Committee reported that ". . . in every province women, including some in strict purdah, came forward as witnesses, either representing organizations or individually, asking for an extension of opinion to the contrary, written or oral, from the women themselves. (Lateef, 1977:1949) Margaret Cousins reporting on the Karachi session of the AIWC, noted that Muslim women held the trump card and could have walked out of the meeting if they had not agreed on a resolution calling for joint electorates, but they did not. Among the Muslim delegates to the conference were Lady Hidayatullah, Mrs. Tyabji, Mrs. Haroon, Mrs. Hamid Ali and Miss Ferojuddin. (Rathbone, 1934:84) This spirit of joint action on women's issues was repeatedly demonstrated. Muslim women in Madras were members of both the Madras Muslim Ladies Association, formed in 1928, and of the Women's Indian Association. (*Stridharma*, 1935:228)

In Madras, the activities of the Women's Indian Association and the Muslim Ladies Association could be co-ordinated because the leaders of the Muslim Ladies Association were also members of the Women's Indian Association. Dr. Muthulakshmi Reddi participated fully in the activities of the Muslim Ladies Association and the two groups jointly collaborated in mobilizing women in the Presidency to influence government policy. (*Stridharma*, 1932:428) The 1933-34 Annual Report indicates that Mrs. Nazir Hussain and Begum Rehmatunissa of the Muslim Ladies Association were on the Executive Committee of the Women's Indian Association, a flourishing organization with 23 centres and 4,000 members. (*Stridharma*, 1934:533)

At the seventh session of the Madras Constituent Conference of Women on Education and Social Reform, Lady Mirza Ismail emphasized the non-communal interests of women. Half the conference delegates were Muslim women who had advocated Swadeshi and Hindu-Muslim unity. (Gedge, 1929:7) On 30 August and 10 September 1932, meetings were held in Madras to deplore the communal differentiation of female electorates. Mrs. Nazir Husain moved the resolution on the use of swadeshi or indigenous cloth. At the Round Table Conference in 1931, women asked only for adult franchise and Begum Shahnawaz declared that whatever men might do, women stood united. (*Stridharma*, 1932:1,14,17) In the same vein, the Bombay Presidency Social Reform Association pointed out that while Hindu castes divided the Hindu community, thus ruling out Hindu-Muslim unity, women leaders of the AIWC belonged to all religions and were both progressive and united. (Hauswirth, 1932:191,227)

The interests of the women's movement were far-ranging. All government policies and legislative action were closely scrutinized and they were able to influence economic and social legislation through their interest and forceful recommendations. This was particularly effective with the Factories Act passed in July 1934, which incorporated many of the suggestions of the AIWC and the Women's Indian Association. (*Social Reform Annual*, 1938:19-20) They supported the rights of women to limit their families and proposed that girls' education be compulsory and free. One of their great successes was increasing the age of marriage through the passage of the Child Marriage Act of 1929. They publicized the issue and educated public opinion in its favour. After its passage, they tried to ensure its implementation by setting up the Sarda Act Committee (*Stridharma*, 1934:536) with chapters throughout the country and they resisted attempts to neutralize its provisions through subsequent amendments. (*Stridharma*, 1932:73) In these and other efforts, the women's movement had the support of the British women's movement, particularly through Eleanor Rathbone, a British Member of Parliament. She and twelve British women's associations lobbied the British parliament against dividing Indian women's electorates communally.

The widely held belief of the time was that Muslim women already enjoyed a number of legal rights granted through their personal laws, and that an improvement in their status was merely a matter of restoring rights eroded through social custom. This was frequently referred to by Hindu and Muslim women leaders. In her presidential address to the AIWC in Lucknow in 1932, Mrs. Hamid Ali urged a solution for the disabilities of Hindu women and the reinstatement of Muslim law to improve the status of Muslim women, which was more equitable than customary law. Among the resolutions passed at the conference were compulsory primary education for girls, urging all parents, particularly Muslim parents, to facilitate their daughters' higher education. They protested against communal electorates for women. They supported the anti-untouchability bill and deplored the prevalence of unilateral divorce among Muslim men, a practice not in accordance with Islamic teaching. They demanded the abolition of all disabilities affecting the rights of women in inheritance, and the recognition of Muslim women's right of divorce by the British courts. (Rathbone, 1934:52) The final AIWC meeting before independence was held at Akela in Berar in 1946, and was attended by many Muslim women. Speeches were made by Princess Durreshahvar of Hyderabad and Masuma Begum, and resolutions passed on communal unity. (*Stridharma*, 1933:56) In the 1935 *Who's Who* of Indian Women only 24 of the 500 women leaders were Muslim. Though Muslim names from all regions were mentioned it can by no means be considered a complete list and many of those mentioned belonged to the same family. Many prominent names from U.P., Calcutta and Madras were omitted. (*Stridharma*, 1932:171- 186). However, even from this limited list, it is clear that Muslim women participated and supported the Indian women's movement. Their collaboration and co-operation continued even as the political chasm widened between the Hindu and Muslim communities.

After 1935, the mobilisation of Muslim women was undertaken by the Muslim League, which somewhat belatedly set up a women's wing. (*Who's Who*, 1935) An all-India Muslim Women's Conference was held in Lahore and presided over by Lady Fazli Hussain. The meeting was attended by 500 women who demanded that customary law be done away with and that Muslim women be accorded their rights according to Muslim Personal Law. Twelve women's committees or anjumans were formed in different parts of the country. (*Stridharma*, 1936:144)

## Feminists after all

Despite the protestations of leaders of the women's movement that they owed their position to men, they were not deterred from making radical demands and they attacked many of the values long cherished in Indian society. Once organized they never lost sight of their goals; they utilized their advantageous position in providing the national movement with broad-based support to wring concessions from political parties while using the support of political parties to obtain concessions from government. The realization that the national movement needed their support provided a leverage which they were quick to use; to link feminist aims to nationalistic aims legitimized their claims. Opposing a foreign government, wresting concessions from it, added lustre to the campaign whether it was a specifically male or female cause. An important factor in the linkage between the feminist and nationalist movements was the familial connection between some male national leaders and key feminists. This speeded the transmission of ideas and the assurance of male support for feminist causes.

Indian feminist rhetoric appeared undaunted by centuries of structural suppression, and was openly and ruthlessly critical of traditions which had assisted this process. At the Alwaye Union Christian College Conference, Mrs. Kalpini Kutti Amma declared, "Modern women will reverence not a Sri Rama who so grievously wronged his devoted wife, but a Raja Ram Mohun Roy, a Lenin or Jawaharlal Nehru." (Shaukat Ali, 1975:66-68)

Begum Shahnawaz Khan, the only woman member of the Third Round Table Conference, speaking at a city dinner in London, said, "Your dictionary describes woman as the better half, in Russia she is the sweeter half. I have yet to discover the dictionary that describes her as the equal half." (*Stridharma*, 1934,271) Chiding the Banaras Hindu University for not allowing women to study the *Karma Kanda* Vedas because they could not become priests, *Roshini*, the magazine of the AIWC, declared, "Men cannot have babies. Does that mean they should not study gynaecology?" (*Stridharma*, 1932:190). In another article *Roshini* commented on Gandhi's article on women, where he had advocated that women ". . . should raise their status through renunciation". *Roshini* declared, "Indian women have a long tradition of renunciation and it has not got us anywhere; we want our rights to improve our status." (*Roshini*, 1946:1)

Mrs. Kamaladevi Chattopadhyaya, a radical feminist, regretted in her Presidential address to the AIWC (7 April 1944), that

> . . . the women's movement is essentially a social movement, and part of the process of enabling a constituent part of society to adjust itself to the constantly changing social and economic conditions and trying to influence these changes and conditions with a view to (merely) minimizing irritations and conflicts . . . Woman power is basic and the woman must be recognized as a social and economic factor on her own and not as assistant to man. Little recognized are the labours of the housewife, she is as much of a working woman as a factory worker — her hours are unlimited and her tools countless, but the non-pecuniary and non-competitive character has lowered the prestige of women's work and role. It is time society recognized that every housewife supports herself by the social labours she performs. Correctly viewed and rightly interpreted, the women's movement is found resting on a scientific basis shaped by a rational ideology and indispensable in the social scheme of things . . . indivisibly linked with economic independence is a woman's sexual independence. (*Roshini*,1946:4)

In an article on the Indian women's movement, Rajkumari Amrit Kaur wrote

> . . . the proper status of women in modern society should,

therefore, be settled not in the light of history but of ethics. It must accord not with the past, but with the general moral ideal which is current at the present time. The treatment of women must be on a level with the general conception of conduct and behaviour which each society seeks to realize . . . therefore, when we women of India today desire a change in outlook as far as our status is concerned, we cannot be criticized, because in every age we have to make the appropriate social venture and we cannot find readymade clothes in the past.

Meherally, 1947:90-92

In 1929, the Junior Maharani of Travancore, presiding at the Calcutta session of the AIWC, stated

> The great difficulty in the way of Indian progress is the divorce between conviction and practice which has been so marked in the past . . . many an ardent social reformer while eloquent on the public platform is perhaps apt to abate his zeal to weaken his advocacy when in his own environment, and he ascribes his feebleness in action mainly to his wife, mother or grandmother . . . we have to make it impossible for men to invoke our name as stumbling blocks to progress . . . it can only be done by a rapid and comprehensive programme of women's education.

Thomas, 1964:31

With independence in sight, the AIWC strategists realized the necessity of preparing and presenting a comprehensive legal and economic plan so that the future Indian government could not overlook their requirements and claims. (*Stridharma*, 1933:236) A Committee was appointed under Kitty Shiva Rao to undertake a survey of changes desired in Hindu law for women. They also drafted an Indian Women's Charter of Rights and Duties which listed fundamental rights which women expected under the new constitution. (Underwood, 1930:119,120) These were: equality before law; no disability due to religion, caste, creed or sex, in public employment, power or dishonour, and in exercise of trade or calling; adult franchise; no difference in education; free health services; equal moral standards for men and women; equal pay for women workers and all amenities (creches for children and maternity benefits); housewives' right to part of husband's income to use as her own; husband should not have the right to dispose of his whole income without the consent of the wife; wife should be the beneficiary of the husband's social insurance; women should inherit equally with men; no polygamy; women's consent to marriage essential; no marriage for girls below 17 years and boys below 21 years; divorce rights; wife should get alimony till she marries or is able to earn; wife should be the equal guardian of the children; court should decide on custody; both husband and wife must decide on adoption; wife has the right to limit the family.

Duties included work in national need; education for good citizenship; fighting social evils; educating children to be good citizens; working for high moral standards and world peace. This document was submitted to the central and provincial legislatures, was signed by Kamaladevi Chattopadhyaya, Hannah Sen, Renuka Ray and Kitty Shiva Rao. (*Roshini*, 1946:22) The scene was therefore well set for the reforms that took place after Independence.

For Muslim women, however, their participation in the Indian women's movement was always overshadowed by Muslim separatist politics, so bitterly fought through the critical decades 1920-1947. Their legal status had been less contested than that of Hindu women and with the passing of the Shariat Act in 1937 and the Dissolution of Muslim Marriages Act 1939, it was considered determined.After Independence two factors affected the prospects of Muslim women. Firstly, the loss of Muslim women leaders due to migration undermined their stature and left them less well placed to deal with economic, social and political changes. Also the exigencies of their minority status impelled their compliance with Muslim Personal Law even where unjustly applied. Secondly, with the passage of the Hindu Code Bill in 1956, the Indian women's movement lost its momentum and leadership. This affected Muslim women adversely since the feminist platform had groomed their leadership and provided an ideology which could unite all women. And worse, the memory of the solidarity forged and nurtured by the women's movement was forgotten.

# 6

## Transition

### Introduction

In the period since Independence Indian social, political and economic structures have undergone organizational and ideological changes. This has had considerable impact on the status and role of women in society and on the many communities, linguistic and religious, that co-exist within the Indian union. Social changes have been induced by legislation and through a process of social education on the rights of women, minorities, etc. Politically, the introduction of a formal constitution, democracy and a variety of political parties has served to educate and guide people regarding their rights. Economic policies aimed at raising the rate of growth and improving income distribution have resulted in diversifying and expanding the economic base and, hence, employment opportunities. The Muslim community and Muslim women have to be considered in the context of these changes. The partition of India made the change institutionally harder to deal with as it solved few problems for the community and almost none for Indian society.

The problems of the community, particularly in the north, were in many ways similar to those it had dealt with a century earlier. Lack of political power made the struggle for economic achievement more difficult which, in turn, made the creation of social institutions, necessary for quickening the pace of change, more problematic. The community's historical antecedents continued to be a complicating factor, and consequently, its need to maintain its identity and preserve its culture increased rather than decreased. For Muslim women the new period of change was complicated, not just by the problems of Indian women but also by the community's minority status. The status of women in India, which has undergone considerable legislative alteration, continues to be subject to the slow pace of social and economic change and is suffering a number of reverses in labour participation rates and in continuing social practices which erode their newly won legislative rights.

## The community

With Independence, and on the insistence of the Muslim political leadership, came the partition of Punjab and Bengal, two Muslim majority provinces which seceded to form the present Pakistan and Bangladesh. But while the partition had a lasting and major political impact, it left almost untouched the problems of coexistence between the Muslim and other communities in India.

The Constitution of the new Republic of India, in an attempt to define the terms of their coexistence stated, that ". . . the State shall strive to promote the welfare of the people by securing and protecting as effectively as it may, a social order in which justice, social, economic and political, shall inform all institutions of national life . . ." (*First Five Year Plan*, 1952). Under the Constitution, India became a secular State: religion and the State function in different areas of human activity, each with its own objectives and methods. All religions are subordinate to as well as separate from the State. The State views the individual as a citizen and not as a member of a particular group, nor is there any compulsion in religion. (Smith, 1963:3)

With Independence, the criteria of achievement for the attainment of wealth or power began to erode the traditional ascriptive nature of Indian society, and new indicators of status based on achievement, consumption, leisure and income began to displace the traditional hierarchies. Education, wealth and consumption, as a result, can no longer be considered the preserve of any one group. (Beteille, 1965:202) This reorientation of social, economic and political structures has affected the Muslim community as much as other communities.

The position of the Muslim community after 1947 has to be re-evaluated, taking into account the full impact of Partition. Zafar Imam has estimated that while migration from the contiguous areas of Punjab was almost total, migration from other regions varied from 10 per cent of the Muslim population from Bihar, Orissa and West Bengal, to 6 per cent from U.P. and Delhi, dropping to 2 per cent from Gujarat and Bombay, one per cent from Madhya Pradesh and Andhra Pradesh, and 0.2 per cent from Madras and Mysore. (Imam, 1975:76) The migrants were the urban young and the educated intelligentsia. This denuded traditional Muslim urban centres such as Delhi, Bhopal, Calcutta, Ahmedabad, Hyderabad, Madras and regions of western U.P. and south Bihar (Imam, 1975:88) while, with the exception of Rajasthan and Punjab, migration to Pakistan from rural areas was negligible. Imam has also noted that the limited migration from the countryside did not change the social and economic structure of the rural Muslim community as did the urban migration. This was despite the outbreak of communal violence and the enforcement of the Evacuee Property Act which resulted in the loss of Muslim property. (Imam, 1975:83) The reduction in the urban Muslim population proved temporary, as rural Muslim migrants replaced them, due perhaps to the displacement of traditional patronage and search for employment. (Imam, 1975:94) This movement of rural families to urban areas should be regarded as an important factor when the response of respondents to the survey is considered, since to some extent it reflects the need for closer identification with their community group, to whom they look for support in urban aeas. (Mines, 1975:413)

The various Indian Muslim economic interest groups must be differentiated when considering the impact of Indian economic and political policies on them. These interests vary between urban and rural Muslims, and between different socio-economic stratum. However, the intention here is not to identify or discuss the nature of different interest groups but to show that, despite this differentiation, they share a commonality of interests which is sustained by emphasizing a distinct Muslim identity through the preservation of certain symbols of unity. (Mazumdar, 1975:186) This unity revolves around the Shariat, which without effective legal and community vigilance, adversely affects the status of Muslim women.

Development programmes in India sought to make major changes in the mobilization and distribution of the country's resources (Ghosh, 1975:206) and the Government has been the prime initiator of development and disbursor of power and patronage. As a result, the importance of mobilizing group interests to obtain a fair share of the limited resources, continues, ensuring a continuation of the communal mobilization of the 19th century. The process of economic development disrupted traditional rural structures, raised the expectations of people beyond the capacity of government to deliver, and intensified the competition for employment and other economic opportunities. This has been a contributory factor in the rise of regional, language, caste and religious nationalisms expressed through the activities of semi-political groups. Ethnicity or communalism has intensified as a result of uneven development and mass politicisation which, it has been demonstrated, can be an important source of power disbursement if successfully manipulated. (Bell, 1975:169) Though these groups are organized around their traditional affiliations, their objectives are directed towards political and economic gain; this process has been demonstrated by Harijans, Muslims, Sikhs and a number of caste groups. It must be kept in mind that these traditional groupings are being used for secular purposes, and there may be both co-operation and support between diverse groups, or divisions within the same group (Lateef, 1980:2087).

These manoeuverings have not been free of violence. There have been frequent clashes between language, caste, regional and religious groups. Though clashes between Muslims and other groups have tended to monopolise attention, the nature of such communal violence and the objectives behind it are quite similar to those of other groups. There have been militant "sons of the soil" movements in Maharashtra, Assam and other regions which demanded that the resources and available employment opportunities be reserved for the people of the state. (Kothari, 1970:114) Other groups agitating for particular language issues also tend to be motivated by the need to promote the group's economic interests, its symbolic unity and its political power. (Brass, 1974:248) These agitations and violent incidents tend to unite groups more closely; Paul Brass has noted that the ideological and political differences which deeply divided the many Muslim groups were set aside to respond to this violence, through the establishment of organizations to represent Muslim grievances and press for demands from the government. (Brass, 1974:249, 250. A number of those interviewed on the field trip were similarly motivated.) The groups could, however, only agree on a few symbolically important issues, such as the need to retain the Shariat or Muslim Personal Law, and the need to gain wider acceptance of Urdu. (Wright, 1963:105, 107)

Many of the demands of Muslims in India have been articulated over time through the Muslim media and through Muslim groups. They have included the preservation of Muslim Personal

Law, a fair share in government employment and access to other economic opportunities. (Rothermund, 1975:60) However, while Muslims are under-represented in the legislature and in government employment, they are also not represented evenly through the socio-economic strata in most regions, which compounds their difficulties when making this representation. The Muslim urban middle class, seeking white collar employment, and Muslim landless labourers have suffered the most as a result of discrimination in the job market; those less dependent on employers are relatively better off. (Rothermund, 1975:59)

The community has had to use all available means of retaining and improving its economic and political position vis-a-vis other communities also engaged in the same struggle. To maintain group cohesiveness and symbolic unity, language and family laws have played their part, although actual usage and practice have varied with community and regional norms. This has affected the perspective and prospects of Muslim women.

## Women in Indian society

The Indian women's movement before Independence was able to realise many of its objectives due to the extraordinary quality of its leadership and its alliance with the national movement. It managed to achieve inter-community coalition, something that was politically elusive at the time. The momentum of the movement and its alliance with the national movement enabled women to gain constitutional equality and, with the passage of the Hindu Code Bill, Hindu women gained legislative equality with Hindu men. This victory, however, tended to diffuse the ideological and organizational content of the movement and it lost much of its momentum at a time when legislative rights were far from being enforced and the country's institutions were being reformulated. The failure to implement legislative changes and the inability of women to act as a pressure group has meant that women have faild to obtain a fair share of the benefits from accelerated economic development.

The content and direction of the present women's movement has to be understood in the context of the history of the movement and of economic, political and social changes in India. The women's movement in India can be considered in three phases; the first, in the latter half of the 19th century, was a process initiated by men for women's education and some expansion of their wholly domestic roles. The second phase in the 1920s was a takeover by women of the movement, imbuing it with specific ideology and content. The earlier phase had already established the collaboration with men and the acceptance of a western ideological orientation to the movement. During the second phase, the leaders of the movement were able to strengthen their organization and use it to gain the support of the national movement for changes in their legislative status. This support was readily extended by the political parties in the national movement, both because they needed the co-operation of the women's movement and because it came to represent a part of the wider struggle. The success of the second phase resulted in constitutional and other legislative equality. The elite orientation of the second phase made the gaining of rights an end in itself without a deeper understanding that the lives of the majority of Indian women would remain unaffected by legislative changes without the infrastructure or the support system to encourage and enable its use. The movement, in fact, had paid little attention to the expectations and requirements of women at different socio-economic levels. (Lateef, 1981:201)

It is only recently and tentatively, and as a result of the impact of development, that the third phase of the movement has begun. The realization that the social and economic problems of Indian women cannot be resolved at the abstract level of legislative and constitutional changes, but require fundamental change in economic and political structures,and in policy planning, has to be reflected in a reorganization of women's groups and strategies if women are not to become a casualty of the development process. The process of social and economic change is being directed at women at the lower end of the socio-economic stratum so that their awareness and response to economic changes can draw them into the developmental process. There are signs that such a re-evaluation and redirection is taking place from the mushrooming of several women's groups, both urban and rural. There is, as yet, no unified women's movement which has articulated the new emphasis and direction in these terms, only a realization that a full-fledged women's movement cannot emerge without the involvement of women at all economic and social levels. Since the major concerns of women from rural and urban areas are economic, one direction of the movement is to provide women with support organizations which can represent them in their struggle for improved employment conditions, childcare and credit. This third phase represents a horizontal movement of ideas and organizational linkages rather than the vertical movement it had earlier been, i.e., a free flow of ideas between women leaders and their constituents, rather than direction from above. The movement represents for the first time the needs and requirements of women at the lower socio-economic level, who have always laboured alongside men for subsistence and under the changes instituted, have not been able to hold their own. By reaching out to this strata of women, and by highlighting their difficulties, the new movement is in fact changing the traditional "ideal" of Indian women through which mother and wife roles were glorified. Protection and seclusion of women became symbols of upper caste and rich women, a status to be sought after and emulated by other castes and classes of women, an ideal which detracted from their productive roles. By focussing on women's economic plight and seeking redress, the new movement is trying to ensure that the neglect of women's productive roles in economic development planning can now be reversed. (Lateef, 1981:201)

Recent social science literature reflects the re-evaluation taking place of the effects of social, political and economic changes on women in all societies. It has been demonstrated that neither economic development nor legislative rights by themselves improve the status of women, unless specific efforts are made in this direction. While this is true to some extent in all societies, it is particularly true in traditional ones where customs and practices are deeply embedded. In such traditional societies, equality is itself contextually difficult to define since the equality of untouchable women with that of their male counterparts hardly constitutes the concept of equality with men as generally understood in the west. (Lateef, 1981:202)

A rudimentary infrastructure for drawing the economically depressed stratum and women into the development process exists in India at many different levels, both in rural and urban areas. However, those well organized or well represented politically are best able to take advantage of this infrastructure. In the case of both women and the poorest sections of society, their very backwardness, and the prevalence of certain social attitudes prevents access to this infrastructure. In the case of women, the view persists that women do not require special consideration since men in the family or community are being helped and, conversely, that women take jobs away from men who have families to support. The government and agencies for women's welfare, therefore, continue to work within the traditional framework of limited participation which has made them increasingly ineffective. The lack of co-ordination and formal articulation of its ideology by the emerging women's movement has left many of the traditional concepts unchallenged. The challenge to prevailing attitudes and misconceptions came from a committee appointed by the government for International Women's Year to go into the economic, social and political condition of Indian women and to report on them. (*Towards Equality*, 1974) The Committee on the Status of Women in India collated statistical and other information on women which, viewed in its entirety, revealed that the condition of women remained almost unaffected by the political and economic progress made by the country. The report questioned the complacency of women's organizations and government and their reliance on legislative measures to solve problems. It provided the evidence, so far lacking in India, of the adverse effects of development on women, particularly in the rural and unorganized sectors, and demonstrated that improvements in urban areas are marginal and cosmetic in relation to the overall social, political and economic condition of Indian women.

The persistence of certain social factors, supported both ideologically and organizationally, can be considered instrumental in effecting the demographic, political and economic reverses suffered by women over the century. Despite religious and regional differences in Indian society, over-riding customs and traditions are followed by most communities and undermine legislative or other gains women may make. The persistence of customs and practices may often be due to the need to maintain unity and cohesion for enabling co-ordinated community action for political and economic ends, with the result that women have, therefore, been subject to contradictory signals from their communities in particular, and society in general. While education and even employment are being encouraged in urban areas, self-determination in marriage, independence in economic matters, separation from the family without marriage, continue to be discouraged. Organizational aspects of community life, kinship, family, marriage and descent, continue to the exclusion of other forms of fulfillment. Thus, taken together, ideology, organization and patterns of economic development continue to compartmentalize women.

The selection of marriage partners is still important for main-

taining hierarchies and community parameters. Despite legislative support for inter-caste and inter-community marriages, arranged and semi-arranged marriages are still the norm (*Towards
Equality*, 1974:62, 63) and one manifestation of this is the continuing importance of dowry payments to ensure that a suitable
partner from the right caste grouping is obtained for women.
This practice has been on the increase in recent years, being
adopted by groups that traditionally did not use the custom, to
improve their *caste status. (Towards Equality*, 1974:70) Legislative
efforts to control the phenomenon have proved futile for a
variety of reasons, among them cases reported under the Dowry
Act, and existing loopholes in the laws of evidence.

The persistence of traditional social attitudes is also responsible for the adverse male-female ratio which has been worsening
in the present century. From 972 women to 1,000 males in 1901
it fell to 930 in 1971. Life expectancy has increased for men, but
not as much for women. (*Status of Women in India*, 1975:7) Factors
such as marriage, fertility, sex of children, lack of health facilities
for women and customs such as eating after men, and the emphasis on self-effacement and subservience affects the ability of
women to seek medical and other help without women's support
organizations.

Social attitudes also affect the educational and literacy levels
of women. While enrolment in primary school has increased,
girls tend to drop out before functional literacy can be achieved.
(*Status of Women in India*, 1975:90) Although literacy rates for
women have been rising more rapidly than for men, in 1971, they
were, at 18 per cent, less than half the literacy rate for men (40
per cent). As a result, the absolute number of illiterate females
outstrips the number of illiterate males. Similarly, social attitudes
that encouraged the reification of women and disparaged their
participation in the labour force have persisted, to exclude
women's participation in the training and education required to
enable them to move into employment in the organized sectors
of the economy, even as traditional avenues of employment for
women are diminishing. In agriculture, they are being reduced
to landless labourers as land holding patterns change and as their
traditional sources of employment have given way to factory
production. (*Status of Women in India*, 1975:68) In the organized
sector their share of employment has improved but not as much
as that of men. The bulk of the expansion has been in service
industries and professions, where certain jobs were already being

identified as low in status and, therefore, suitable for women. This increased dependence on government employment and patronage has made them vulnerable to cuts in government spending. (*Towards Equality*, 1974:204)

This reduced role in the economy is mirrored in the inadequate representation in legislative bodies and in the political hierarchy of political parties. While the participation of women voters has been rising, their representation in legislatures has sharply declined, both at the national and state level. (*Status of Women in India*, 1975:104, 105) In the present political climate, where political office represents not only access to the power structure but a forum where different comunities display their political power as they make demands on behalf of their communities, it has been difficult for women in legislatures to adequately represent women's interests. The struggle for power, regionally and nationally, between different communities has also made the securing of nominations and contesting of elections expensive and difficult for women, quite apart from the difficulties which beset women candidates in a restrictive social milieu. The lack of an active women's movement with a definite ideology has meant that unlike the earlier phase, women politicians have been unable to find a feminist platform and work in conjunction with women's groups; instead, they are obliged to follow party policies which do not encourage the taking up of controversial issues. (Lateef, 1981:206)

## Muslim women: an analytical framework

Muslim women have been affected by the economic, social and political situation facing different Muslim communities in India, and by those facing Indian women as a whole. There has, however, been little acknowledgement of this similarity by Indian social scientists or even the Committee on the Status of Women in India (Hate, 1969; Mitra, 1978; *Towards Equality*, 1974:393-453), which treat Muslim women as an undifferentiated mass, irrespective of differences in socio-economic strata or regional customs and practices, as a phenomenon apart from the experiences of other women in Indian society. This is because Islam has been regarded as the primary factor in any analysis of the social, political and economic problems of Muslim women. This detracts from the real problems and their origins. The analytical separation between the status of Muslim and other women is a continuation of the distinction made between the rise of ethnic politicization between the Muslim and other communities. By this separation it has been possible to attribute the blame for the social, political and economic problems of Muslim women on Islam; this however, does not further our understanding of the complexities of change for the Muslim and all other communities and women, or the social policy solutions to them. Whereas, in all societies women play secondary roles to men, specific studies require an acknowledgment of regional and other factors as a basis of analysis.

Such an approach has also been used in a number of recent studies on the effects of social, political and economic changes on women (Tinker, 1976; Boserup, 1970; O'Barr, 1976) and communities, (Cohen, 1969; Beteille, 1965; Mines, 1975; Enloe, 1971; Glazer, 1975) irrespective of differences in culture or religion. Rosaldo, for instance has found that ". . . everywhere, from those societies we might want to call egalitarian, to those in which sexual stratification is most marked, men are the locus of cultural values". (Rosaldo, 1974:20) And though technology has to some extent freed women from the seemingly inevitable ties to child-bearing and rearing, it does not eliminate a universal constant "being female" (O'Barr, 1976:3); even as the underlying demographic, technological, economic and ecological conditions to which these sex-linked roles are adapted become modified or cease to exist, new cultural definitions of sex-linked roles may begin to emerge. (O'Barr, 1976:7) Therefore, ". . . we should be alert, whenever we come across a definition of female and male roles inflected with a heavy ideological or moral component. The biological or sexual difference in female and male performance is invariable; variations on the theme are cultural or a matter of gender." (O'Barr, 1976:52). Irene Tinker has observed that western stereotypes should be avoided because social and cultural differences are perceived differently by societies. Nuclear families are cited as liberating women in India; in the west they are regarded as oppressive. Purdah, which is regarded as oppressive in the west, is seen as an alternative to hard labour in the fields by some societies, and therefore liberating. The process of Sanskritization has had a similar effect on women in Hindu communities. In western societies children belong to the mother; in Muslim and some African societies to the father; this enables women to remarry.

Development can have a positive effect if the problems of women in their particular cultural milieu are considered in the planning of economic change. Lack of education limits women's options, particularly in urban areas, where they are confronted by better qualified competitors. (Tinker, 1976:72) Padma Desai has compared the labour participation rates for women in north Africa, west Asia and Asia to show that active female economic participation as a percentage of total female population was 57 per cent for Turkey, 15 per cent for Pakistan, 12 per cent for Iran, 18 per cent for Bangladesh, 40 per cent for Indonesia, 24 per cent for Sri Lanka and 13 per cent for India. (Desai, 1975:38) Ester Boserup has noted that ". . . in regions where Muslim women take no part in trade, it is often taken for granted that it is because women's trading is supposed to be incompatible with the Muslim religion. But this is an unwarranted inference, for in regions with female predominance in trade, religion does not prevent women from taking part in it." (Boserup, 1970:92) Nor did Muslim religion send Indonesian and Malay women into domesticity. (Boserup, 1970:182) Dorothy Remy has noted that in developing countries, the possibilities of obtaining satisfactory employment are related to the growth of the economy and the socio-economic structure; education may overcome these difficulties but the structural constraints continue. (Remy, 1975:370) Even when judicial equality for women is conceded, discrimination and socio-economic factors and traditional prejudices still have a decisive influence. (Salazar, 1976:184, 197)

Perdita Huston's interviews with women in Mexico, Sri Lanka, Kenya, Sudan, Egypt and Tunisia demonstrate very clearly that despite wide-ranging differences in culture, religion and the pace of economic development, the essential problems of women were the same in content, if not in specificity. Socio-economic strata appeared to be the primary cause of differentiation. The aspirations of women everywhere indicate a universal desire for an improvement in their social and economic condition; this desire is expressed through their desire for education and employment. (Huston, 1979:118)

Despite this universal desire for freedom, equality and achievement on the part of women, social realities bolstered by cultural norms transmit conflicting images, and the country's cultural environment and its definition of fundamental male-female spheres are important factors that affect women's participation. These disadvantages can be intensified by ethnic differences, in which women can face discrimination both on account of sex and race. (Almquist, 1975:142)

The experience of minorities, with some exceptions, has been that their labour is regarded as marginal and that if the economy does well, they prosper; otherwise their ability to earn remains limited. (Anderson, 1975:130) Social and cultural factors, however, are most important when considering the status and role of women. Gore has pointed out that attitudes towards the employment of Hindu women in India involve a number of considerations from family status and concept of appropriateness, to innate feminine qualities and disabilities, and caste and class variants which are particularly important in urban areas. (Gore, 1968:198) Smock has shown that in Bangladesh, despite strongly differentiated Hindu and Muslim identities, cultural values, customs and practices pertaining to women are shared. The concept of women as symbols, for example, is shared by both communities. (Smock, 1977:85, 89)

The status of Muslim women in India can, therefore, be viewed as subject to a number of factors; the political and economic position of the community; social, cultural and economic factors current in Indian society and the socio-economic strata to which they belong. The pressure that religion exerts, in the experience of other developing countries, is subject to and often overruled by the universality of certain phenomena, customs and practices in society, economic factors, urbanisation and social, political and economic changes.

The legal aspect of change is perhaps the single factor which differentiates Muslim women from women of other communities in India, and it has been constantly used to characterise the community and women as backward and conservative, implying that legal changes have improved the real status of women of other communities in India and in other societies; a premise not borne out by experience. This also overlooks the mass of secular legislation on the family that already exists in India which can and is being used by members of all communities. The use of this can be encouraged and will increase with education and with the re-emergence of the women's movement.

### Conclusion

The Muslim community and Muslim women, particularly after the institution of political, social and economic changes in India, need to be considered within the framework of Indian society. These changes had a far-reaching impact on the social structure and the economic and political participation of all communities, which in turn affected the perception, interaction and competition for benefits among all. To consider the response of a community or group of women separately rather than vis-a-vis the totality of communities or groups of women, tends to detract from the real problems the community and its women face. An integrated analysis may well prove that the solutions to their situational problems are similar to those of other communities and other groups of women.

# 7

## Findings

Placing Muslim women firmly in the Indian social, political and economic context, the survey sought to relate the experiences of the Muslim community and of Indian women to those of Muslim women. The basic data on Muslim women was gathered through a stratified survey that covered nine cities. Together with the field trip, the survey provided an empirical basis for evaluating the status of Muslim women and the community's attitudes towards women in juxtaposition with those of other Indian communities. While the survey provided an insight into the attitudes, practices and levels of participation of Muslim women, the field trip furthered the understanding of social and political pressures that confront minority communities and widen the distance between private and political religion. Such pressures and the occupational structure of the Muslim community in different regions affected responses differently. While the survey sought to differentiate between regions and categories, the field trip presented an overview of the community's regional and national concerns.

### The survey

The primary objective of the survey was to evaluate the status and role of Muslim women in the context of changes taking place in India. In most existing studies any reference to Muslim women has been based less on empirical evidence and more on the already prevalent stereotype of Muslim women regarding purdah, lack of formal education and familial conservatism. (Hate, 1969) However, different regional studies have suggested that great differences exist between women in different socio-economic strata. (Roy, 1979: XIII) This survey was designed to differentiate between region, socio-economic strata and fields of activity in order to ensure a realistic appraisal of Muslim women's status. It also took into account the extent to which they were affected by the Indian, woman and Islamic factors.

The study is entirely urban. Initially, it was hoped that rural areas could be included in each region and accordingly, a modified questionnaire was prepared, but resources of time, finances and personnel could not be extended beyond the nine cities already covered. There are area studies on rural or semi-urban Muslim communities, particularly those of Cora Vreede de Stuers, Leela Dube, P.C. Aggarwal, Mattison Mines and Rothermund's edited volume of a conference on South Asian Muslim communities, (de Stuers, 1968; Dube, 1969; Aggarwal, 1971, Rothermund, 1975; Mines, 1975) that suggest as this one does, that, while Muslim communities absorb local customs and adapt to social and political change, their preoccupation with identity and differentiation remains constant. Aggarwal's study of Meos in Rajasthan indicates the changes that can take place in a community due to politically induced pressures; Mines' study demonstrates that the shift from rural to urban areas by community members induces perceptual changes that influence group behaviour, particularly in urban areas. Both types of pressure lead to greater emphasis on maintenance of group identity and differentiation. In India both Muslim communities referred to in Aggarwal's and Mines' studies were greatly affected by communal political mobilization before 1947. After 1947 continuing instances of ethnic strife between Muslim and other communities have created uncertainties which serve to emphasize the need for collective security and reinforce group differentiation. For the purpose of this study, it can be argued that although customs, practices and attitudes towards women in the community may vary and depend on regional communities, the minority character of the community as a whole makes the maintenance of community identity important to all members, in all its institutional aspects. Due to language and cultural differences between Indian Muslim communities no generalizations on customs, practices or attitudes of rural Muslim women are possible, except that as members of a minority community, they like urban women, are affected by the emphasis on institutional differentiation.

The questionnaire was designed to explore familial relationships, interaction with the Muslim community and other communities and the responsiveness of Muslim women respondents to conditions and trends in society. The survey was stratified since the community in eight of the nine cities surveyed ranged only from 8-16 per cent of the population, the only exception being Srinagar. Without stratification it would be difficult to ensure representation for certain categories of women. The number of respondents in each was specified since adequate data was not available to weight them. Within the specified number of respondents in each category electoral rolls were used to identify respondents, mainly housewives and wage-earners living in mohallas or inner city areas, and every fifth name was picked. For students, college rolls were similarly used. In the case of middle class housewives and career women, since Muslim women were thinly scattered through these categories, respondents were typically chosen on the basis of availability.

Stratification was based on fields of activity; two categories of housewives, two categories of women engaged in economic activity outside the house, and students at college or university. A distinction has been made between housewives in mohallas in predominantly Muslim areas and those living in integrated middle class neighbourhoods. The study by de Stuers had indicated that, though women living in mohallas may vary in socioeconomic composition, the close proximity of community neighbours ensures the continuation of practices and rituals and imposes certain behavioural norms on men and women. (de Stuers, 1968) Respondents in this category were expected to conform more closely to the Muslim woman stereotype which would also include non-participation in activities outside the home, lack of interest in daughters' education and the education of sons at the local mosque school. Housewives in the middle class were expected to reflect changes in purdah customs; greater interest in their daughters' education; education of children at secular schools and greater participation in outside activities. They were expected to parallel Rama Mehta's western educated Hindu woman (Mehta, 1970). The prototype is adaptable to change but conscious of the community's heritage, traditions and customs.

Wage-earners reflect the tradition of labour among women in lower socio-economic strata as well as economic opportunities in urban areas. They were unlikely to observe purdah or if they did, to do so flexibly, to have no formal education and to participate in family decision making, reflecting their monetary contribution to the family income. Career women would be educated with a defined career (as in Promilla Kapur's study) and representative of changing urban practices and attitudes (Kapur, 1974). Students would represent both the households from which they were drawn and the options and opportunities available to their generation as reflected in a student study by Rhoda Goldstein (Goldstein, 1972).

The survey was conducted in Delhi, in the capital cities of Tamil Nadu, Maharashtra, Andhra Pradesh, West Bengal, Uttar Pradesh, Gujarat, Jammu and Kashmir and Cochin in Kerala in 1973-74. There were 1,332 respondents. The regions to be surveyed were chosen on three criteria: (a) Homogeneity of culture between the Muslim and other communities, since regional studies, particularly those of Leela Dube and Mattison Mines and Karim (Mines, 1975; Dube, 1969; Karim, 1963; Nanda, 1976; D'-Souza, 1975; SNDT, 1975; Report of the Committee on the Status of Women in India, 1974; Boserup, 1978; Mitra, 1978; Jain, 1975; Mehta, 1970; Ross, 1961; Gore, 1968; Kapadia, 1956; Kapur, 1974) had suggested that Muslim communities were frequently closer to the regional community than to other Muslim communities in matters of language, customs, food and dress. West Bengal, Kerala and Tamil Nadu reflect this homogeneity. (b) Areas noted for communal tension or communal harmony; communal conflict has been indigent in Uttar Pradesh, while Maharashtra, Gujarat and Andhra Pradesh had traditionally been harmonious; this has been eroded in the last two decades. In Jammu and Kashmir, Kerala and Tamil Nadu communal conflicts and tensions are not endemic, though present. (c) A Muslim majority state, the only example being Jammu and Kashmir.

Class variations are significant determinants of status and the role of women in a society where economic deprivation is the norm rather than the exception. Economic class differentials determine levels of nutrition, education and training which can help women increase control over their lives and permit easier exploitation of limited economic opportunities. Fields of activity of respondents in conjunction with housing and regional differentials, were used to evaluate socio-economic strata, an important factor in determining this control. The fields of activity selected differentiated between respondents who routinely interacted with outside society i.e., students, career women and wage earners, and the two housewives categories in order to determine their responsiveness to societal change. In the case of wage earners and career women their financial contribution to the family would, it was expected, be reflected in a greater say in family decision making. A distinction was made between purdah and non-purdah respondents to establish the extent to which purdah affected decision making, control and social attitudes. The initial analysis was based on the importance of this distinction but stratification and to some extent, regional factors were to provide a more decisive basis of differentiating responses on the major issues.

Regional differences proved to be important with respect to purdah observance and education. Stratification emerged as the most important factor determining responses. The analysis, therefore, focuses primarily on stratification categories to evaluate responses to factual and attitudinal questions. Regional responses are presented only where they indicate significant differences.

Providing satisfactory indices for establishing socio-economic differentials between respondents proved difficult. Income, the obvious indicator, was considered unsatisfactory since it could be misreported by respondents or reflect only temporary earnings. Housing was considered more reliable, but here allowances have to be made for urban housing constraints where both mohallas and middle class housing can vary in size and in the availability of utilities and conveniences. The following housing indicators were used:

1. Rented or owned thatched hut, kerosene, public tap.
2. Rented or owned masonry building, 1-2 rooms, electricity, public tap.
3. Rented or owned masonry building, 1-2 rooms, electricity, private tap, 1-2 durable consumer goods, eg., cycle, sewing machine, etc.
4. Rented or owned masonry building, more than three rooms, electricity, private tap, two or more consumer goods, car, telephone, etc.

Table 1 indicates that respondents were almost equally divided among the four categories. While students, career women and middle class housewives were mainly drawn from 3 and 4, housewives from mohallas ranged over all four categories indicating the economic contrasts that can categorize inner city areas; wage earners were mainly confined to the two lower housing categories.

**Table 1**

Socio-economic stratum based on type of accommodation

| Respondents | 1 | 2 | 3 | 4 | No response | Total | Value N |
|---|---|---|---|---|---|---|---|
| Students | 2.7 | 9.3 | 39.1 | 47.2 | 1.7 | 100 | 209 |
| Housewives in mohallas | 24.2 | 41.9 | 28.8 | 3.2 | 0.9 | 100 | 477 |
| Wage earners | 47.9 | 30.3 | 9.4 | 10.2 | 2.3 | 100 | 123 |
| Housewives in upper strata | — | 28.9 | 28.0 | 42.2 | 0.8 | 100 | 342 |
| Career women | 4.6 | 16.8 | 28.8 | 48.0 | 1.8 | 100 | 181 |
| Total | 14.1 | 28.9 | 28.8 | 26.8 | 1.2 | 100 | 1,332 |

Tables 2a-2d indicate the nature of the respondent's husband's employment (employer, employee, self-employed, unemployed). There was very little unemployment and very few employers, with the exception of respondents' husbands in Bombay. Among husbands of housewives in mohalls 41 per cent were employees, with the exception of Ahmedabad at 64 per cent. This could reflect the greater employment opportunities available due to the textile industry. A further 31 per cent in this category were self-employed husbands, with Lucknow and Srinagar indicating percentages above average. Discrimination in employment and greater reliance on semi-skilled work could be responsible for greater self-employment in Lucknow. In Srinagar the large number of arts and crafts, the greater demand for artisans, and tourism could partly account for this. Husbands of housewives in the upper strata tended to be mainly employees (48 per cent) particularly in Delhi, Bombay and Cochin. Consistent with the earlier findings were 38 per cent self-employed husbands in Lucknow and Srinagar.

Husbands of career women tended to be equally distributed among self-employed and employees, except in Hyderabad and Ahmedabad where the self-employed were more numerous, and Delhi and Srinagar where the number of employees was higher.

Although there is no supporting evidence, the low proportion of those shown as unemployed could imply that the term self-employed was frequently used as a euphemism for an unemployed or underemployed husband.

## Field trip

The field trip was undertaken well after the survey and the initial analysis of data. It became a means of verifying the results of the survey, which had refuted many of the long-held beliefs that Muslim women remained apart from the many changes that had taken place in the status and role of women in India. From the survey results it was clear that, while the behaviour and attitudes of Muslim women were based primarily on their socio-economic strata, the need to maintain their identity and survival as a group was also reflected. This need for identity did not appear to have interfered with their capacity to comprehend and adapt changes to their particular requirements. The key question was why, if the traditional image of Muslim women both in practice and in attitudes had undergone considerable change, were there no overt manifestations of this change? Such manifestations could

## Table 2a

Respondents whose husbands are employed by city
(per cent of total number surveyed in each category)

| Respondents | Delhi | Bombay | Cochin | Madras | Hyder-abad | Calcutta | Ahmed-abad | Lucknow | Srinagar | All India |
|---|---|---|---|---|---|---|---|---|---|---|
| Students | — (N=22) | — (N=21) | — (N=23) | — (N=29) | 7.4 (N=27) | — (N=17) | — (N=27) | 3.4 (N=29) | — (N=28) | 1.7 (N=209) |
| Housewives in mohallas | 41.3 (N=63) | 46.8 (N=77) | 40.0 (N=35) | 41.9 (N=43) | 35.5 (N=76) | 42.9 (N=28) | 63.6 (N=33) | 31.0 (N=29) | 24.1 (N=58) | 40.8 (N=477) |
| Wage earners | 11.8 (N=17) | 42.9 (N=7) | — (N=1) | 100.0 (N=2) | 38.7 (N=31) | 22.2 (N=9) | 54.2 (N=24) | 14.3 (N=21) | — (N=10) | 32.8 (N=123) |
| Housewives in upper strata | 63.3 (N=49) | 54.5 (N=44) | 70.0 (N=30) | 37.5 (N=40) | 44.4 (N=36) | 47.4 (N=19) | 44.4 (N=27) | 31.9 (N=69) | 42.0 (N=50) | 47.6 (N=342) |
| Career women | 57.9 (N=19) | 20.6 (N=34) | — (N=0) | 31.3 (N=16) | 31.6 (N=19) | 18.8 (N=16) | — (N=2) | 28.6 (N=21) | 43.8 (N=32) | 29.3 (N=181) |

*Note:* The total of those surveyed in each category includes those who failed to respond. N denotes the total number of respondents in each category, in each city, who responded to the question.

**Table 2b**

Respondents whose husbands are employers, by city
(per cent of total number surveyed in each category)

| Respondents | Delhi | Bombay | Cochin | Madras | Hyder-abad | Calcutta | Ahmed-abad | Lucknow | Srinagar | All India |
|---|---|---|---|---|---|---|---|---|---|---|
| Students | —<br>(N=22) | —<br>(N=21) | —<br>(N=23) | —<br>(N=29) | —<br>(N=27) | —<br>(N=17) | 3.7<br>(N=27) | —<br>(N=29) | —<br>(N=28) | 0.4<br>(N=209) |
| Housewives in mohallas | —<br>(N=63) | 16.9<br>(N=77) | 5.7<br>(N=35) | —<br>(N=43) | 7.9<br>(N=76) | —<br>(N=28) | —<br>(N=33) | —<br>(N=29) | 3.4<br>(N=58) | 7.8<br>(N=477) |
| Wage earners | —<br>(N=17) | 14.3<br>(N=7) | —<br>(N=1) | —<br>(N=2) | 3.2<br>(N=31) | —<br>(N=9) | 4.2<br>(N=24) | —<br>(N=21) | —<br>(N=10) | 3.4<br>(N=123) |
| Housewives in upper strata | 4.1<br>(N=49) | 2.3<br>(N=44) | 13.3<br>(N=30) | 5.0<br>(N=40) | 5.6<br>(N=36) | —<br>(N=19) | 7.4<br>(N=27) | —<br>(N=69) | —<br>(N=50) | 3.1<br>(N=342) |
| Career women | —<br>(N=19) | 2.9<br>(N=34) | —<br>(N=0) | —<br>(N=16) | 5.3<br>(N=19) | —<br>(N=16) | —<br>(N=2) | —<br>(N=21) | —<br>(N=32) | 1.9<br>(N=181) |

*Note:* The total of those surveyed in each category includes those who failed to respond.

**Table 2c**

Respondents whose husbands are self-employed, by city
(Per cent of total number surveyed in each category)

| Respondents | Delhi | Bombay | Cochin | Madras | Hyder-abad | Calcutta | Ahmed-abad | Lucknow | Srinagar | All India |
|---|---|---|---|---|---|---|---|---|---|---|
| Students | — (N=22) | 4.8 (N=21) | 4.3 (N=23) | 3.4 (N=29) | 3.7 (N=27) | 5.9 (N=17) | 3.7 (N=27) | 6.9 (N=29) | 3.6 (N=28) | 3.2 (N=209) |
| Housewives in mohallas | 33.3 (N=63) | 19.5 (N=77) | 34.3 (N=35) | 30.2 (N=43) | 34.2 (N=76) | 35.7 (N=28) | 21.2 (N=33) | 58.6 (N=29) | 44.8 (N=58) | 30.6 (N=477) |
| Wage earners | 41.2 (N=17) | — (N=7) | 100.0 (N=1) | — (N=2) | 25.8 (N=31) | — (N=9) | 8.3 (N=24) | 52.4 (N=21) | 30.0 (N=10) | 22.1 (N=123) |
| Housewives in upper strata | 22.4 (N=49) | 34.1 (N=44) | 13.3 (N=30) | 42.5 (N=40) | 27.8 (N=36) | 36.8 (N=19) | 37.0 (N=27) | 62.3 (N=69) | 48.0 (N=50) | 37.6 (N=342) |
| Career women | 10.5 (N=19) | 32.4 (N=34) | — (N=0) | 12.5 (N=16) | 42.1 (N=19) | 6.3 (N=16) | 50.0 (N=2) | 28.6 (N=21) | 18.8 (N=32) | 26.0 (N=181) |

*Note:* The total of those surveyed in each category includes those who failed to respond.

## Table 2d

Respondents whose husbands are unemployed, by city
(per cent of total number surveyed in each category)

| Respondents | Delhi | Bombay | Cochin | Madras | Hyder-abad | Calcutta | Ahmed-abad | Lucknow | Srinagar | All India |
|---|---|---|---|---|---|---|---|---|---|---|
| Students | — (N=22) | 4.8 (N=21) | — (N=23) | — (N=29) | — (N=27) | — (N=17) | — (N=27) | — (N=29) | — (N=28) | 0.9 (N=209) |
| Housewives in mohallas | 4.8 (N=63) | 5.2 (N=77) | — (N=35) | 4.7 (N=43) | 6.6 (N=76) | 3.6 (N=28) | 6.1 (N=33) | 6.9 (N=29) | 5.2 (N=58) | 5.3 (N=477) |
| Wage earners | 11.8 (N=17) | — (N=7) | — (N=1) | — (N=2) | 9.7 (N=31) | — (N=9) | 4.2 (N=24) | — (N=21) | — (N=10) | 5.2 (N=123) |
| Housewives in stratta | 2.0 (N=49) | — (N=44) | — (N=30) | 5.0 (N=40) | 5.6 (N=36) | — (N=19) | 3.7 (N=27) | 1.4 (N=69) | 8.0 (N=50) | 2.9 (N=342) |
| Career women | — (N=19) | 2.9 (N=34) | — (N=0) | — (N=16) | 5.3 (N=19) | 31.3 (N=16) | — (N=2) | — (N=21) | — (N=32) | 5.4 (N=181) |

*Note:* The total of those surveyed in each category includes those who failed to respond

have been evident through the pronouncements of Muslim leaders, in the emergence of women leaders or in institutions. It was hoped that the field trip through the nine cities already surveyed would provide some of the answers.

The field trip focused on Muslim women and men leaders who were actively involved in community projects or in politics. Few women or men leaders interviewed were nationally known. However, their involvement in the community and in the region gave them a special perspective on the problems and prospects of the community in the region. Some leaders of other communities were also interviewed for their assessment of the Muslim community, its leaders, problems and prospects. Community institutions were visited so that their role and effectiveness could be evaluated.

The field trip provided additional insights into the regionally specific economic, social and political problems of different Muslim communities. All interviewers were asked the same questions about legal changes in the status of Muslim women; their economic participation; the economic position of the community; the incidence of polygamy and unilateral divorce; the advantages of using a standardized Nikahnama or marriage contract form to overcome secular discrepancies in marriage practices; education and literacy in the community and, lastly, institutions and their role in promoting economic and social change. Different regions had dealt differently with these social and economic problems, due to the lack of a national social organization and because economic opportunities differed, depending on occupational structures. Politically, of course, there is no unity between communities or regions in terms of support for a particular political party.

The field trip showed that while the significant factors which moulded Muslim attitudes and actions were similar to those affecting other communities in the same region, there were innate factors such as communal tension, concern for preservation of identity and survival as a community that were specific to the Muslim community. Muslim women were affected both by regional conditions, attitudes towards women and by pressures on the community.

The distinction between political and private religion was emphasized across the country, and respondents' attitudes and practices differed significantly from the rhetoric of conservative leaders of the community. This was particularly noticeable in the progressive attitudes towards purdah, women's education, the language in which respondents were literate or educated, supportive attitudes towards women working outside the home, reflecting pragmatism and responsiveness to change in society. The overweening concern with identity and the emphasis on nationally uniting symbols reflected the economic, social and political insecurity of a minority community.

Regional Muslim communities tended to be more influenced by local norms of social behaviour than by other Muslim communities. Throughout the cities surveyed there was evidence of adaptation and change in private religion as attitudes and family practices responded to modern urban pressures and its attendant ideology. Practices such as purdah, more prevalent in northern cities, tended to be flexibly observed. There was evidence of greater emphasis on secular education for women in response to economic necessity and the search for employment. In Madras it was pointed out that women in lower socio-economic strata were better educated than those in the upper strata so they could compete more effectively for jobs. There was little evidence on the field trip of polygamy or unilateral divorce.

In Delhi, Calcutta, Lucknow and Ahmedabad there were fewer Muslim institutions that could provide social guidance or support to the community. In Ahmedabad and Bombay there were sectarian organizations specific to the Khojas and Bohras which were well organized to deal with and guide their communities but did not include the rest of the Muslim community. This, however, was not an unmixed blessing because these organizations are rather conservatively run, with little thought given to innovation or adaptation particularly as far as women are concerned. In Bombay and Trivandrum there were attempts by the community to create organizations which could address women's and other social problems. In Bombay the Bazm-e-Niswan to some extent symbolizes an attempt to deal with social issues that specifically concern women. In Trivandrum, in keeping with regional trends, the age at marriage for Muslim women is higher and a better understanding of religion is promoted through a Malayalam translation of the Quran. The Palayam Mosque Committee, consisting of two members of different Muslim sects, provides a forum for the presentation and possible resolutions of various family disputes, though its decisions are not legally binding. The Kerala High Court, under the leadership of Justice Krishna Iyer, sought to interpret Quranic laws favourably for women. In recent years the maintenance case filed by Shah Bano Begum against her husband was successfully fought up to the Supreme Court which used secular legislation to award her maintenance, although this did not violate the Shariat, since it was circumvented by using a secular criminal law to insist on destitute women being supported by their husbands. This led the politically well organized conservatives in the community to mount a vociferous defence of the Shariat, a classic display of political religion. They sought the repeal of the secular laws under which Muslim women had been granted maintenance and asked for assurances from the government that Muslim law would no longer be open to interpretation by the courts. Muslim women on the other hand demonstrated in favour of the judgement and on their part sought assurances from the government that the laws which helped Shah Bano would not be repealed and the courts not prevented from interpreting the Shariat. For the first time there was an issue which brought out the differing interests of Muslim men and women. It established that Muslim women who had so far acquiesced with men in the continuance of social laws were prepared to take a stand and fight for their legal rights and to break rank with the community. The government, however, chose political expediency and passed a Muslim Women's Protection Bill in 1986 that gave in to the conservatives while ignoring the protests of the women. It met the conservative demands by disallowing any further legal attempts by Muslim women to get maintenance and disposed off the problem of divorced Muslim women by forcing them to seek help from their families or from Muslim waqfs which are neither able nor geared to such usage. There has been an appeal filed by a group of divorced Muslim women in the Supreme Court against the Bill on the grounds that it violated their constitutional rights. The outcome is still awaited.

The political exigencies of a minority community, particularly one with a past, creates its own tensions. The need to present a united front was evident as all community leaders, prior to the Shah Bano case, on the field trip, reiterated their support for the Shariat and the Urdu language, even though there was direct evidence that regional language schools are being used for children's education and that Shariat laws are being more generously interpreted to meet women's needs. As one leader put it, the desire for symbolic religious unity was necessary ". . . because a fearful minority is a conservative minority". (Kamilla

Tyabji, Bombay, 23 August, 1977), while another felt that "... the government should be more concerned with ameliorating the economic conditions of the community before they try to change their laws; changes in law and the growing stress against their language and culture threaten the community." (Justice Basheer Ahmad Sayed, Madras, August 1977.) Political religion continues to be a strongly motivating force as different Muslim communities struggle to maintain or improve their political and economic position. To improve this position there was general recognition of the importance of secular education, though discrimination in the job market and the increasing frequency of communal riots directed at the economic base of the community were a disincentive.

Leaders felt the need for Muslim social institutions which could fulfil the community's desire to institutionalize and transmit changes to all sections of the community, and to represent their interests to the rest of society. The absence of such institutions was really marked during the Shah Bano case, where other than the conservatives no other organizations representing liberals or women were in evidence. While a number of organizations were hastily formed, including a Muslim women's organization, it was too late to put up an adequate defence. The primary reason for this lack has been apathy and money within the community which could have been utilized for social purposes. The importance of political representation in order to safeguard the community's economic interests was important to all regional Muslim communities and one to which they had paid the most attention.

Muslim women were affected by the ever present communal tensions since it restrained them from actively lobbying legal and other changes either within the community or politically. The ruinous financial consequences of communal riots on the community also tended to adversely affect the ability of women to achieve economic independence, or to improve the education and career prospects of younger women of the community. The lack of well-trained Kazis or interpreters of Muslim law and of Muslim or state organizations to monitor such laws left Muslim women without much legal or social protection. Standardization of the marriage contract form could alleviate some of these problems by specifying conditionality without affecting Shariat laws.

The lack of a dynamic women's movement has affected Muslim women as much as other women, as has the lack of a substantive Muslim middle class. There is little leadership to provide the community or women with clear objectives or guidelines or to improve social or economic conditions. However, Muslim communities did display a certain degree of resilience and pragmatism in dealing with social and economic issues. While they acknowledged the importance of Urdu and Muslim Personal Law as providing important linkages between disparate communities they devised internal regional solutions to deal with social problems, and secular education has been given preference over religious or Urdu education.

The survey and the field trip sought to establish a methodological basis for evaluating the status of minority Muslim women, rejecting the unidimensional approach of studies that based it on Islamic tenets, relating it instead to the reality of Indian political, economic and social conditions as they affected Indian women and communities.

The difficulties of initiating such a study, only marginally assisted by other studies, is apparent. The field trip gave many concerned Muslim men and women a chance of expressing the community's fears and hopes. The pressures of maintaining identity while effectively dealing with economic and political changes by the community are evident in its response to the unequal legal position of Muslim women. This question was discussed by leaders on the field trip, as were questions relating to education and employment, since the preservation and survival of Muslim culture and identity was clearly identified with the community's ability to become economically effective and viable.

The survey and field trip served to relate the experience and reactions of different Muslim communities to the experience of other regional communities in dealing with changes in India.

# 8

## Marriage, Family and Purdah

The institutional importance of the family as a structure in which male and female roles are played out and new generations are reared and socialized, has led to its regulation by all religions and, over time, a proliferation of customs and practices that direct these relationships. The emphasis on child-bearing and rearing served to underscore the role of women and, in India, purdah or the ideology of the seclusion of women was one of the customs used to perpetuate this role. In this chapter attitudes and practices relating to marriage and the extent to which purdah influences Muslim women's lives are examined.

### Marriage and family

In India, forms of marriage vary, but although it is a sacrament for Hindus and a contract for Muslims, both cummunities agree on the importance of marriage for women. (Ross, 1961:61) Other similarities, depending on region and socio-economic circumstances, include age at marriage, reificataion of women and the specified behaviour of brides towards the husband and his family. (Karim, 1963:304) Keeping these differences and similarities in mind we examine both the extent to which women respondents shared activities with their husbands and their role in family decision making. This contrasts with the traditional family structure based on segregation, with specific roles and responsibilities for men and women; these roles were always conceived of within the framework of the extended family and its interests, rather than the interest of the two persons directly involved. The cultural parameters of male-female roles are evaluated through the responses of housewives and reflects their estimation of their role in decision making and inter-familial relationships. Some sociologists have argued that this presents only one side of the marriage mosaic. (Wilkening, 1963:349-350) In the Indian context the approach is justified since the role of marriage partners seems to be sharply differentiated and the views of the traditionally less powerful member on decision making and participation are significant. It also indicates the extent to which private religion has adapted to urbanization and change. Perceptions and attitudes of respondents are affected by the role of the extended family in arranging marriages and controlling aspects of family life. (Heer, 1963:133) Stratification takes into account women from different socio-economic strata, and it differentiates between respondents engaged in economic activity outside the home and housewives; both of which affect the respondent's family situation. (Cartwright, 1959:109) Urban respondents can be presumed to have experienced some easing of both the extended familial ties and traditional caste and religious structures, giving them more choice and independence. (Gore, 1968:151) Women in minority communities are subject to a number of discriminatory factors which make it difficult for them to overtly diversify their role playing, while symbolically maintaining their traditional identity. Thus women tend to suffer a double disadvantage when they belong both to a minority community and to the female sex (Almquist, 1975:129)

The institutional importance of marriage and family and its centrality in women's lives is an enduring belief in India. This is demonstrated by cultural practices and religious and social traditions which continue to support role differentiation, marriage and family. While concessions to modernity have raised the age of marriage, increased educational levels and extended the available career opportunities for women, the desirability of marriage as the pre-eminent goal for women continues to be stressed. (Kapur, 1974:9) There has been no real questioning of the validity of role differentiation between men and women, even among social scientists. The expansion of women's rights and roles is, therefore, considered within this framework of role differentiation. While the expansion could be considered as a first step towards greater equality, it has actually meant that women are bearing an additional burden since male support and complementary accommodating roles have not gained wide acceptance. It has also meant that marriage is still considered the first and most desirable goal of a woman's life; the attendant problems of widowhood, dowry and social acceptability of single career women continue to be important, while the implementation of equality in many different spheres has remained elusive.)

Family relationships in India are intricately defined. The definitions approximate to the degree of authority that can be exercised over relatives; the courtesy and obedience to be extended; the relatives before whom a female may appear unveiled and whom she may address directly. The system tends to formalize both relationships and women's roles. Marriage, through the elimination of other alternatives, used to be the only option open to women. Within marriage, the husband and his family controlled all outside relationships. Women were entirely dependent on the goodwill of men as they had no independent financial standing. It was only after a few years of marriage and children, particularly a son, that a woman's position in the family improved and her participation in family decision making increased.

This should not imply that men in the family exercised total control over women's lives. The woman's influence was a function of age and seniority in the family hierarchy. It was also contingent upon the control exercised by the head of the family. In a joint family, males were also subject to control by the head of the family and were not always free to support their wives financially or in a bid for independence. (Gore, 1968:150) They were not able to direct their own lives although as a rule men had more control over them and more options to choose from.

The increase in the number of nuclear families due to urbanization, has helped to make marriage more of a relationship between two persons, involving the rest of the family much less. Family ties are still strong, however, and still exercise considerable control over choice of marriage partner.

There has been a modification of traditional restrictions and behavioural constraints, but they have not been discarded. M.S. Gore has shown that the urban nuclear family is only marginally less restrictive in maintaining customs and practices controlling women than the traditional joint family. (Gore, 1968:168) The traditional prescribed behaviour of wives towards husbands which emphasized their total dependence, economic, social and spiritual, and which manifested itself in daily rituals such as touching of feet, fasting for the husband's health and longevity, and eating only after men had eaten, is being less rigidly enforced and more liberally interpreted. (Kapadia, 1956; Thapar, 1963) There has, however, been no redefinition of equality in male-female status. While many of these customs applied only to Hindu women, the general acceptance of dependency and subservience characterized all communities.

Many attitudes towards women and marriage are supposed to be based on religious beliefs and prescriptions. Studies have detailed the religious basis for these beliefs. (Dube, 1969) While such a basis does exist this study demonstrates that ethnic diversity and regional differences between members of the same religious group have meant that actual practices differ from region to region. Neighbours belonging to different religious groups may be closer, in practices and attitudes, to each other than to community members in other regions.

Initially, Hindu women lacked the right to inheritance, divorce and remarriage. Muslim women had these rights but almost never invoked them; the system fused to produce regional patterns of female rights and roles. After the passage of the Hindu Code Bill the legal inequality between the rights of Hindu men and women was eliminated, while the marginal inequality between the rights of Muslim women and men remained. Despite these differences in the legal status of Hindu and Muslim women and the extent to which legal rights helped and hindered them before 1947, the lack of equality or the extent of inequality that restricts them today depends on custom and practice in different regions. Thus, it is important here to examine both marriage and family relationships and regional customs and practices relating to women, rather than to focus solely on religious dogma. Prior to 1947, some attempts were made by women leaders to shift the ideological emphasis from marriage to economic independence, but these were muted. While Mahatma Gandhi deplored the more iniquitous customs hampering women, he appealed to their traditional conditioning of self-effacement and self-sacrifice, even as he called on their help in the national struggle. (*Towards Equality*, 1974:231)

This lack of structural change in male-female relations and attitudes has placed a great strain on women, particularly on educated ones. The family is no longer the social security system it once was for women. The pace and scale of change in India has placed an additional burden on women who now face competition for jobs (teachers, nurses, doctors) which had initially been their domain as a result of seclusion. (O'Barr, 1976:12) In the past Indian men and women lived separate lives with defined social obligations; now women find themselves called upon to play a variety of roles, while still trying to conform to the traditional concept of the wifely role. However, the situation of Indian women is by no means unique. Legal, religious and social prescriptions have provided justification for the subordination of women in western and other eastern societies. Asymmetry in male-female roles exists even in those societies where women are not in seclusion. Even when their labour contributes directly to the subsistence of the family and the group, their relative position continues to be inferior. (Kapur, 1974:9)

In traditional societies the changes in the social structure induced by social, economic and political factors have been of particular concern and the desire to blend tradition with modern requirements is reflected in social policy commentaries. Community leaders see changes in women's roles as inevitable, but are concerned that a too open break with tradition may diffuse group differentiation. Concern for the maintenance of Indian tradition has been voiced by feminists and academics in India, who hoped that the progress of Indian women would not be at the expense of the family. Concerns have also been voiced in the specific context of Muslim families and societies. One commentator felt that

> ... the Muslim family today faces many challenges from modern society for the reason that the traditional status of women (in our society) has not been revised in the light of original Islamic teachings. We stick to ... medieval notions of women's status in society and offer resistance to the changes called forth by modern needs; most of those who interpreted Islam belonged to the medieval period and they tried to justify their notions of the rights of women in Muslim society from the Quran and the Hadith. But these interpretations do not appeal to the modern mind and there is urgent need to reinterpret Islam and its original spirit, so as to exclude medieval notions fostered on it. This is a task which should seriously be undertaken by Muslim scholars, thinkers and intellectuals.

> Niazi, 1976:10,11

Their desire to maintain certain aspects of tradition and integrate them into modern structures is not exclusive to India, and it is parallel in other societies which are experiencing change. (Giele, Smock, 1977:49) Thus it is important to see the reiteration of traditionality as maintaining a facade of countinuity, even where actual practices may have been abandoned.

In Table 1, 70.2 per cent of respondents, as expected in a stratified survey, were married. The majority of those single were students, while only 7.7 per cent were divorced or widowed. Married respondents were asked whether they shared leisure time activities with their husbands. The sharing of such activities is considered important by sociologists since it is widely accepted that couples should value such time together. (Ortner, 1975:91) This is of course, contrary to the traditional Indian pattern of segregated roles and, therefore, there are few joint activities between men and women, even married ones. Traditionally, women shared their activities with other women in the family and, when they went beyond the family, it was with women of a similar caste and class background. The concept of women and men meeting socially is relatively new. Also, social activities imply a certain financial outlay, beyond the means of many in India. Nevertheless, a clear majority of respondents (55 per cent) indulged in a wide variety of social activities with their husbands. A further 21 per cent accompanied their husbands only to the doctor or to visit relatives; and a mere 18 per cent reported on joint activities with their husbands at all.

While the majority of respondents go everywhere with their husbands, the socio-economic stratum is an important factor in determining the extent of this activity. Among housewives in mohallas and wage earners those reporting joint social activities were a much smaller proportion of the total than housewives and career women in the upper strata. The domination of men in this lower strata affects home and outside relationships for their wives thus increasing women's dependency. (Blood, 1972:57) The fact that 46 per cent of housewives in mohallas and wage earners participated in activities with their husbands should be considered an advance on the traditional separation of activities.

Respondents were asked whether their husbands took an active interest in the house and the children, and whether or not they helped with household chores and child care. The majority of respondents said their husbands helped them with household chores; this was particularly true for housewives in the upper strata and for career women.

In Table 2, while a clear 69 per cent responded positively to the question, it must be noted that, traditionally, men did participate in chores that involved interaction with the outside

**Table 1**

Leisure-time activities with husbands

| | Cinema, friends everywhere | Relatives, doctor | Does not go out | No response | Total |
|---|---|---|---|---|---|
| Students | 10 | 1 | - | 8 | 19 |
| | (52.6) | (5.3) | (-) | (41.1) | (100.0) |
| Housewives in mohallas | 194 | 105 | 96 | 21 | 416 |
| | (46.6) | (25.2) | (23.0) | (5.0) | (100.0) |
| Wage earners | 35 | 14 | 23 | 5 | 77 |
| | (45.4) | (18.9) | (29.9) | (6.4) | (100.0) |
| Housewives in upper strata | 196 | 60 | 48 | 9 | 313 |
| | (62.6) | (19.5) | (15.3) | (2.8) | (100.0) |
| Career women | 86 | 14 | 6 | 6 | 111 |
| | (77.4) | (12.6) | (5.4) | (5.4) | (100.0) |
| Total | 521 | 193 | 173 | 49 | 936 |
| | (55.5) | (20.6) | (18.4) | (5.2) | (100.0) |

*Note:* Figures in brackets are percentages of the total of each row.

**Table 2**

Whether husband shares in household chores

| | Yes | No | No response | Total |
|---|---|---|---|---|
| Students | 7 | 2 | 10 | 19 |
| | (36.8) | (10.5) | (52.6) | (100.0) |
| Housewives in mohallas | 282 | 110 | 24 | 416 |
| | (67.7) | (26.4) | (5.7) | (100.0) |
| Wage earners | 42 | 29 | 6 | 77 |
| | (54.5) | (37.6) | (7.7) | (100.0) |
| Housewives in upper strata | 232 | 73 | 8 | 313 |
| | (74.1) | (23.3) | (2.5) | (100.0) |
| Career women | 83 | 26 | 2 | 111 |
| | (74.7) | (23.3) | (1.8) | (100.0) |
| Total | 646 | 240 | 50 | 936 |
| | (69.0) | (25.6) | (5.3) | (100.0) |

world. This was necessitated by the norms of segregation and their response may not reflect participation in chores within the house.

Table 3 indicates that 48.2 per cent felt that budgetary decisions involved both respondents and their husbands; 28.4 per cent felt they had entire control over the family budget. This indicates closer interaction and co-operation on matters which were traditionally considered to be a male prerogative. Among career women and wage earners the majority had a greater say in financial decision making compared with the two housewife categories.

Students were asked to pick careers that they were interested in. Such choices reflect changes in attitudes towards women's employment and students' perceptions of their options in the job market. Table 4 shows that students still tilted heavily towards teaching, which is a traditionally favoured occupation for women because teaching at a primarily female institution continues to segregate women and men; moreover it is considered to be a flexible career, easily adapted to family moves and changes. Only 23.8 per cent of students did not know or did not respond to the question. Therefore, while the majority planned careers, they did not appear to have well defined aims or goals. This reflects the continued conditioning of women towards marriage and family, the lack of career counselling at women's institutions and the inherent limitations of the Indian economy.

While there has been a definite change in women's attitudes towards employment, it is clearly not sufficient to overcome the tradition of arranged marriages, required to maintain caste and

**Table 3**
Expenditure decisions

|  | I decide | He decides | We decide | No response | Total |
|---|---|---|---|---|---|
| Students | 4 | 2 | 6 | 7 | 19 |
|  | (21.0) | (10.5) | (31.5) | (37.0) | (100.0) |
| Housewives in mohallas | 105 | 90 | 210 | 11 | 416 |
|  | (25.2) | (21.6) | (50.4) | (2.8) | (100.0) |
| Wage earners | 33 | 12 | 32 | — | 77 |
|  | (42.8) | (15.5) | (41.5) | (—) | (100.0) |
| Housewives in upper strata | 84 | 67 | 136 | 26 | 313 |
|  | (26.8) | (21.4) | (43.4) | (8.3) | (100.0) |
| Career women | 40 | 3 | 68 | — | 111 |
|  | (36.0) | (2.7) | (61.2) | (—) | (100.0) |
| Total | 266 | 174 | 452 | 44 | 936 |
|  | (28.4) | (18.6) | (48.2) | (4.7) | (100.0) |

### Table 4
Careers students wish to pursue
(percentages)

| | |
|---|---|
| Teaching | 46.4 |
| Secretarial | 8.1 |
| Executive | 10.0 |
| Government | 2.3 |
| Air-hostess }<br>Modelling } | 3.3 |
| Professions | 5.7 |
| Don't know | 3.8 |
| No response | 20.0 |
| Total | 100.0<br>(N=209) |

endogamy rules. The pattern of employment, too, depends on caste and regional norms, while socialization continues to reinforce gender roles. However, the very consideration of a career represents a positive change and lack of expectations can be seen to be a result of limitations of the economic structure. Religion appears to have little bearing on responses and in this respect upholds the findings of other studies. (Goldstein, 1972:109; Lamar, 1969:291, 295, 298) Aileen Ross has pointed out that in urban areas, on issues of education and employment, caste, language and social class have little bearing on the behaviour of families, who tend to reflect similar ambitions, conflicts and tensions, the homogenizing effects of urbanization and industrialization. (Ross, 1961:61)

## Purdah

Purdah has been characterized as an extreme form of sex role differentiation (Saifullah Khan, 1974:1) and as providing "separate worlds and symbolic shelter", (Papanek, 1973:289-325) It has been pointed out that, even where the custom as symbolized among Indian Muslim women by the wearing of an outer garment is discarded, the "purdah mentality" continues to affect the attitudes of women, (Papanek, 1971:529) and to limit their public roles.

Attitudes propagating the seclusion of women are quite general in India, even where they have not been formalized by an extra piece of clothing. Family structures, bolstered by socio-religious customs, help to maintain hierarchy and authority within the family. For all women, whether Hindu or Muslim, seclusion was a method of exercising this control. In practice there is greater purdah within certain upper caste Hindu families, while Muslim purdah is practised vis-a-vis outsiders, and is much less rigid within the family. (Papanek, 1973:304) In either case, purdah limits the freedom of women and confines them to domestic roles. The ability of a family to keep its women in purdah is directly related to their socio-economic status, i.e., where the family is not dependent on the woman's earning capacity. Status of families and communities is, therefore, linked to their ability to protect their women through purdah. Ironically, upwardly mobile groups often find it necessary to practice purdah when they aspire to a higher social level. (de Stuers, 1968:98) To women forced to work, purdah can be both liberating and a status symbol. (Tinker, 1974:66) The practice has an important effect on men as well, since on them devolves the sole responsibility for the economic and physical well being of the family. As with women, the family structure tends to impose limitations on men restricting change. (Mazhar ul Khan, 1972:69)

Even today attitudes towards "suitable" roles for women reflect traditional limitations and moderate both the expectations of women and the realities of their status. In effect, the functioning of the "purdah mentality" continues to influence the status and role of women. However, purdah has not been entirely negative in its effects on women; it enabled them to move into fields of activity such as teaching and medicine and, through these, to other areas.

In India, among urban Muslims, the survey indicated that women do not regard purdah as religiously binding; nor are they compelled by their husbands or families to observe the custom. The present continuation of purdah emphasized by the wearing of an outer garment does not, therefore, appear to be the extreme form of sex role differentiation which it was at an earlier period. The pattern of seclusion depends on a number of factors, including the social origins of the family; the place and region where they live; education and maintenance of the family's honour, a concern which goes beyond specific religion in India. (Giele, Smock, 1977:49) Purdah reflects the socio-economic environment in which there are limited opportunities for employment; it also reflects regional and class differentials and the need for symbolic Islamic differentiation. These factors have obscured the extent to which changes in the attitudes of women in the community have reduced the importance of purdah.

In differentiating the responses of purdah and non-purdah women, the primary focus of the study was on those aspects which, due to seclusion, most affect women in purdah. The immediate impact of purdah is reduced access to other women and to the rest of society. Comparing the responses of purdah and non-purdah women to questions on family decision making, contacts with the community and society and awareness of changing social, political and economic conditions provides an insight into the extent to which purdah women are institutionally insulated from social changes occurring in society. It also provides evidence of the adaptiveness of the community.

Almost 50 per cent of respondents who observed purdah themselves or came from families that observed it were from the two housewives categories. Personal purdah practised by the respondents was negligible in the case of students, wage earners and career women. This is also the case of families in purdah in these categories in Table 5. Only 34.5 per cent of respondents in purdah felt that it was a religious requirement, mainly from the two housewives categories. Some 34 per cent felt it was a family custom and only 3.4 per cent observed it because their husbands insisted on it.

## Family relationships

Family relationships, particularly those relating to income disbursement and decision making, tend to reflect the constraints facing women in purdah compared to women not so encumbered. Lack of purdah implies greater control over all aspects of their lives, overcoming the traditional restraints imposed on women through intensely regulated family structures. The following discussion examines the responses of purdah and non-purdah women to social activities with husbands, their role in family decision making, knowledge of family income and their say in its disbursement.

In making an assessment of the activities of purdah and non-purdah women, it must be borne in mind that the concept of social activities is still relatively new in India. While such activities are gaining acceptability in urban areas, they are still more a function of socio-economic status and dependent on what is considered "acceptable" behaviour in the strata to which respondents belonged: in the case of non-purdah women it may

**Table 5**
Who observes purdah?

| | Respon-dent | Respon-dent's daughter | Respon-dent's in-laws | Entire family | No-one | No response | Total |
|---|---|---|---|---|---|---|---|
| Students | 20 | 1 | 9 | 63 | 92 | 24 | 209 |
| | (9.5) | (0.4) | (4.3) | (30.1) | (44.0) | (11.4) | (100.0) |
| Housewives in mohallas | 141 | 6 | 13 | 102 | 162 | 53 | 477 |
| | (29.5) | (1.2) | (2.7) | (21.3) | (33.9) | (11.1) | (100.0) |
| Wage earners | 19 | 2 | 3 | 23 | 58 | 18 | 123 |
| | (15.4) | (1.6) | (2.4) | (18.6) | (47.1) | (14.6) | (100.0) |
| Housewives in upper strata | 70 | 4 | 9 | 98 | 142 | 19 | 342 |
| | (20.4) | (1.1) | (2.6) | (28.6) | (41.5) | (5.5) | (100.0) |
| Career women | 21 | 1 | 8 | 28 | 104 | 19 | 181 |
| | (11.6) | (0.5) | (4.4) | (15.4) | (57.4) | (10.4) | (100.0) |
| Total | 271 | 14 | 43 | 314 | 558 | 132 | 1332 |
| | (20.3) | (1.1) | (3.2) | (23.5) | (41.9) | (9.9) | (100.0) |

(Figures in parentheses are percentages.)

be an extension of the "purdah mentality" that continues to place limits on their activities, and among purdah women, the actual constraints imposed by seclusion. As might be expected, women not in purdah were much more likely to go everywhere with their husbands, than women in purdah as indicated in Table 6. This was true of all categories other than wage earners. Conversely, women in purdah were much more likely to not accompany their husbands anywhere than women not in purdah. However, nearly 25 per cent of respondents in purdah did accompany their husbands everywhere, and a further 15 per cent to the doctor and relatives, implying that the traditional demarcation between the domestic realm of the wife and the public realm of the husband was beginning to blur.

Table 7 compares purdah and non-purdah respondents' responses to how decisions were made regarding the disbursement of household income. About 39 per cent of purdah and 47 per cent of non-purdah respondents felt that decisions were jointly made; 26 per cent non-purdah and 20 per cent purdah respondents felt the husband decided. Non-purdah respondents were therefore, only marginally better off. It is particularly noteworthy that very few wage earners or career women felt that the decision was made solely by the husband, a reflection perhaps of their own earning capacities.

## Table 6

Comparison of social activities with husband of married women[a]

| | Not in purdah | | | | | In purdah | | | | |
| --- | --- | --- | --- | --- | --- | --- | --- | --- | --- | --- |
| | Every-where | Doctor/relatives | Nowhere | No response | Total | Every-where | Doctor/relatives | Nowhere | No response | Total |
| Housewives in mohallas | 83 (51.4) | 30 (18.5) | 21 (12.7) | 28 (17.3) | 162 (100.0) | 87 (35.8) | 57 (23.5) | 67 (27.6) | 32 (13.1) | 243 (100.0) |
| Wage earners | 12 (20.2) | 7 (12.8) | 14 (23.6) | 25 (43.4) | 58 (100.0) | 12 (28.3) | 5 (11.0) | 9 (21.2) | 16 (39.5) | 42 (100.0) |
| Housewives in upper strata | 92 (64.7) | 21 (14.7) | 10 (7.0) | 19 (13.2) | 142 (100.0) | 78 (46.5) | 37 (21.8) | 36 (21.4) | 17 (10.3) | 168 (100.0) |
| Career women | 50 (48.0) | 4 (3.8) | – (-) | 50 (48.3) | 104 (100.0) | 18 (37.5) | 8 (17.1) | 5 (10.8) | 18 (34.5) | 49 (100.0) |
| Total | 237 (50.8) | 62 (13.5) | 45 (9.7) | 122 (26.1) | 466 (100.0) | 195 (38.8) | 107 (21.3) | 117 (23.3) | 83 (16.5) | 502 (100.0) |

[a] Excluding students.

**Table 7**

Income disbursement decision

| | Not in purdah | | | | | In purdah | | | | |
| --- | --- | --- | --- | --- | --- | --- | --- | --- | --- | --- |
| | I decide | He decides | We decides | No response | Total | I decide | He decides | We decide | No response | Total |
| Housewives in mohallas | 37 (22.8) | 31 (19.1) | 88 (54.3) | 6 (3.7) | 162 (100.0) | 63 (25.9) | 52 (21.3) | 96 (39.5) | 32 (13.1) | 243 (100.0) |
| Wage earners | 17 (29.3) | 10 (17.2) | 14 (24.1) | 17 (29.3) | 58 (100.0) | 15 (35.7) | 2 (4.7) | 14 (33.3) | 11 (26.1) | 42 (100.0) |
| Housewives in upper strata | 48 (33.8) | 20 (14.0) | 67 (47.1) | 7 (4.9) | 142 (100.0) | 35 (20.8) | 42 (25.0) | 63 (37.5) | 20 (16.6) | 168 (100.0) |
| Career women | 21 (20.1) | 2 (1.9) | 39 (37.5) | 42 (40.3) | 104 (100.0) | 14 (28.5) | 2 (4.0) | 22 (44.8) | 11 (22.4) | 49 (100.0) |
| Total | 123 (26.3) | 63 (13.5) | 208 (44.6) | 72 (15.4) | 466 (100.0) | 127 (25.2) | 98 (19.5) | 195 (38.8) | 82 (16.3) | 502 (100.0) |

Table 8 compares the level of education among purdah and non-purdah respondents. The number of purdah respondents without formal education was substantially larger than those not in purdah among all strata of respondents. Similarly, the proportion of respondents with secondary education and university degrees was higher among non-purdah respondents. Table 9 compares respondents' education; literacy was much lower among purdah respondents and, when literate, they were more likely to be literate in Urdu. While 11 per cent of non-purdah respondents knew no written language, 21 per cent of purdah respondents were literate only in Urdu but only 12 per cent of non-purdah respondents fell into this category. Of those not in purdah among the two housewives categories, 29-35 per cent knew regional and other languages compared to 9-15 per cent respondents in purdah. This distinction also appears among non-purdah and purdah career women, but not among students or wage earners.

Table 10 compares daughters' education among purdah and non-purdah respondents. Very few purdah or non-purdah respondents had daughters in denominational schools. The largest proportion among both purdah and non-purdah respondents was in secular schools. There were few differences between purdah and non-purdah respondents with regard to daughters' education, though more non-purdah respondents had daughters in private schools and colleges.

In Table 11 comparing the response of purdah and non-purdah respondents to questions probing their knowledge of Muslim Personal Law, particularly with regard to inheritance rights—an important factor considering that so many of their problems revolve around the knowledge and exercise of those rights—the vast majority did not know their specified share of patriarchal property (i.e., one-third); only 17 per cent of non-purdah and 23 per cent of purdah responded correctly.

The number of women who read newspapers or journals was not substantial among either purdah or non-purdah respondents. Table 12 indicates that only 26 per cent of non-purdah and 11 per cent of purdah respondents read journals; non-purdah career women and students were more likely to read newspapers than other categories.

Participation in elections by respondents was considered another indication of their involvement in the political process which could have been affected by purdah. Few respondents did not vote in elections, except in the case of purdah students, the

**Table 8**
Literacy

| | Not in purdah | | | | | | In purdah | | | | | |
|---|---|---|---|---|---|---|---|---|---|---|---|---|
| | Urdu only | Urdu + | Regional + | None | No response | Total | Urdu only | Urdu + | Regional + | None | No response | Total |
| Students | — (—) | 19 (20.6) | 66 (71.7) | — (—) | 7 (7.6) | 92 (100.0) | 3 (2.6) | 18 (21.6) | 54 (65.0) | — (—) | 8 (9.6) | 83 (100.0) |
| Housewives in mohallas | 41 (25.3) | 13 (8.0) | 70 (43.2) | 26 (16.0) | 12 (6.7) | 162 (100.0) | 65 (26.7) | 23 (9.4) | 40 (16.4) | 102 (41.9) | 13 (5.3) | 243 (100.0) |
| Wage earners | 1 (2.1) | 3 (5.1) | 20 (34.4) | 19 (30.6) | 15 (36.6) | 58 (100.0) | 2 (1.8) | 4 (9.5) | 10 (23.8) | 27 (63.1) | — (—) | 42 (100.0) |
| Housewives in upper strata | 25 (17.7) | 35 (24.6) | 56 (39.4) | 15 (10.5) | 11 (7.7) | 142 (100.0) | 48 (28.4) | 30 (17.8) | 31 (18.4) | 49 (29.1) | 11 (6.5) | 168 (100.0) |
| Career women | 1 (0.9) | 9 (8.6) | 90 (86.5) | — (—) | 4 (4.8) | 104 (100.0) | 3 (6.1) | 5 (10.2) | 27 (55.1) | — (—) | 12 (24.4) | 49 (100.) |
| Total | 68 (12.1) | 79 (14.1) | 302 (54.1) | 60 (10.7) | 49 (8.7) | 558 (100.0) | 121 (20.6) | 80 (13.6) | 162 (27.6) | 178 (30.4) | 44 (7.1) | 585 (100.0) |

## Table 9
### Education

| | Not in purdah | | | | | | In purdah | | | | | |
| --- | --- | --- | --- | --- | --- | --- | --- | --- | --- | --- | --- | --- |
| | No formal education | Primary | Secondary | BA+ | No response | Total | No formal | Primary | Secondary | BA+ | No response | Total |
| Students | - (-) | - (-) | 18 (19.5) | 62 (67.3) | 12 (13.0) | 92 (100.0) | - (-) | - (-) | 7 (8.4) | 73 (87.9) | 3 (3.6) | 83 (100.0) |
| Housewives in mohallas | 58 (35.8) | 41 (25.2) | 36 (22.3) | 19 (11.9) | 8 (5.2) | 162 (100.0) | 157 (64.8) | 40 (16.6) | 24 (9.8) | 5 (2.0) | 17 (6.3) | 243 (100.0) |
| Wage earners | 23 (40.2) | 3 (5.2) | 4 (6.3) | 15 (25.8) | 13 (22.3) | 58 (100.0) | 29 (69.0) | 1 (3.1) | 4 (8.9) | 5 (11.9) | 3 (5.6) | 42 (100.0) |
| Housewives in upper strata | 27 (19.4) | 27 (19.4) | 53 (37.7) | 26 (18.3) | 9 (5.0) | 142 (100.0) | 70 (41.8) | 25 (15.0) | 33 (19.9) | 12 (7.1) | 28 (16.2) | 168 (100.0) |
| Career women | - (-) | - (-) | 19 (18.4) | 81 (77.8) | 4 (3.8) | 104 (100.0) | 10 (20.4) | 3 (6.1) | 10 (20.4) | 21 (42.8) | 5 (10.6) | 49 (100.0) |
| Total | 108 (19.5) | 71 (12.8) | 130 (23.3) | 203 (36.5) | 46 (8.0) | 558 (100.0) | 266 (45.4) | 69 (11.7) | 78 (13.3) | 116 (19.8) | 56 (9.5) | 585 (100.0) |

## Table 10

### Daughters' education

| | Not in purdah | | | | | | In purdah | | | | | |
|---|---|---|---|---|---|---|---|---|---|---|---|---|
| | Denomi-national | Govern-ment | Private | College | No resp-onse | Total | Denomi-national | Govern-ment | Private | College | No resp-onse | Total |
| Housewives in mohallas | — (—) | 41 (24.4) | 39 (24.1) | 6 (3.7) | 76 (47.1) | 162 (100.0) | 7 (3.0) | 71 (29.7) | 25 (10.3) | 3 (1.4) | 135 (55.6) | 243 (100.0) |
| Wage earners | — (—) | 13 (21.5) | 1 (1.1) | 8 (12.9) | 36 (64.6) | 58 (100.0) | 1 (2.3) | 16 (38.1) | 1 (2.3) | 1 (2.3) | 23 (57.5) | 42 (100.0) |
| Housewives in upper strata | 1 (0.7) | 40 (28.4) | 31 (21.7) | 12 (8.6) | 58 (40.9) | 142 (100.0) | 1 (0.6) | 50 (29.5) | 7 (4.2) | 11 (6.5) | 98 (58.1) | 168 (100.0) |
| Career women | — (—) | 10 (9.4) | 12 (11.7) | 7 (6.6) | 75 (72.4) | 104 (100.0) | 3 (5.8) | 6 (11.5) | 1 (1.9) | 1 (1.9) | 40 (78.9) | 49 (100.0) |
| Total | 1 (0.2) | 104 (18.4) | 83 (14.9) | 33 (5.9) | 245 (60.4) | 466 (100.0) | 12 (2.1) | 143 (24.5) | 34 (6.2) | 16 (2.7) | 296 (64.6) | 502 (100.0) |

**Table 11**

Respondents' knowledge of share in father's property

| | Not in purdah | | | | | In purdah | | | | |
|---|---|---|---|---|---|---|---|---|---|---|
| | One-third | Half | Don't know | No response | Total | One-third | Half | Don't know | No response | Total |
| Students | 14 (15.0) | 3 (3.2) | 73 (79.3) | 2 (2.8) | 92 (100.0) | 23 (28.1) | 6 (7.7) | 48 (57.8) | 6 (7.2) | 83 (100.0) |
| Housewives in mohallas | 19 (11.7) | 9 (5.7) | 95 (58.4) | 39 (24.7) | 162 (100.0) | 40 (16.5) | 7 (3.0) | 144 (59.2) | 52 (21.4) | 243 (100.0) |
| Wage earners | 7 (11.6) | 5 (9.4) | 34 (58.6) | 12 (20.6) | 58 (100.0) | 10 (23.7) | 4 (8.8) | 23 (54.7) | 5 (12.4) | 42 (100.0) |
| Housewives in upper strata | 37 (26.3) | 8 (5.6) | 77 (54.5) | 20 (14.0) | 142 (100.0) | 47 (27.8) | 18 (10.5) | 87 (51.8) | 16 (9.5) | 168 (100.0) |
| Career women | 19 (18.2) | 9 (8.6) | 54 (51.9) | 22 (21.2) | 104 (100.0) | 16 (33.5) | 5 (11.1) | 18 (36.7) | 10 (19.3) | 49 (100.0) |
| Total | 96 (17.4) | 34 (6.3) | 333 (59.6) | 95 (16.8) | 558 (100.0) | 136 (23.4) | 40 (6.9) | 320 (54.6) | 89 (15.2) | 585 (100.0) |

### Table 12
Newspaper or journal reading

| | Not in purdah Yes | In purdah Yes |
|---|---|---|
| Students | 33.5 (N=92) | 31.1 (N=83) |
| Housewives in mohallas | 11.2 (N=162) | 5.2 (N=243) |
| Wage earners | 5.9 (N=58) | 6.2 (N=42) |
| Housewives in upper strata | 26.8 (N=142) | 8.0 (N=168) |
| Career women | 53.1 (N=104) | 19.4 (N=49) |
| Total | 26.1 (N=558) | 11.0 (N=585) |

majority of whom had not voted; among wage earners and housewives in mohallas there was greater vote participation among purdah observers. However, on the whole, Table 13 indicates that non-purdah respondents tended to participate marginally more in the voting process than those in purdah.

Respondents were asked what changes they would like to see among women of the community to assess their attitudes regarding the role and position of Muslim women in a society that is undergoing economic and social change. Tables 14a and 14b indicate the changes respondents would like to see among women in the community as measured by responses to an open-ended question. About 62 per cent non-purdah and 54.5 per cent purdah respondents wanted more education or careers for women in the community. This is an indication of the importance of education and economic independence in improving status and widening the roles women can play in society. Only 6-9 per cent of respondents in both categories mentioned the need for women to give up purdah, indicating that it was not an important issue and that if economic or educational circumstances warranted it, purdah would not be the factor holding women back. Few respondents mentioned dowry abolition indicating that because it was not widely practised, it was not an important issue in the community. Few respondents wanted women in the community to become more religious or to participate more in national life. Less than one per cent mentioned equal rights or

**Table 13**
Participation in elections (%)

| | Not in purdah | | In purdah | |
|---|---|---|---|---|
| | Voted | Did not vote | Voted | Did not vote |
| Students | 89.1 (N=92) | 9.3 | 19.2 (N=83) | 78.8 |
| Housewives in mohallas | 71.1 (N=162) | 24.2 | 80.5 (N=243) | 15.4 |
| Wage earners | 58.1 (N=58) | 34.9 | 71.2 (N=42) | 23.2 |
| Housewives in upper strata | 75.9 (N=142) | 21.8 | 69.6 (N=168) | 30.1 |
| Career women | 91.3 (N=104) | 4.9 | 84.4 (N=49) | 15.6 |
| Total | 77.7 (N=558) | 18.6 | 68.4 (N=585) | 27.1 |

abolition of unilateral divorce, implying that the Shariat remains important to the respondents and that the issue of unilateral divorce was not of great significance. The emphasis was entirely on education and careers, both of which if attained would mean independence and greater control of their lives for women.

The traditional segregation of women in purdah involved elaborate social rules and living spaces within the home and in public areas, such as parks, cinema-seating etc., and the rigidity of segregation kept purdah women separate from the mainstream of ideas and activities. (Papanek, 1973:291,294) A comparison here between purdah and non-purdah respondents indicates a break from the traditional pattern of segregation. Segregated living space is no longer the norm and the present purdah system no longer connotes strictly demarcated public and private spaces. Purdah Muslim women are now no longer non-participants in education or public life, since they are involved in political, economic and social activities.

Family relationships between respondents and their husbands are affected to some extent by purdah, but cooperation and discussion on important decisions and in the allocation of family income was usual among both purdah and non-purdah respondents. This is also reflected in the small number of respondents who attributed the continuation of the custom of purdah to their

## Table 14a

### Changes hoped for among women in the community

#### Not in Purdah

| | Leave purdah | Education | Careers | Abolition of dowry | Participation in national life | No changes | Must become more religious | No unilateral divorce women's rights | Religious moderation | Education and career | Equal rights | Don't know | No response | Total |
|---|---|---|---|---|---|---|---|---|---|---|---|---|---|---|
| Students | 13 (14.1) | 47 (51.3) | 3 (3.2) | 3 (3.2) | 9 (10.1) | - (-) | - (-) | 1 (0.7) | 1 (1.0) | 9 (9.3) | 1 (1.6) | 1 (0.7) | 4 (5.5) | 92 (100.0) |
| Housewives in mohallas | 3 (1.7) | 47 (29.4) | 9 (5.4) | - (-) | 10 (6.4) | 5 (2.9) | 6 (3.5) | 1 (0.5) | - (-) | 35 (21.8) | 3 (1.8) | 18 (11.2) | 25 (15.5) | 162 (100.0) |
| Wage-earners | 3 (5.6) | 17 (29.4) | 8 (14.3) | - (-) | 2 (2.7) | 3 (5.6) | - (-) | - (-) | - (-) | 14 (23.5) | 1 (1.7) | 3 (4.5) | 7 (12.4) | 58 (100.0) |
| Housewives in upper strata | 17 (12.1) | 54 (38.7) | 11 (7.8) | 1 (0.9) | 10 (6.8) | 7 (4.8) | 3 (1.8) | - (-) | 1 (0.5) | 22 (15.4) | 1 (0.5) | 4 (2.9) | 11 (7.9) | 142 (100.0) |
| Career women | 15 (14.9) | 35 (33.5) | 2 (1.5) | 1 (1.2) | 8 (8.1) | - (-) | 1 (0.6) | - (-) | 2 (1.9) | 34 (33.2) | 3 (2.5) | - (-) | 3 (2.4) | 104 (100.0) |
| Total | 51 (9.2) | 200 (36.1) | 33 (5.8) | 5 (0.9) | 39 (7.0) | 15 (2.6) | 10 (1.6) | 2 (0.3) | 4 (0.7) | 114 (20.4) | 9 (1.6) | 26 (4.6) | 50 (9.2) | 558 (100.0) |

**Table 14b**

Changes hoped for among women in the community

**Not in purdah**

| | Leave purdah | Education | Careers | Abolition of dowry | Participation in national life | No changes | Must become more religious | No unilateral divorce women's rights | Religious moderation | Education and career | Equal rights | Don't know | No response | Total |
|---|---|---|---|---|---|---|---|---|---|---|---|---|---|---|
| Students | 19 (22.8) | 21 (25.4) | 5 (6.6) | 2 (2.2) | 11 (13.5) | 1 (0.8) | 3 (4.1) | - (-) | 3 (3.5) | 10 (12.0) | 2 (2.4) | 4 (4.3) | 2 (2.4) | 83 (100.0) |
| Housewives in mohallas | 7 (2.8) | 49 (20.2) | 25 (10.3) | 1 (0.5) | 7 (2.8) | 8 (3.5) | 15 (6.1) | 1 (0.2) | 1 (0.5) | 62 (25.4) | 10 (4.3) | 26 (10.9) | 31 (12.0) | 243 (100.0) |
| Wage-earners | - (-) | 8 (19.6) | 6 (13.8) | - (-) | 1 (2.2) | 3 (7.4) | 1 (3.1) | 1 (2.2) | - (-) | 16 (38.7) | - (-) | 2 (4.7) | 4 (8.3) | 42 (100.0) |
| Housewives in upper strata | 5 (3.2) | 47 (28.4) | 24 (14.6) | 4 (2.5) | 12 (7.2) | 9 (5.3) | 18 (10.7) | - (-) | 2 (1.2) | 14 (8.6) | 2 (1.1) | 16 (9.5) | 15 (7.5) | 168 (100.0) |
| Career women | 4 (7.8) | 18 (36.7) | 7 (13.7) | 3 (6.1) | 2 (4.0) | - (-) | 3 (5.5) | - (-) | - (-) | 5 (10.6) | - (-) | 4 (7.4) | 3 (7.2) | 49 (100.0) |
| Total | 35 (6.0) | 143 (24.5) | 67 (11.6) | 10 (1.8) | 33 (5.8) | 21 (3.6) | 40 (7.0) | 2 (0.3) | 6 (1.1) | 107 (18.4) | 14 (2.4) | 52 (8.8) | 55 (8.7) | 585 (100.0) |

husbands' insistence.

The practice of purdah in urban areas tends to affect the work women can do outside the house. This was pointed out by Ela Bhatt (personal interview, Ahmedabad, 24 August 1977), the Secretary and organizer of SEWA (Self-Employed Women's Association) a union of women labourers. Muslim women labourers constituted 25 per cent of the membership, were enthusiastic participants at union meetings and conscientious in repaying loans. While purdah was not an impediment to their union participation or their economic activity, it tended to affect the type of work they did. Other union members were vegetable vendors, head-loaders etc., while Muslim women members tended to work at home as garment makers and patchwork workers.

This is the pattern in the northern states where Muslim women work contractually at home at beedi making (rolling indigenous cigarettes), carpet weaving and embroidery. In Kashmir, however, women also work in the fields. Muslim women are usually skilled workers and if well organized, could derive enormous benefit but, because they do not conduct business themselves, the benefit of their labour frequently accrues to men—and to middlemen. They are precluded from being able to unionize, except in Gujarat, to form a cooperative to realise the full worth of their skills.

The field trip indicated that most Muslim communities were now turning their attention to solving their social and economic problems through the formation of associations and women's groups. Examples of these are the Muslim Education Society in Kerala, various educational societies in other states, and a variety of Muslim women's organizations which all emphasize education as an avenue to progress. This is in keeping with the new social and cultural concerns of the community and the views of the majority of respondents who emphasized the importance of education and jobs for Muslim women as well as increased participation and social interaction with other communities.

The purdah mentality continues to separate the activities of men and women, irrespective of community, region or class, though the formal manifestations no longer operate. Purdah is given great emphasis by social scientists who attribute to it Muslim women's lack of political and social participation: ". . . purdah is still followed by Muslim women, so how can they decide whom to marry and whom to vote for?" (Hate, 1969:36).

In fact the survey shows that, despite purdah, Muslim women's participation in the political process has been substantial both in casting their vote and deciding whom to vote for. The decision to marry and the choice of marriage partners for women in India is still very much under the family's control, even for educated women not in purdah. This lack of choice is reflected by the continuance of the dowry system which tends to reduce women to barter items, cuts across communities and regions and is not specific to the Muslim community.

Among associations started by Muslim women, particular mention needs to be made of the Basm-e-Niswan in Maharashtra. It was started in response to a severe communal riot in 1958 requiring community rehabilitation, by Mrs. Khatija Khateeb, (personal interview, Bombay, 23 August, 1977) who had been in purdah most of her life, even through boarding school in Poona and college in Bombay. The organization has ten rural centres in Maharashtra which provide primary education to children and involve Muslim women in social welfare activities. It has also met some specific community needs, such as textbooks which integrate Marathi, English and Urdu along with other instruction. While Mrs. Khateeb does not practice purdah in Bombay any more, she still uses it when she visits the rural centres, since the conservative image helps her to gain greater support for her work. She felt that purdah need not prevent women from being actively involved in economic or social activities, and that with sufficient economic opportunities the remnants of the purdah system would go. She did not feel there were any inconsistencies between her many activities and interests and her use of purdah.

This attitude was reflected throughout the field trip in interviews with men and women. They no longer regarded purdah as a brake on mobility or achievement; with the breakdown of the traditional structure which made it viable, there appeared to be little concern for the institution or its continuance. Time and better economic conditions would, it was felt, take care of the problem. Most men and women interviewed on the field trip mentioned that their mothers or, in some cases, their grandmothers had been in purdah, but over the period of their lives, had been increasingly less protected and more involved in social and economic changes. In some cases, respondents had themselves started life in purdah but this had not prevented them from being educated or involving themselves in public life. This was the pattern with respondents from Lucknow, Srinagar,

Calcutta, Delhi and Hyderabad, rather than from cities in the south where purdah was not such an important factor. The comparison between purdah and non-purdah respondents makes it clear that socio-economic circumstances materially affect responses and that they reflect educational and economic limitations which implicitly influence the perceptions of both types of respondents. However, the responses of housewives in both socio-economic categories frequently were closer than responses of other respondents.

Family relationships portray changes almost irrespective of purdah, reflecting the closer interaction and dependencies of nuclear families. However, the economic independence of wage earners and career women was reflected in their responses on monetary decision making. Non-purdah respondents tended to be more involved in all aspects of family life and decision making than purdah respondents; but only a small percentage of purdah respondents were entirely cut off from this process. While non-purdah respondents were better able to respond to modern economic and social requirements, purdah respondents no longer appear subject to traditional constraints; they reflect instead the new and flexible form of purdah current in India which is shaped more by social pressures and less by deep conviction. The purdah mentality which continues to moderate the activities of Indian women generally, and perhaps Muslim women particularly, could be said to limit their achievement horizons, but this will be increasingly widened as social and economic conditions change.

## Conclusion

Family relationships and purdah observance among survey respondents tended to reinforce the importance of stratification and region for identifying factors that most affect attitudes and behaviour. The importance of marriage and the bearing of children for women has led to various customs which supported and encouraged marriage to the exclusion of other options. Over time, purdah, the curbing of education for women and early marriage were customs developed to limit women's options. In the 19th century the plight of young widows emphasized the necessity of widening employment and other opportunities for women through education, and removal of purdah. Such changes sought to improve the status of women in society and within the family; this chapter is indicative of the piecemeal nature of such changes, for while there have been changes in marriage relationships as segregation broke down, such changes have been limited by economic and social developments. This was true in leisure time activities with husband, decision-making for all respondents and a comparison between purdah and non-purdah respondents. However, the similarity between purdah and non-purdah respondents is an indication of the extent to which purdah has been breached. While differences did exist between different categories of respondents, particularly career women, wage earners and the two housewives categories, it was found that purdah respondents were no less involved and concerned with issues that confront Muslim women.

# 9

## Education And Literacy

To some extent, the ability of women to participate in modern economic, political and social structures remains contingent upon their ability to acquire the skills needed for this participation. Traditionally, women did and could participate in economic activities without necessarily requiring sophisticated modern skills; it is increasingly evident however, that for entry into the current job market the necessary training and skills required need social organization and education. (Salazar, 1975) Women, thus, tend to be self-employed, in domestic or other service employment, as labourers in small workshops or in agriculture. (Chaney, 1975:169) But even these limited opportunities can be eroded as the economy adopts technologically advanced techniques (Chaney, 1975:163) for which women are not trained. Though education may not ensure the entry of women into the required job market it remains an important factor in their ongoing struggle to deal with and adapt to changes in the economy.

Education, therefore, is necessary both in rural and urban areas if women are to effectively improve their participation rate in economic activities. In urban areas women find it even more important to acquire the skills needed to compete against already skilled competitors. (Tinker, 1976:72; *Towards Equality*, 1975:90) This is not to overstate the case for education; it is a necessary *but not sufficient* condition for the greater participation of women in modern economies.

### Indian educational realities

Though social reformers and successive governments have emphasized the importance of women's education, and while considerable progress has been made, education and literacy for

women remains low. In **1947** primary school enrolment constituted 83 per cent for all girls in the educational system, middle
school enrolment was 9 per cent and secondary school enrolment
only 7 per cent, with hardly any university enrolment. By 1970-71
73 per cent were enrolled in primary schools, 14 per cent in
middle schools, 7.3 per cent in secondary schools, 2.4 per cent in
universities and colleges and 3.3 per cent in professional schools
(*Towards Equality*, 1975:90). Despite this progress the drop-out
rate for girls remains high. Of 100 girls enrolled in the first grade
only 30 reach grade five, dropping out before they gain functional literacy, primarily because they are useful to the family as
household help and in contributing to the family income. Socio-
economic factors make these options more attractive than continuing with education. In higher socio-economic strata the
education of women has been boosted by the education of men
and their preference for educated wives. (*Towards Equality*,
1975:95).

Regional factors too, affect women's education and roles. This
is amply demonstrated by the enormous differences, between
regions, of women literates. Urban literacy varies from 62 per
cent in Kerala to 29 per cent in Jammu and Kashmir. Table 1
represents women literates as a percentage of total female
population for the states covered by the survey.

This table shows not just the extent of literacy among women
currently, but mirrors their historical background. Kerala's high
literacy is a result of progressive policies followed by the State

**Table 1**

Female literates as a percentage of total female population, 1971

| State | Female literates |
|---|---|
| Kerala | 62.50 |
| West Bengal | 47.82 |
| Maharashtra | 46.58 |
| Tamil Nadu | 45.55 |
| Gujarat | 44.33 |
| Andhra Pradesh | 33.27 |
| Jammu and Kashmir | 28.89 |
| Uttar Pradesh | 33.27 |
| Delhi | 55.56 |

*Source:* Census of India, 1971.

of Travancore before 1947. West Bengal was among the first states to introduce western forms of education in the 19th century, followed by Maharashtra and Tamil Nadu during the days of the Presidency. Uttar Pradesh, while fairly quick to introduce education among men, was tardy on the education of women. At the present time most urban parents are convinced of the need for women's education. According to a survey conducted by the Committee on the Status of Women in India, (*Towards Equality*, 1974:261) only 16.8 per cent felt girls should not be educated; 64.5 per cent felt that while they should be educated they should not go in for higher education. The Committee also noted that the middle class is committed to education as a sign of modernization, while the lower middle class regarded it as a means of economic mobility. However, they faced financial and other difficulties which constrained the education of daughters (*Towards Equality*, 1974:261,262). In Andhra Pradesh, Maharashtra and Uttar Pradesh there has been great progress in women's education at the primary level; in Delhi, Jammu and Kashmir, Kerala and Tamil Nadu progress has been both at the primary and middle level. In West Bengal, female enrolment at the primary level was maintained, but not at the middle school level, while only in Kerala, Tamil Nadu and Delhi was there definite progress at the secondary school level.

The National Committee on Women's Education, 1958-59, advocated separate institutions for girls to break down the prejudice against their education. In 1947-48 only 10.3 per cent of educational institutions were exclusively for women. By 1967-68 this had increased to 29 per cent; in 1947 only 14.4 per cent of school teachers were women; this had risen by 1967-68 to 26 per cent in primary, 30 per cent in middle schools and 37 per cent in secondary schools; in universities and colleges it has risen from 8.5 per cent in 1950-51 to 15 per cent in 1970-71. The lower proportion in primary school teaching is due to the difficulties faced by single teachers in rural areas. On the field trip Mrs. Khateeb of the Bazm-e-Niswan noted that she had to overcome local prejudice against single women teachers living alone in villages. She had to persuade Muslim women in rural areas to teach and to use her own traditional image and background to gain support and credibility for them. (*Towards Equality*, 1975:92; Khatija Khateeb, Bombay, 1977). Since family wealth and status are no longer considered guarantees of financial security, middle class families regard education as a prime instrument of social mobility (Mehta, 1970:164). A similar desire for vertical mobility exists among lower middle class families who are willing to make sacrifices for their children's education. Education is also increasingly regarded by these classes as a way of meeting unforeseen contingencies in women's lives (Mehta, 1970:94). However, traditional attitudes of hostility or indifference to higher education could be one of the contributory factors holding girls back from higher education. (*Towards Equality*, 1975:94).

Female literacy in India has increased from 0.9 per cent in 1901 to 18.4 per cent in 1971. The number of literate females per thousand males has increased from 68 to 435. However, the total number of illiterate women has increased from 161.9 million in 1951 to 215.3 million in 1971 due to the increase in population. In the age group 15 to 24, 29.8 million or 87.5 per cent of women are illiterate; in the age group over 25, illiterate women total 74.5 million or 86.8 per cent of female population. Of the literate women in the 25+ age group the majority have only primary level education. (*Towards Equality*, 1975:94)

The findings of the survey tend to correspond with these national statistics. Respondents' education and literacy has been considered separately to provide for informal schooling and this is borne out by the number of respondents who, while they have received no formal education, were in fact literate.

## Survey

The formal educational level of respondents takes into account primary, secondary and college or university, and also covers those without formal education. Since respondents were stratified, much of the information on education, socio-economic categories etc., tended to coincide with the categories, i.e., students and career women were by definition better educated than wage earners or housewives in lower socio-economic strata. The majority of respondents had received some formal education, a high proportion with secondary or university degrees. Around one half of housewives in mohallas and wage earners had no formal education. About 22.5 per cent of wage earnes were "overqualified" as wage earners, perhaps a reflection of the lack of economic opportunities, or of enterprise on the part of respondents. Among career women, a small number are listed without formal education. This may be because they are Urdu or Quran teachers for which they need not be formally trained, but for our purposes are considered career women. Housewives in mohallas appear to be the least educated reflecting the prevalence of traditional socio-economic factors in these neighbourhoods. Due to stratification this sample may not be representative of the rest of the female Muslim population.

Table 3, when read in conjunction with Table 2, clearly shows that there is some informal education among respondents. Most respondents were literate in Urdu, English and a regional language. The 15.8 per cent of respondents literate only in Urdu probably form the bulk of those not formally educated but literate. All other language combinations imply some formal education. Apart from students and career women there was some illiteracy in all categories. It was particularly high among housewives in mohallas. Very few students were literate just in Urdu, evidence of the move away from their language of identification to languages which can provide them with better employment opportunities. Similarly, for career women, the majority are literate in a combination of languages rather than just Urdu. Only among the two housewives' categories are about 24 per cent of respondents literate only in Urdu.

The respondents' commitment to education, as enabling social mobility and providing career opportunities, was further tested in their responses to questions about the education of their sons and daughters. The questions were designed to establish whether

**Table 2**
Respondents' level of education

|  | Primary | Second-ary | Univer-sity | No formal education | No res-ponse | Total |
|---|---|---|---|---|---|---|
| Students | — | 45 (21.4) | 146 (69.9) | — | 18 (8.7) | 209 (100.0) |
| Housewives in mohallas | 87 (18.3) | 75 (15.6) | 28 (5.9) | 261 (54.7) | 26 (5.4) | 477 (100.0) |
| Wage-earners | 7 (5.7) | 11 (9.0) | 28 (22.5) | 59 (48.5) | 18 (14.2) | 123 (100.0) |
| Housewives in upper strata | 61 (17.8) | 94 (27.5) | 45 (13.1) | 105 (10.9) | 37 (30.0) | 342 (100.0) |
| Career women | 3 (1.6) | 32 (17.9) | 122 (67.1) | 11 (6.6) | 12 (6.6) | 181 (100.0) |
| Total | 158 (11.8) | 257 (19.2) | 369 (27.6) | 437 (32.8) | 111 (8.3) | 1,332 (100.0) |

(Figures in brackets are percentages of the total of each row.)

## Table 2a

Respondents whose husbands are employed by city
(per cent of total number surveyed in each category)

| Respondents | Delhi | Bombay | Cochin | Madras | Hyder-abad | Calcutta | Ahmed-abad | Lucknow | Srinagar | All India |
|---|---|---|---|---|---|---|---|---|---|---|
| **Students** | —<br>(N=22) | —<br>(N=21) | —<br>(N=23) | —<br>(N=29) | 7.4<br>(N=27) | —<br>(N=17) | —<br>(N=27) | 3.4<br>(N=29) | —<br>(N=28) | 1.7<br>(N=209) |
| Housewives in mohallas | 41.3<br>(N=63) | 46.8<br>(N=77) | 40.0<br>(N=35) | 41.9<br>(N=43) | 35.5<br>(N=76) | 42.9<br>(N=28) | 63.6<br>(N=33) | 31.0<br>(N=29) | 24.1<br>(N=58) | 40.8<br>(N=477) |
| Wage earners | 11.8<br>(N=17) | 42.9<br>(N=7) | —<br>(N=1) | 100.0<br>(N=2) | 38.7<br>(N=31) | 22.2<br>(N=9) | 54.2<br>(N=24) | 14.3<br>(N=21) | —<br>(N=10) | 32.8<br>(N=123) |
| Housewives in upper strata | 63.3<br>(N=49) | 54.5<br>(N=44) | 70.0<br>(N=30) | 37.5<br>(N=40) | 44.4<br>(N=36) | 47.4<br>(N=19) | 44.4<br>(N=27) | 31.9<br>(N=69) | 42.0<br>(N=50) | 47.6<br>(N=342) |
| Career women | 57.9<br>(N=19) | 20.6<br>(N=34) | —<br>(N=0) | 31.3<br>(N=16) | 31.6<br>(N=19) | 18.8<br>(N=16) | —<br>(N=2) | 28.6<br>(N=21) | 43.8<br>(N=32) | 29.3<br>(N=181) |

*Note:* The total of those surveyed in each category includes those who failed to respond. N denotes the total number of respondents in each category, in each city, who responded to the question.

there was discrimination between boys and girls in education and whether only traditional education was being imparted through denominational schools and whether secular schools were being used by respondents. Only respondents with children are considered; students' responses have not been considered because few had children.

Table 4 on daughters' education is representative of respondents with daughters of an appropriate educational age. The high level of no responses would indicate that the respondents either had no daughters or they were not of the appropriate age or circumstances. Very few respondents appear to be educating their daughters at denominational institutions; the majority attended secular government schools or other educational institutions. Few respondents' children combined work with study, except at home. Respondents were further asked if they would try to overcome any difficulties that may arise in continuing their daughters' education. Of those who responded the majority would make the effort to overcome any such difficulties. Only wage earners took a more cautious view. In the Indian context the response to this question is not automatically positive, because various customs and traditions enforce attitudes that regard the education of girls as unimportant and unnecessary. The positive response, therefore, indicates a change from tradition. This commitment to education may have been more complete had there been a direct correlation between education and

### Table 4
Daughters' education

|  | Denomi-national | Govt. school | Private school | College | Work+ school/college | No response | Total |
|---|---|---|---|---|---|---|---|
| Housewives in mohallas | 7 (1.7) | 124 (29.8) | 77 (18.0) | 6 (1.4) | 16 (3.9) | 186 (44.7) | 416 (100.0) |
| Wage-earners | 1 (1.2) | 23 (29.8) | 7 (9.0) | 1 (1.2) | 6 (7.7) | 39 (50.6) | 77 (100.0) |
| Housewives in upper strata | 3 (1.0) | 90 (28.7) | 46 (14.6) | 21 (6.7) | 6 (1.9) | 147 (46.9) | 313 (100.0) |
| Career women | 3 (2.7) | 15 (13.5) | 16 (14.4) | 8 (7.2) | 1 (0.9) | 68 (61.2) | 111 (100.0) |
| Total | 14 (15.2) | 252 (27.4) | 146 (15.9) | 36 (3.9) | 39 (3.1) | 430 (46.8) | 917 (100.0) |

employment and social mobility for women. In reality, expenditure on education beyond literacy may not always be justified if the perception is of limited economic opportunities for women.

## Conclusion

The discussion on Muslim women's education or on Muslim education generally, has so far tended to include all Muslims without regard to the individual community's occupational or socio-economic structure, a distinction usually made for other communities; an article by A.R. Kamat (Kamat, 1981:1031-1033) is an indication that there is some realization of the need to make such distinctions in the Indian context. Earlier studies such as Krishan and Madhav's *Pattern of City Literacy* (Krishan, Madhav, 1974:795) and C.A. Hate's *Changing Status of Women in Post-Independence India* (Hate, 1969) provide evidence of the educational backwardness of Muslims using such overall statistics. While Krishan and Madhav correlate size of Muslim population to illiteracy in cities, Hate notes that of an overall population of 7.6 per cent Muslim women only 2.9 per cent are educated or engage in non-manual work. (Hate, 1969:36)

Specific area studies such as S.P. Jain's *The Social Structure of the Hindu Muslim Community* (Jain, 1975) and Rhoda Goldstein's study of students in Bangalore (Goldstein, 1972) indicate that socio-economic differences are important factors in determining education and aspirations. Jain has noted that among Muslims there was a correlation between education, class and caste similar to that for Hindus. (Jain, 1975:177) Goldstein noted that Muslim women in Bangalore were either studying, employed or seeking employnment. (Goldstein, 1972:103) Similarly, Shibani Roy's study of Muslims in north India notes that income and higher education were closely linked and that from mother to daughter illiteracy has decreased by 16.5 per cent; informal education has decreased by 31.36 per cent; school education has increased by 14.9 per cent and college education by 32.67 per cent (Roy, 1979:63). Further, she found no illiteracy among Muslim men and, except for a few older women, women supported the education of daughters. (Roy, 1979:68,69)

This study, by differentiating between socio-economic strata and by probing attitudes, can further the argument that a definite correlation exists between education and class and that while education is often a means of achieving employment and upward mobility, lack of economic opportunities and discrimination can render higher education dysfunctional.It is also important to consider Muslim women's education in the context of both the education of women in India and development. Ester Boserup, in comparing educational levels for women in different countries, has noted that the percentage of women students to all women is almost the lowest in India, compared to other Asian countries. (Boserup, 1970:120) This is further borne out by a later study by Padma Desai which indicates that among Asian nations India has the highest female illiteracy and that women involved in economic activities outside the house are, as a percentage of total female population, the lowest in Asia. (Desai, 1975:33,23) In India, the correlation between education and economic achievement is less readily made for women due to the persistence of both discrimination in employment, and of certain social traditions which continue to regard employment for women of secondary importance to marriage and family. These attitudes and traditions are widely prevalent and affect all communities.

Due to stratification this survey is not representative of the Indian Muslim community as a whole. However, despite the limitations of respondents' own educational background, their attitude towards daughters' education and the lack of discrimination between sons' and daughters' education is encouraging. Also the predominance of secular education is evidence of an understanding of the schooling required to improve future employment opportunities. The main obstacle, cited by respondents, to further education for girls was monetary, rather than anticipated difficulty in finding marriage partners for educated daughters as noted by respondents to the Committee's survey *(Towards Equality*, 1974:261). Students, too, noted th at they had been supported by both parents in their decision to continue their education.

# 10

## Within the Mainstream

The Muslim community lost much of its urban middle class at Partition; this consequently affected the community's ability to overcome the economic, social and political difficulties that beset it after 1947. Politically it lost credibility and its efforts to reorganize were regarded with suspicion and hostility. Its economic base was eroded and its ability to recoup impaired by the migration of entrepreneurial talent and by the loss of political power. As has been established, social changes in the Muslim community, particularly in relation to women, education and social practices, had evolved over time. However, with Partition and the loss of broad-based leadership of both sexes, political parties tended to nominate party members, designating them community leaders, to symbolically represent the community. These leaders were unable to reflect the community's aspirations or to provide the leadership required for it to take its place in the new social, economic and political order. The established political leadership did not encourage the formation of fresh grassroots Muslim leadership for historic reasons; they preferred the convenience of appointing pliable leaders who could be utilized to benefit the party or the leadership without raising controversial or difficult questions either within the community or in national forums. Most Muslim leadership has, therefore, been used to symbolically represent the community, without tackling any of the more difficult issues confronting it. Their attention is thus focussed on the lowest common denominator—the need to maintain the identity of the community through support for Muslim Personal Law (Lateef, 1978), but without seeking to genuinely implement its tenets or its regulations (except negatively) for women. Efforts to organize politically on a communal basis have not only been regarded with suspicion by other communities but have not been popular within the community, whose members have wisely opted to work through established political parties. The lack of a middle class has affected the community's ability to create and maintain social organizations that would represent the community, and provide a forum in which community issues can be debated and find resolution.

The cumulative effect of Muslim separatist politics and the subsequent loss of male and female leadership has been two-fold. Firstly, historians and political scientists, in analysing Muslim separatist politics, have concentrated on Islam as being the primary factor determining Muslim behaviour, without relating the response of the Muslim community to the response and strategies adopted by other communities to the political struggles being waged in India prior to 1947. This also does not take into account the regional and ideological differences that existed within the community, while the ideologically and regionally specific responses of other communities were all considered under the canopy of Indian nationalism (Karandikar, 1969; Lal Bahadur, 1954). This had resulted in a certain stereotyping of the Muslim community as being uniquely unable to accept modern political structures the way other communities have done. Sociologists using the same approach in the post-Independence period have not linked the responses of the Muslim community to those of other communities, taking into account regional and socio-economic factors. (Jain, 1975) Thus the stereotype of Muslim lack of responsiveness to social change and modern political, economic and social structures has been perpetuated.

Secondly, the loss of leadership after independence and the lack of social organizations since, have made it more difficult to address the specific social and economic needs of Muslim women both within the community and in relation to other communities. Token leadership has caused these requirements to be ignored· since supporting them would necessitate politicians' supporting causes which conservative sections of the community would resist. The lack of feminist leaders, both in the Indian women's movement and in the community, leaves Muslim women without direction and support. This lends credibility to the social scientists' stereotype of Muslim women being in purdah, uneducated and unresponsive to social, political and economic changes. (Hate, 1969:36,61) The Muslim community, generally, and Muslim women in particular, are considered to be outside the

Indian mainstream by academics and commentators even though, conceptually, an Indian mainstream is hardly credible since, at best, it applies only to a small fraction of the urban educated population and, even among them, there is no real rejection of caste, regional or religious affiliations.

This chapter attempts to analyse the responses of Muslim women to questions relating to their rights under Muslim Personal Law and the Indian Constitution. It also looks at their interaction with non-community members and their activities in order to determine their participation or distance from the so-called mainstream.

## Knowledge of rights

As has been pointed out earlier, Muslim women's rights to divorce, inheritance, repudiation of arranged marriage and dower had been eroded over time and their restitution was urged by all leaders of the women's movement. In fact, it was hoped that this restitution would lead to legislative changes for women's rights in other communities. The passage of the Shariat Act or Muslim Personal Law in 1937, and the Dissolution of Muslim Marriages Act of 1939 was, therefore, regarded as having advanced the rights of women. However, with the passage of the Hindu Code Bill in 1956, the drawbacks of the Shariat Act have been highlighted— specifically the continuing permissibility of polygamy and unilateral divorce, whether practised or not, as these detract from the ascriptive status of Muslim women. Though changes in Muslim Personal Law continue to be resisted by the community, there have been secular legislative changes made after 1947 which can be used by any citizen. The Special Marriages Act is one such, which entitles women to use special divorce and inheritance laws. In keeping with previous policy, legislative changes have been left to the internal decision of the Muslim community, and the passage of the Muslim Women's Protection Bill in 1986 emphasizes this, though it is possible to challenge the government's assumption that this represented the majority community opinion. This legal differentiation has left intact the male option of polygamy and unilateral divorce, both of which have been banned in several Muslim countries but continue to remain legal in India. One complicating factor in orchestrating support for such changes is the nature of Islam, which has pronounced on both the spiritual as well as the social structure that should define Muslim society. The theological

implementation was left to individuals while the pronouncements on marriage, divorce, custody of children and inheritance,
etc., aspects which require legal implementation, have been left
to the State. Islam sought to bring women into the community
of believers and to invest them with duties and rights, though
no systematic definition of their role or status is attempted in the
Quran. (Giele, Smock, 1977:37) These rights were called the
Shariat (Anderson, 1971:16), and represented a system of moral
values rather than legally enforceable laws. Customary laws had
always existed in different Muslim countries and had legal
validity, while Shariat rights served as a counterpoint to them.
Courts were regulated not by Qazis or interpreters of the Quran,
but by rulers and the government, which did not consider itself
bound by the Shariat. The rise of nationalism with its Islamic
symbols in different Muslim societies gave the implementation
of the Shariat greater importance, but laws like the family, have
been evolving in Muslim societies. And while there have been
some efforts to provide a socio-religious basis for women's inheritance and other family laws they have been based on a
*reinterpretation* of the Shariat (Anderson, 1971:18-29) rather than
a reconsideration of it.

Among the rights accorded to Muslim women are inheritance
of property from father and husband. Muslim women also had
the right to repudiate a marriage contracted without their consent on their behalf by their guardians; they have the right to
dower or mehr, a part of their husband's property, at the time
of marriage. Muslim women as well as men could get a divorce,
even a unilateral divorce (Minaltur, 1975:99-100). Polygamy was
permitted on specific conditions which, if complied with, would
be impossible to fulfil. The socialization process of women has
been such that rights accorded to them have seldom, if ever, been
complied with. This was particularly the case if they conflicted
with the rights of men over polygamy; with the family over
dower or inheritance, or with the community over the enforcement of women's rights. In India, social structures effectively
preempted the rights of all women, including Muslim women.
Dower, the right of the bride to a portion of the husband's
property, could rarely be claimed at marriage since it would
make marriage alliances more diffcult to arrange, would indicate
greed and detract from family honour. (Giele, Smock, 1977:100)
It was felt that if dower was set at an impossibly high figure, it
would ensure against divorce or ill treatment and would afford

the wife security, since it is the first claim levied on a deceased husband's property. In reality, women seldom gained control over the dower property. (Pastner, 1975:5) Although remarriage, due either to divorce or widowhood, is permitted under Islam, Muslim women in certain regions could not easily remarry due to the prevailing social prejudice against remarriage, to which the Muslims also subscribed. (Giele, Smock, 1077:101) Therefore, despite the intention of Islamic laws and secular laws that seek to enforce changes in the status of women, the only way there can be any change is through individual women or organized women's groups seeking their implementation.

Muslim law makes specific inheritance provisions for all degrees of female relatives, so that their security is not jeopardized. Though this share is usually less than that of men, women seldom got their share of immovable family property. (Pastner, 1975:7) In India this lack of a share in immovable property is compensated by marriage gifts and continuing support by the family. Even when marriages are arranged within families between cousins, women seldom inherit their share of the property without resorting to protracted law suits, and even where Muslim law has been superseded, as in Turkey, women's inheritance has not significantly benefited. In fact, women's access to property is always at the convenience of male members of the family rathe than on legal grounds even when those exist. The passage of the Shariat Act in 1937, once expected to help Muslim women better their legal prospects, has singularly failed to benefit them either with regard to property or dower, since social attitudes have not changed sufficiently for them to be able to demand their rights. This has also been the experience after the passage of the Hindu Code Bill which ensured Hindu women's inheritance legally, but not actually. (*Towards Equality*, 1974:135) In the course of the field trip, men and women leaders were asked to comment on Muslim women's rights and their ability to use them, and on the prevalence of polygamy and unilateral divorce. Most respondents bemoaned the lack of organizational or individual awareness among Muslim women of their rights, and while polygamy in the experience of the respondents was rare, there was a feeling that unilateral divorce was often invoked among lower socioeconomic groups to get rid of unwanted wives.

Respondents were asked whether they were aware of their inheritance rights, rights in divorce and in the Constitution, to assess awareness and usage. Table 1 indicates that the majority

**Table 1**

Muslim women's share of father's property

| Respondent | One-third | Half | Goes to son | Don't know | No response | Total |
|---|---|---|---|---|---|---|
| Students | 43 | 10 | 1 | 143 | 12 | 209 |
| | (20.6) | (4.7) | (0.3) | (68.3) | (6.1) | (100.0) |
| Housewives in mohallas | 80 | 19 | 8 | 271 | 99 | 477 |
| | (16.7) | (4.1) | (1.7) | (56.7) | (20.9) | (100.0) |
| Wage earners | 25 | 10 | — | 67 | 21 | 123 |
| | (20.2) | (8.0) | (—) | (54.7) | (17.1) | (100.0) |
| Housewives in upper strata | 93 | 26 | 1 | 180 | 42 | 342 |
| | (27.2) | (7.6) | (0.3) | (52.6) | (12.3) | (100.0) |
| Career women | 44 | 15 | — | 88 | 34 | 181 |
| | (24.1) | (8.2) | (—) | (48.7) | (19.0) | (100.0) |
| Total | 285 | 80 | 10 | 749 | 208 | 1332 |
| | (21.3) | (6.0) | (0.8) | (56.2) | (15.8) | (100.0) |

(Figures in parentheses are percentages.)

of respondents did not know of their rights to one-third of the patriarchal family property, although among career women and housewives in the upper strata, approximately half were aware of this right. However, respondents were clearly aware that the property did not all go to the male line.

Respondents were further asked whether they knew how they could obtain their rights in property, and were also asked about the agency through which this right could be obtained: the courts, family or community. The majority of respondents may not have known their share of inherited property rights, but they were aware of the efficacy of courts should they require redress. Table 2 indicates that respondents were also aware of the role that family and community can play in assisting them. Housewives in mohallas laid particular emphasis on intervention by the family. Very few respondents felt that women could not receive their inheritance; those who did not know probably reflected indecision on the method rather than a conviction that women cannot be recompensed. Among students and career women there appears to be greater reliance on legal procedures than on other agencies. Taken together the two tables are indicative of the manner in which women's rights are regarded in society and by women themselves. While actual details of rights are hazy, there is considerable awareness that legal disputes are

### Table 2
How to obtain family inheritance

| Respondent | Courts | Family & commu- nity | Court & commu- nity | No re- course | Don't know | No res- ponse | Total |
|---|---|---|---|---|---|---|---|
| Students | 117 | 42 | 6 | 6 | 14 | 24 | 209 |
|  | (55.8) | (20.0) | (3.0) | (2.9) | (6.7) | (11.5) | (100.0) |
| Housewives in mohallas | 203 (42.5) | 114 (23.9) | 22 (4.5) | 22 (4.5) | 52 (10.8) | 64 (13.6) | 477 (100.0) |
| Wage earners | 53 (43.1) | 24 (19.5) | 10 (8.1) | 5 (4.0) | 19 (15.0) | 12 (10.4) | 123 (100.0) |
| Housewives in upper strata | 146 (42.6) | 92 (26.9) | 7 (2.0) | 16 (4.8) | 21 (6.3) | 60 (17.5) | 342 (100.0) |
| Career women | 123 (67.9) | 30 (16.3) | 3 (1.5) | 2 (1.1) | 8 (4.2) | 16 (9.0) | 181 (100.0) |
| Total | 642 (48.1) | 302 (22.7) | 48 (3.6) | 51 (3.8) | 114 (8.5) | 175 (13.2) | 1332 (100.0) |

inevitably settled through courts or through the good offices of the family and community. Without the ready support of the women's movement or economic independence, women find it difficult to call attention to their rights and, in the process, alienate members of their family.

Since the passage of the Dissolution of Muslim Marriages Act of 1939, the right of Muslim women to divorce has been fairly liberally interpreted. The Act combines the most liberal features of different schools of Islamic jurisprudence to assist women seeking a divorce. The grounds for divorce are (i) whereabouts of the husbands not known for four years; (ii) failure of husband to provide maintenance for two years; (iii) sentence of imprison- ment of husband for seven years; (iv) failure without cause to perform marital obligation for four months; (v) impotence; (vi) insanity; (vii) if a minor is married, she can repudiate the mar- riage at puberty; (viii) cruelty of husband i.e., habitual assault, associating with women of ill repute, attempting to force his wife to lead an immoral life, disposing of her property or preventing her from exercising her legal rights over it, obstructing her in the observance of her religion or has more than one wife and does not treat her equitably.

Respondents were asked if they knew how they could get a divorce, a right Muslim women have always enjoyed. In Table 3 the majority of respondents were aware that they could get a divorce through the courts; few respondents placed their reliance on persuading the husband to give them a divorce or on intervention by a Muslim clergyman who had performed the wedding. The intervention of the family or community remained important. The nikahnama or marriage contract can serve as an important document to protect the rights of the wife, since it can contain clauses which prohibit unilateral divorce, polygamy, etc. There have been suggestions in recent years that the contract form should be standardized to routinely include protective clauses. Respondents seemed aware of the importance of the contract form and its ability to protect their rights; the majority, however, were aware of the legal protection offered by the courts and few respondents were completely ignorant of how they could secure a divorce. However, if we include the don't knows with no responses and categories other than courts and nikahnama, almost 40 per cent of respondents appear unsure of their ability to secure a divorce.

When asked to name some of the rights given to them under the Indian Constitution the majority of respondents, as Table 4 demonstrates, were unaware of their constitutional rights. Here the distinction between career women and students and other

## Table 3

Conditions under which divorce can be obtained

|  | Courts | Nikah-nama | Family & community | Persuade husband |  | Don't know | No response | Total |
|---|---|---|---|---|---|---|---|---|
| Students | 100 | 24 | 12 | 7 | 5 | 45 | 17 | 209 |
|  | (47.6) | (11.4) | (5.7) | (3.4) | (2.4) | (21.7) | (7.9) | (100.0) |
| Housewives in mohallas | 200 | 61 | 64 | 33 | 10 | 71 | 38 | 477 |
|  | (42.0) | (12.7) | (13.4) | (7.0) | (2.1) | (15.0) | (9.9) | (100.0) |
| Wage-earners | 51 | 18 | 13 | 8 | 21 | 3 | 9 | 123 |
|  | (41.7) | (15.0) | (10 9) | (6.5) | (17.4) | (2.4) | (7.9) | (100.0) |
| Housewives in upper strata | 160 | 42 | 37 | 12 | 13 | 49 | 28 | 342 |
|  | (46.7) | (12.4) | (10.9) | (3.6) | (3.9) | (14.2) | (8.2) | (100.0) |
| Career women | 103 | 17 | 22 | 3 | 2 | 15 | 19 | 181 |
|  | (56.9) | (9.5) | (12.0) | (1.5) | (1.1) | (8.2) | (10.8) | (100.0) |
| Total | 614 | 162 | 148 | 63 | 51 | 183 | 111 | 1332 |
|  | (46.1) | (12.2) | (11.1) | (4.6) | (2.4) | (15.1) | (8.2) | (100.0) |

respondents is quite sharp. Among housewives of both categories and wage earners, less than one-third could mention any rights. Education and interaction at institutional levels would account for the greater awareness among respondents who knew their rights.

## Interaction

Respondents were asked a series of questions to determine the extent of their awareness and involvement in women's organizations and in general political and social activities. These questions, while not in themselves decisive, do cumulatively provide an insight into the participation of Muslim women in a variety of institutions.

Firstly, respondents' membership of women's organizations is considered an indication of their ability to be reached by women's groups and made more conscious of their rights and opportunities. However, as has been pointed out earlier, the women's movement during the 1920s was unable to attract women from all sections of the socio-economic range primarily because of their initial orientation towards legislative rights, and because social pressures prevented women's participation in activities outside the house. Since Independence, there has been greater focus on economic issues which most affect the majority of women, but the lack of a coherent women's movement still preempts their ability to act as an effective pressure group.

### Table 4
### Rights in constitution

|  | One right | Two + | Don't know | No response | Total |
|---|---|---|---|---|---|
| Students | 29 | 90 | 71 | 19 | 209 |
|  | (14.1) | (42.9) | (33.7) | (9.1) | (100.0) |
| Housewives in mohallas | 49 | 38 | 322 | 68 | 477 |
|  | (10.4) | (7.8) | (67.7) | (14.1) | (100.0) |
| Wage earners | 7 | 23 | 77 | 16 | 123 |
|  | (5.7) | (18.3) | (62.0) | (14.0) | (100.0) |
| Housewives in upper strata | 36 | 41 | 230 | 35 | 342 |
|  | (10.5) | (12.0) | (67.2) | (10.3) | (100.0) |
| Career women | 18 | 83 | 64 | 16 | 181 |
|  | (9.7) | (45.8) | (35.4) | (9.1) | (100.0) |
| Total | 139 | 275 | 764 | 154 | 1332 |
|  | (10.5) | (20.5) | (57.3) | (11.7) | (100.0) |

However, quasi women's groups have sprung up in the form of cooperatives, social welfare and educational groups which try to reach women through a range of services.

From Table 5 it is clear that less than 10 per cent of respondents appear to be involved in women's groups or organizations. Few students, wage earners or middle class housewives are involved in such activities; housewives in mohallas and career women are perhaps involved with groups connected to their economic activities; or in the case of housewives in mohallas, to informal groups operating in the neighbourhood. The lack of Muslim women leaders in groups or organizations may perhaps account for this.

Respondents were asked if they knew where and how to look for a job, should they need one (Table 6); nearly 7 per cent said they would consult women's organizations. These responses cover most avenues through which employment may be sought in India: through the good offices of a women's group which may have information or channels to employment opportunities; through the general employment exchange; through community or family contacts. Few respondents other than the two housewives categories said they did not want to work. However, two-thirds of all respondents did not respond or did not know how to set about obtaining employment. This reflects the difficulties of entering the urban labour market in India.

**Table 5**
Membership of women's organizations

|  | Yes | No | No response | Total |
|---|---|---|---|---|
| Students | 12 | 173 | 24 | 209 |
|  | (5.7) | (82.7) | (11.9) | (100.0) |
| Housewives in mohallas | 38 | 381 | 58 | 477 |
|  | (7.9) | (79.8) | (12.1) | (100.0) |
| Wage earners | 12 | 94 | 17 | 123 |
|  | (9.7) | (76.4) | (13.8) | (100.0) |
| Housewives in upper strata | 26 | 281 | 35 | 342 |
|  | (7.6) | (82.3) | (10.1) | (100.0) |
| Career women | 39 | 137 | 5 | 181 |
|  | (21.7) | (75.4) | (2.9) | (100.0) |
| Total | 127 | 1066 | 139 | 1332 |
|  | (9.5) | (80.0) | (10.0) | (100.0) |

**Table 6**

Seeking employment

| | Women's groups | Emp-loy ex-change | Comm-unity, family | Apply every where | Don't want to work | Don't know | No res-ponse | Total |
|---|---|---|---|---|---|---|---|---|
| Students | 28 | 34 | 20 | 17 | 2 | 11 | 97 | 209 |
| | (13.2) | (16.1) | (9.5) | (8.1) | (0.9) | (5.2) | (46.9) | (100.0) |
| Housewives in mohallas | 30 (6.2) | 37 (7.8) | 47 (9.9) | 6 (1.4) | 74 (15.4) | 53 (11.1) | 230 (48.2) | 477 (100.0) |
| Wage earners | 4 | 4 | 7 | 1 | 1 | 9 | 97 | 123 |
| | (3.5) | (3.5) | (5.9) | (1.2) | (1.2) | (7.5) | (77.9) | (100.0) |
| Housewives in upper strata | 26 (7.6) | 22 (6.3) | 23 (6.7) | 4 (1.3) | 51 (14.9) | 33 (9.7) | 183 (53.4) | 342 (100.0) |
| Career women | 4 (2.2) | 7 (3.6) | 1 (0.4) | — (—) | — (—) | — (—) | 169 (93.9) | 181 (100.0) |
| Total | 92 (6.9) | 104 (7.8) | 98 (7.3) | 28 (2.0) | 128 (9.6) | 106 (8.0) | 776 (58.3) | 1332 (100.0) |

Respondents were asked if they had friends, other than members of the family or community. They were further asked if they visited them and vice versa, to establish the degree of contact at a social level with members of other communities. However, it must be noted that social contact is limited by economic factors and by tradition which traditionally reserved social interaction for men, confining women to the house. Table 7 indicates that respondents who visited friends from other communities were drawn from all categories. In the case of students and career women, most respondents did visit friends, as did the majority of housewives and wage earners. This indicates both contact and interaction between respondents and women friends, representing support and involvement outside the home.

Respondents were also asked whether they listened to the radio, to confirm their exposure to the media. As Table 8 indicates, the majority of respondents are exposed to the radio in every category. Among housewives in mohallas and wage earners, approximately 40 per cent of respondents are not, and are possibly prevented from owning a radio due to economic circumstances. For the majority, however, the radio was a source of entertainment and information, both. Respondents were asked to name the prime minister and ruling party in order to assess their awareness of current political events; the majority were able

**Table 7**
Visiting friends

|  | Yes | No | No response | Total |
|---|---|---|---|---|
| Students | 163 (77.9) | 37 (17.7) | 9 (4.3) | 209 (100.0) |
| Housewives in mohallas | 227 (47.5) | 221 (46.3) | 29 (6.0) | 477 (100.0) |
| Wage-earners | 65 (52.8) | 53 (43.0) | 5 (4.0) | 123 (100.0) |
| Housewives in upper strata | 192 (56.1) | 128 (37.4) | 22 (6.4) | 342 (100.0) |
| Career women | 159 (87.8) | 20 (11.0) | 2 (1.1) | 181 (100.0) |
| Total | 806 (60.5) | 459 (34.4) | 67 (4.9) | 1332 (100.0) |

**Table 8**
Listen to the radio (per cent)

| | |
|---|---|
| Students | 92.8 |
| Housewives in mohallas | 59.8 |
| Wage earners | 55.6 |
| Housewives in upper strata | 70.5 |
| Career women | 84.4 |
| Total | 70.7 |
| | (N=1332) |

to name both while all could name at least the prime minister (Table 9). Only among housewives in mohallas did respondents require prodding; among career women and students, very few were ignorant of the political leader or the party. These findings are significant, considering that the survey covered a number of different states, many of which are dominated by parties other than the one in power in the central government.

Traditionally it has been assumed that women's participation in the electoral process has been a reflection of the voting pattern of the family or the community, rather than a decision arrived at independently. Respondents were asked if they had voted in the last election and how they had decided which candidate to

### Table 9
Prime minister and ruling party

| | Prime Minister | PM + party | Party | Prodded | Don't know | No res-ponse | Total |
|---|---|---|---|---|---|---|---|
| Students | 25 | 175 | 1 | — | 3 | 5 | 209 |
| | (11.9) | (83.8) | (0.4) | (—) | (1.4) | (2.4) | (100.0) |
| Housewives | 138 | 225 | 6 | 15 | 77 | 16 | 477 |
| in mohallas | (28.9) | (47.1) | (1.2) | (3.1) | (16.1) | (3.7) | (100.0) |
| Wage-earners | 41 | 57 | — | — | 24 | 1 | 123 |
| | (33.1) | (45.8) | (—) | (—) | (19.1) | (2.0) | (100.0) |
| Housewives | 111 | 178 | 2 | (—) | 39 | 12 | 342 |
| in upper strata | (32.6) | (52.0) | (0.6) | (—) | (11.5) | (3.2) | (100.0) |
| Career | 10 | 157 | 1 | 0 | 7 | 6 | 181 |
| women | (5.4) | (86.9) | (0.7) | (—) | (3.9) | (3.0) | (100.0) |
| Total | 325 | 792 | 10 | 15 | 150 | 40 | 1332 |
| | (24.4) | (59.4) | (0.7) | (1.2) | (11.2) | (3.1) | (100.0) |

vote for. The majority had exercised their right to vote (Table 10) with the exception of students, some of whom may have been too young to do so. This may also have been true of housewives in mohallas and wage earners but, on the whole, the participation of Muslim women in the electoral process across socio-economic categories and throughout the country is substantial. Moreover the overall participation of Muslim women in voting compares favourably with women in India generally. (*Towards Equality*, 1974:446) On making the decision on which way to vote (Table 11) most respondents said they had not been influenced by the family or the community, although it would be difficult to gauge the accuracy of this response.

Finally, respondents were asked what changes they would like to see among women in the community. This question, as has already been mentioned, was open-ended and the responses recorded fully. It was posed in order to allow respondents to express all their concerns (Table 12). Over 60 per cent favoured education and employment over other aspects of change. Very few respondents appeared concerned with unilateral divorce, implying that its incidence was not part of their experience and, therefore, not of much interest to them. Dowry, too, was of little interest as it is not widely practised in the community. Respondents showed scant interest again, in equal legislative rights,

### Table 10
Casting their vote

|  | Yes | No | Too young | No response | Total |
|---|---|---|---|---|---|
| Students | 34 | 145 | 13 | 17 | 209 |
|  | (16.5) | (69.2) | (6.3) | (8.1) | (100.0) |
| Housewives in mohallas | 380 | 75 | 0 | 22 | 477 |
|  | (70.6) | (15.7) | (—) | (4.6) | (100.0) |
| Wage-earners | 81 | 34 | — | 8 | 123 |
|  | (65.7) | (27.3) | (—) | (6.9) | (100.0) |
| Housewives in upper strata | 242 | 94 | — | 6 | 342 |
|  | (70.7) | (27.6) | (—) | (1.7) | (100.0) |
| Career women | 141 | 31 | 3 | 6 | 181 |
|  | (77.9) | (17.0) | (1.5) | (3.6) | (100.0) |
| Total | 878 | 379 | 16 | 59 | 1332 |
|  | (65.9) | (28.4) | (1.2) | (4.1) | (100.0) |

### Table 11
Decision on voting influenced by

|  | Husband | Party | Community | I decided | No res- | Total |
|---|---|---|---|---|---|---|
| Students | 3 | 12 | 1 | 18 | 175 | 209 |
|  | (1.3) | (5.5) | (0.5) | (8.4) | (84.4) | (100.0) |
| Housewives in mohallas | 125 | 81 | 9 | 173 | 89 | 477 |
|  | (26.1) | (16.9) | (1.8) | (36.2) | (18.9) | (100.0) |
| Wage earners | 24 | 18 | 7 | 38 | 36 | 123 |
|  | (19.3) | (14.3) | (5.4) | (30.9) | (30.1) | (100.0) |
| Housewives in upper strata | 110 | 30 | 5 | 89 | 108 | 342 |
|  | (32.3) | (8.8) | (1.5) | (26.1) | (31.4) | (100.0) |
| Career women | 18 | 32 | 3 | 83 | 45 | 181 |
|  | (9.8) | (17.6) | (1.7) | (46.0) | (24.8) | (100.0) |
| Total | 280 | 173 | 25 | 401 | 453 | 1332 |
|  | (21.0) | (12.9) | (1.8) | (30.1) | (33.7) | (100.0) |

perhaps because, in their experience, rights per se have not significantly improved the status of women. Few respondents advocated religious moderation or greater religious practice; a tiny minority did not want to see changes in the situation of women in the community or did not know the kind of changes desired. Purdah did not appear to be of much concern to respondents, despite its high incidence in the community and among respondents themselves. Regional diversity in the usage of purdah and the flexibility with which it is used i.e., frequently only within the parameters of Muslim mohallas makes it most vulnerable to change. Respondents regarded education and employment opportunities to be the most liberating factors. Greater participation in national life, too, appeared to be secondary to the importance of education and employment which in themselves would lead to greater representation and participation. Education was accorded most importance by those respondents who distinguished between employment and education; this indicates the importance given to women's education in the community and a recognition of its fundamental role in improving the prospects of women in employment and in the realization of their rights and status. The emphasis on education is consistent with the general opinion on the importance of education for women (*Towards Equality*, 1974:443).

While the lack of emphasis on legislative rights reflects the continuing support for symbolic differentiation exemplified by Muslim Personal  Law, it also indicates a dramatic decline in polygamy and unilateral divorce (borne out by the field trip) which most threaten marriages. In the case of dower and inheritance rights respondents' clearly emphasised education and employment strengthening their ability to fight for their rights. Muslim women's concern with education and employment and not with legislative rights reflects an understanding of the requirements of status in the modern context. Education continues to be an important avenue for achievement which respondents felt should be utilized by women to become economically independent since this would represent genuine emancipation from traditional constraints and would serve to equalize existing inequalities in women's status.

## Conclusion

Exposure to several forms of media and a certain amount of active political participation have served to create an awareness among Indian Muslim women of the changes underway in society. In dealing with them Muslim women are subjective, a response not unlike that demonstrated by women in different caste, linguistic or regional groups within the mainstream.

The concept of individual rights and freedom of choice is almost innovative in Indian society, which has traditionally sub-

## Table 12.
### Changes sought among Muslim women

| | Leave purdah | Education | Employment | Abolish dowry | Participate more | More religious | Education employment | No unilateral divorce | Moderation in religion | Equal rights | No change | Don't know | No response | Total |
|---|---|---|---|---|---|---|---|---|---|---|---|---|---|---|
| Students | 37 (17.7) | 80 (38.5) | 12 (6.0) | 5 (2.2) | 24 (11.7) | 5 (2.6) | 21 (9.9) | 1 (0.3) | 4 (1.8) | 3 (1.6) | 2 (0.7) | 4 (2.0) | 11 (5.0) | 209 (100.0) |
| Housewives in mohallas | 11 (2.4) | 111 (23.3) | 40 (8.4) | 4 (0.8) | 18 (3.8) | 20 (4.3) | 118 (24.9) | 3 (0.6) | 3 (0.6) | 15 (3.1) | 15 (3.2) | 48 (10.2) | 71 (14.6) | 477 (100.0) |
| Wage earners | 5 (3.8) | 30 (24.0) | 21 (17.3) | — (—) | 2 (2.0) | 1 (1.1) | 37 (30.1) | 1 (0.3) | — (—) | 1 (1.0) | 7 (5.7) | 6 (4.9) | 12 (9.4) | 123 (100.0) |
| Housewives in upper strata | 26 (7.6) | 112 (33.0) | 37 (10.9) | 6 (1.8) | 23 (6.7) | 23 (6.8) | 39 (11.5) | — (—) | 3 (0.8) | 2 (0.7) | 17 (4.9) | 22 (6.6) | 32 (8.6) | 342 (100.0) |
| Career women | 20 (11.0) | 63 (34.8) | 8 (4.6) | 5 (2.9) | 17 (9.5) | 3 (1.9) | 45 (24.8) | — (—) | 2 (1.2) | 3 (1.5) | — (—) | 6 (3.3) | 9 (4.8) | 181 (100.0) |
| Total | 99 (7.4) | 396 (29.8) | 118 (8.9) | 20 (1.5) | 84 (6.4) | 52 (4.0) | 260 (19.6) | 5 (0.3) | 12 (0.8) | 25 (1.8) | 40 (3.0) | 86 (6.4) | 135 (10.1) | 1332 (100.0) |

jugated individual rights and desires to the preservation of familial and societal hierarchies. The concept of individualism, however, is better established in male activities: in the realm of female activities the message has always been subdued and even confused. Women's rights were traditionally derived through male relatives, and women were conditioned to support such a view. Even under the current growth of nuclear families women are encouraged to keep their rights and demands subservient to those of the family and men. The knowledge and exercise of rights is, therefore, only gradually gaining ground, even in the case of Muslim women who traditionally have had the right to inheritance, divorce, etc. To increase awareness and usage of women's rights a forum is required through which the message can be transmitted and support provided for the struggle which must be waged if women are to inherit, gain equal wages, and abolish dowry.

With changing economic and political structures, the traditional ties of caste, community and language tend to lose much of their relevance in daily life. However, identification with traditional groups remains important for better representation in government and availing economic opportunities. Traditional ties help communities' transition to current practices by incorporating them into community causes or projects. This was amply demonstrated by many communities, including the Muslim community, in the 19th century on the question of education and social reform. However, in the case of women's issues, community signals remain mixed, since all communities encourage education and employment, but try to retain control by emphasizing the family and the role of mother and wife. For women in a minority community which is under pressure, there is all that and more, as is evident from the question of rights and change. In the urban setting, with exposure to many different forms of information and the media, respondents appear well able to understand and respond to the exigencies of survival in India, and such solutions centre around education and employment, both necessary conditions for improving their real status. Their rejection of legislative changes, even when many practices have already changed, is an indication of their implicit support for maintaining the community's exclusive identity through an unchanging Muslim Personal Law. There seems to be an implicit understanding of the slow process of change in a traditional society, particularly as legislative changes have not proved effective without a positive assertion  by women of their legal rights or their economic independence. Respondents, therefore, emphasized education and employment as changes which would make women both economically independent and more assertive of their rights. In real terms, therefore, Muslim women share the achievements, goals and expectations for the future with other women in India.

# 11

## Confronting the Issues

This study has evaluated the status and role of Muslim women in India within the framework of their Indian environment, their religion and their female condition. It has been set against a historical background to show the underlying continuities and constraints of Muslim women's status and role, and has distinguished between the ascribed and achieved status of women. This is an important distinction for, while the legislative components of status differentiates between Hindu and Muslim women, their achieved status reflects distinctions more of class and region, on the basis of which real parallels or differentiation can be demonstrated. Historical research has indicated the continuities and re-evaluation which the status and role of Muslim women have undergone over time. These are related both to conditions in India as a whole and to different regions, and related also to ethnic perceptions and concerns, to the economic and political situation of the community over time, and to the evolution of Indian women from traditional roles to being full participants in Indian society.

For Muslim women, the situation of the community is an important factor because economic and political conditions determine social attitudes and perceptions. Religion, while extremely important for commonly held beliefs and worship, is different in public and private usage, though traditionally these did converge. This study has demonstrated the dichotomy between the private and public usage of Islam; it has also demonstrated the historical circumstances which led to this dichotomy. In western societies the split between private and public usage of religions has been woven into the fabric of life; in more traditional societies, a separation of the two did not occur till much later, due to traditional social structures and the relative lack of economically induced social mobility. In India, with the introduction of new political rules in the 19th century, the Muslim community experienced a distancing between public and private religious customs and practices which previously had been fused. Changing political and economic structures made this inevitable. All communities were similarly affected and as traditional ties to the community and village weakened, the dichotomy between public and private religion became sharper. Public religion was used to unite disparate communities for secular and political ends.[1] Private religion continued to moderate the actions of community members to conform to broad tenets, while simultaneously accommodating and incorporating new elements which were introduced as a result of social, political and economic changes. This separation between public or political and private religion remained, at best, unclear for those who used religion as a political adhesive and for their followers. Religious communities divided by language and custom united for political purposes, while secularizing to acquire skills and reorganising customs to cope with contemporary political and economic life. Resolution of these contradictions is precluded by the disparate educational and socio-economic level of community members, to whom differentiation became an end in itself.

[1] In recent years the political use of religion has been aptly demonstrated by sections of Harijan villagers in Tamil Nadu, who have publicly converted to Islam. In interviews in the *Hindustan Times* (July 17, 1981) Harijan leaders claimed "...that all 21 crore Harijans of India would convert to Islam once the concessions are withdrawn," referring to the special concessions made to the Harijan community in education and employment. The article noted that several decades earlier other villagers had converted to Christianity to improve their education and job prospects. A Member of Parliament from the area, Mr. Arunachalam, had converted to Christianity and then back to Hinduism to get the ticket for the reserved constituency. The Muslims in the area are not elated by the conversions which have caused considerable hostility and anger, and while accusations of foreign money have been made, it appears to be more an ultimate form of protest than anything else. Uttam and Anuradha Bhoite have also pointed out that to communities or groups, modernization means equality, but that despite some modernization there has been no change in caste elitism. Conversions to Buddhism took place among untouchables to register protest. The Dalit movement in Maharashtra was an effort to create a sense of identity and pride among Neo-Buddhists. "The Dalit Sahitya Movement in Maharashtra: A Sociological Analysis,"*Sociological Bulletin*, Vol 26, No.1, March 1977.

For women, this was a setback since the politicization of religion implied the outward retention and sometimes even the reenactment of customs and practices specific to women. This emphasized differentiation, but did not interfere with the community's political and economic progress. The status of minority women, therefore, has to take into account ascriptive and achievement factors, since status is linked to the political and economic situation of the community at any given time. In the case of Muslim women and the Muslim community this link to the community's historical, political and economic situation is critical to an understanding of their position in Indian society.

## Community links

In multi-ethnic societies, different religions, languages and cultures are expected to coexist. Egalitarian ideologies have aroused expectations of power-sharing between communities rather than the traditional dominant and subordinate relationship. While the majority community has a numerical edge over the minorities in claiming power, this can be counteracted by cohesive minorities bargaining for power and position.[2] This egalitarian ideology determines and necessitates public, political religion to unify communities for joint action to derive maximum political leverage and economic gain. The Muslim community in India represents an example of the constraints and pressures that minority communities ecounter particularly in traditional societies with limited economic resources.

The historical background discussed in Chapters 2, 3 and 4 provides evidence of the development of this process both in the Muslim and other communities. A number of studies have indicated the dichotomy between religious beliefs and actual customs and practices. Imtiaz Ahmad has summed it up in describing the process of Islamization taking place in India, a process through which different Muslim communities or sects endeavour to divest themselves of unorthodox practices and beliefs in order to identify more closely with Islamic ideals and

[2] Yogendra Malik has demonstrated that Hindus in Trinidad have organized themselves for economic reasons. Hinduism has been used by politicians to bring different Hindu groups together. Daily religious classes organized for children, and the celebration of festivals and customs has helped to emphasize group differentiation and unity. Sub-group loyalties have to some extent been overcome because of this pressure of external forces. (*Sociological Bulletin*, No. XIII, Vol I, Bombay, March 1963)

to differentiate themselves and other communities ". . . But this does not always result in Islamic beliefs replacing existent ones . . ."; the course of this process depends on the exigencies of the local situation. Mattison Mines has shown that this change occurred only when members of the community moved from the traditional village, with its established community status and relationships, to the urban areas where such ties with their own and other communities have to be reworked. Common religious ties were used to establish links with the Muslim community in town, through a reiteration of ideal beliefs often in conflict with actual practices. P.C. Aggarwal has noted that, while Meos have made a conscious effort to Islamize, their traditional practices continue, despite the rhetoric. Similar conflict between rhetoric and practice has been noted by Ellikson for Bengali Muslims; ". . . therefore," as Imtiaz Ahmad says, "where Islam clashes with local beliefs, it is ignored. And local councils which interpret Islam for the benefit of their constituents merely reflect their version of its precepts." (Ahmad, 1975:6, 7)

Basing a study of Muslims merely on Islamic injunctions is, therefore, unrealistic. (Aggarwal, 1966; Mines, 1975; Dube, 1969) It is this tendency among authors writing on the Muslim community and Muslim women to place inordinate emphasis on Islam, to the exclusion of other factors based on the culture and tradition of different Muslim communities, which distorts the realities on which this behaviour is based. Specific studies indicate considerably more cultural mingling between different religious communities sharing the same cultural environment in different Indian regions. This is not to say that religious communities do not share certain qualities; merely that, if overstated, it can misrepresent the primary orientation of the community (Ahmad, 1975:5).

This study has established that political and economic changes in the 19th century induced a reorganization of community structure and ideology. A number of commentators have attributed these changes to the educational backwardness of the Muslim community (Lal Bahadur, 1954; Prasad, Subedar, 1974:10; Thorpe, 1965), the ambitions of their leaders and their inability to accept minority status. (Sen, 1939:97, 211) Gail Minault, however, has made the point that the Muslim political movement of the 1920s was an effort to unite different Muslim communities in India by using religious and cultural symbols meaningful to all strata of the community, in the hope that community unity would strengthen their minority bargaining position.

Minault shows that the Khilafat leadership used the dismemberment of Turkey by Britain and the displacement of the Khalifa or titular head of Islam, to unite the community against British rule in India. Like Mahatma Gandhi, they were interested in national freedom and tried to ensure this through unity within their own various communities. (Minault, 1975:37-38) Judith Brown's study of Gandhi's rise to power makes the point that Sikhs, Muslims and Hindus had the same end in view, namely to define the identity of their community and safeguard its position. To this end, cultural and educational associations became agencies for demands made by communities. (Brown, 1972:35) In his study of Brahmins in Sripuram, Andre Beteille has suggested that other communities are affected by the reorganisation of neighbouing communities. The rise of non-Brahmin castes and their structural and ideological reorganization created a feeling of insecurity among Brahmins; the result was that sectarian differences between Brahmin communities were forgotten and a common identity was forged. This politicization was necessary to consolidate the community's position, and caste provided a viable basis for political mobilization. (Beteille, 1965:212, 214, 222)

In the modern Indian context, the Muslim community can be said to have reorganized ideologically and structurally in response to political, economic and social changes in the 19th century, and the activities of other communities. It cannot however, be regarded as unique or unusual in this regard. That political activism rather than simple political gain led to Partition was coincidental, and in fact split the Indian Muslim community into three and proved fatal to the interests of the Muslims who remained in India. The process, a reaction to modern structures, continues in all communities; the costs of such a process are frequently borne by women.

## Women as catalysts

The position of Muslim women in India over the last century has reflected the travails of the community as a national and regional entity. It has also reflected the travails of Indian women and to a lesser degree, religious factors. Muslim women constitute only about 6 per cent of the total Indian population and are a minority within a minority community. While there are Muslims in every region, they are not represented in every socio-economic stratum, an important factor in any consideration of women's status and role. Generalizations, therefore, with regard to education, purdah or labour participation, are misleading. Also women's responses to social, political or economic stimuli are affected by their lack of economic representation. Nevertheless, generalizaions abound, and the notion persists among academics and administrators that by statistically aggregating the responses of widely disparate Muslim communities and classes it is possible to distinguish between the "modern" responses of communities disaggregated by caste and the aggregated "non-modern" Muslim response (*Towards Equality*, 1974:395-450).

Religion as a factor has played an important part in the misconception that has characterized references to Muslim women. Their actions and reactions are examined not vis-a-vis other neighbouring communities with similar practices or beliefs, but in the light of Islamic practice. Thus the apparent backwardness of Muslim women in education and non-manual employment is attributed to the fact that they were in purdah and, therefore, incapable of deciding whom to marry or vote for, that their marriages were still traditionally arranged, and that a distinction was made between the education of sons and daughters. (Hate, 1969:36, 38, 56) Yet the same studies also noted that Hindu marriages are based on considerations of astrology and dowry in which women have no say, and that Christian marriages are also arranged. (Hate, 1969:57, 66, 73)

The main factor used to highlight the "backwardness" of the Muslim community is the legal status of its women, which has been based on the Shariat Act of 1937 and the Dissolution of Muslim Marriages Act of 1939. *Towards Equality* has made an impassioned plea for the passage of a uniform legislative act for all communities to overcome the abuses of polygamy and unilateral divorce, rejecting the view of Justice Krishna Iyer of the Indian Supreme Court that such legislation was unnecessary since the incidence of either practice is negligible if not non-existent (*Towards Equality*, 1974:121) and overlooking the mass of secular legislation which can readily be used by any community, which would preclude any such abuses. In the Committee's Report on the Status of Women in India, references were made to the lack of education of Muslim women in Kerala, where generally the educational level of women was high without reference to their socio-economic difference (*Towards Equality*1975:96). The Committee's report also deplored the lack of uniform legislation, continuing to pin its hopes on it despite its evident disenchantment with legislation as a means of elevating the status of women.

In a study on population in India, Ashok Mitra has also drawn the link between religion and the status of women, to the exclusion of other factors. While noting that there is higher female mortality than male mortality among Muslims than among Hindus, he links it to lack of inheritance rights, divorce and maintenance rights rather than to socio-economic strata or the pervasive poverty of the community in certain regions, which may perhaps be responsible for poor housing, health and related conditions. (Mitra, 1978:29, 31) Thus, in another context, Muslim households in the Delhi region are shown to be extremely poor; some 56 per cent have a monthly income of Rs.200-299; only 11.6 per cent have an income of Rs. 500-599 and only 0.6 per cent have an income over Rs.1,500. Caste Hindus and Sikhs are much better off financially, yet religion and not socio-economic factors is blamed for lower educational levels. (Mitra, 1978:322)

Shibani Roy's study on Muslim women in north India, too, used the premise that Islam is the pre-eminent factor in determining status (Roy, 1979:xii), and further states that orthodoxy led to social evils which are holding Muslims back. (Roy, 1979:56) Even as the book demonstrated that higher income among Muslims had led to higher education (Roy, 1979:62), that Muslim girls are being formally educated (Roy, 1979:63), her study found no illiteracy among the Muslim men (Roy, 1979:68), and in her sample men supported their wives leaving purdah (Roy, 1979:40) and encouraged the education of women. (Roy, 1979:68) Moreover 27 per cent of the women in her sample were employed (Roy, 1979:40). Similarly, Zarina Bhatty looks at the status of Muslim women not vis-a-vis other regional communities or the situation of Indian women generally, but in terms of whether the Muslim community in India is able to provide opportunities to women for their self-realisation so that ". . . they can make their contribution to national development and world peace. . ." implying thereby that other communities were able to do this. The author is then emphatic about the negative attitudinal and legal limitations the community has imposed on its women. (Bhatty, 1976:101) It would indeed be a miracle if the Muslim community, small, fragmented and economically non-viable, were able to achieve what other Indian communities and Indian society as a whole have not been able to achieve for women.

Barbara Ward similarly links the status of Muslim women to religion when she finds only "Islam is inevitably resistant to change in general and change in the position of Muslim women in particular". (Ward, 1963-67) Empirical studies, however, have indicated that socio-economic conditions rather than religion are the primary cause of differentiation between groups of women (Boserup, 1970; Huston, 1979; Geile, Smock, 1977; Nash, Safa, 1976). D'Souza has noted that the pattern of employment in India is more reflective of regional norms and that socialization rather than religion reinforces gender roles. (D'Souza, 1975:xiv) Aileen Ross felt that caste, language and even social class made little difference in India, where all groups felt the consequences of modern tensions and  conflicts and shared similar ambitions. (Ross, 1961:281)

The findings of this study based on the survey, the field trip and historical material tend to confirm that the response of women to various questions is dependent on their socio-economic strata rather than on some arbitrary "Muslim" position, as well as on the norms prevalent in the region.

From the historical material discussed in Chapter 5 it is apparent that since the expansion of women's roles took place well after the initial impact of social, political and economic changes had been absorbed, all communities were able to endorse the expansion. Muslim women, depending on their socio-economic strata, were similarly affected. Muslim women's ability to organize as a group was demonstrated with the formation of the Muslim Ladies Conference and their subsequent activities in the Indian women's movement. Muslim women rose beyond their specific community interests to cooperate with women of other communities and collaborate in the effort to win franchise and legislative changes in their rights. They were also vocal in their condemnation of purdah, polygamy and pre-puberty marriages, and in their subsequent support for joint electorates and women's rights, despite growing Muslim support for separate electorates and eventually, Partition. Legislative changes in 1937 and 1939 ensured better rights for Muslim women, and as such, were regarded as a progressive step. That they also symbolically united the community should be kept in mind.

After Independence, the Muslim community in the north was depleted and deprived of much of its middle class leadership due to migration. This adversely affected its political, economic and social position, particularly in the north. The survey and the field trip tend to confirm the importance of socio-economic factors and the role of public religion as having a critical effect on the status and role of women in general, and on minority women in particular. Socio-economic strata proved to be a much more compelling influence on status than region or religion, since they affected education, purdah, family relationships and children's education. This tends to confirm Ross's observation that the desire for change and progress is shared by all families; the concerns expressed by the survey respondents for the kind of changes they hoped to see among women of the community overwhelmingly included education and employment; only their own socio-economic conditions and perceptions of the expected returns from education may temper this support.

In education and literacy, in purdah, in activities undertaken with husbands, respondents tended to conform to the pressures of their socio-economic stratum rather than some arbitrary "Muslim" position. On the field trip the main concern of Muslim leaders was the economic survival of the community; poverty and unemployment were always cited as being responsible for the continuation of purdah. For economically active Muslim women purdah was not a hampering factor, as borne out by the experience of Muslim women members of SEWA (Self-employed Women's Association) in Gujarat. Survey respondents, too, appeared much less concerned with the removal of purdah and equal legislative rights, than they were with the need for education and employment. In this, their concern reflected those of other Indian women. On the field trip, Muslim educational institutions in Lucknow, Srinagar and Madras tended to confirm the casual nature of purdah observance, both in attitude and practice by Muslim girls and their parents; they also noted that the practice had declined over time. Patricia Jeffery's study of purdah in a Muslim cleric's family in Delhi reflects the dilemma of young women in purdah, conscious, despite restrictions, of the changes taking place, and desirous of participating in them. (Jeffery, 1979:128, 129) This pattern may be repeated in conservative households, but the exigencies of poverty and the aspirations of women themselves rule out any return to the traditional pattern of purdah observance.

The status of Muslim women is therefore greatly affected by social, political and economic conditions in India and by customs and practices, modified over time. In any case, with sectarian differences and cultural overtones in the many cultures of Islamic influence, rigid definitions can hardly be meaningfully invoked. Muslim communities throughout the world tend to follow their own traditions, and there being no church in Islam, each culture has interpreted and even legislatively modified traditional "Islamic" practices, apart fom the five basic tenets enjoined on all Muslims. In legislative changes too, no uniform interpretation has been evolved, and the extent and manner of change have been dependent on cultural requirements, and recently, political expediency. The latter tends to utilize Islam as a unifying symbol and as an alternate ideology to traditional left and right wing ideologies, which due to colonialism came to symbolize specific cultures.

The Muslim communities in India have, along with other religious, language and caste communities, long used a form of political religion to maintain a distinct identity and unity for political and economic gain. Many of the symbols used in this process have become immutable over time and this symbolism has, as in many other societies, come to rest on laws pertaining to family and women. The survey and the field trip while testifying to the desire of the community for economic, social and political progress, indicated the continuing importance of political religion in the lack of support for legislative change in the status of women and support for Urdu, both emphasizing community differentiation  and unity. The Shariat laws have thus come to signify this symbolic unity. However, since many writers tend to emphasize legal rights, the continuation of Shariat laws has been regarded as a contributing factor to the backwardness of the community and to remaining outside the Indian mainstream (Haq, 1974; Bhatty, 1976; Weekly Round Table, 1973; Shah, 1969; *Towards Equality*, 1974; Derret, 1968).

Since legal rights, even when not enforced, are nevertheless regarded as contributing to status in India, the distinction between ascribed and achieved status becomes important in the case of Muslim women. For while Muslim women do not have the full protection of the law to equalize their status with that of Muslim men, their achieved status nevertheless conforms to that of women of other communities in similar socio-economic strata, since these reflect general regional norms  and practices. That this is indeed the case has been conceded in the comprehensive study done by the Committee on the Status of Women in India, from which it is clear that an improvement in the status of women can only come about if official development programmes paid particular attention to the requirements of women and improved their ability to participate in the labour market. The Committee also noted that legislative rights had in fact not improved the economic, social or political status of women, and in the 25 years since legislation (viz. The Hindu Code Bill, 1956) came into effect social conservatism had increased to negate the laws on dowry, inheritance and widow remarriage *(Towards Equality*, 1974:71, 79, 135). This is not to deny the importance of legislative change, but to point out that the status of Muslim women should not be judged on the sole criterion of legislative equality, particularly as there are a variety of secular legislative enactments which can be invoked to overcome shortfalls in religious law.

Two factors could bring about changes in the status of Muslim women and indeed of all women in India. Firstly, specific economic programmes to educate and train women to move into the job market would improve their labour participation rates, and add impetus to the acquisition of literacy and education. Muslim women skilled at handicrafts in a number of regions could benefit from such training and from the formation of co-operatives to develop and market their goods. Secondly, or-ganizations with specifically feminist goals, or social organiza-tions which encourage Muslim membership would make a considerable difference to the ability of Muslim women to cope with changes in society. It would also strengthen their ability to bargain for structural reorganization within the community to enable them to improve their position.

Women in the Muslim community are scattered through socio-economic strata and face problems similar to those con-fronting all women in organizing as a group to utilize newly available economic opportunities. Being scattered also means that they lack leadership which would enable them to organize as quickly as other groups; this was particularly evident during the Shah Bano case when only towards the end of the crisis was a Muslim women's organization formed to protest the passage of the iniquitous Muslim Women's (Rights of Protection on Divorce) Act.

In India the issue of women's rights and their maintenance has been considered peripheral to overall changes in the economy and in politics. There has been relatively little realiza-tion that social, political and economic changes bolster each other and are equally if not more important for genuine, equitable progress. The reason for this lies in the fact that social changes in India were not part of an evolutionary process, but were induced by the political and economic changes of the 19th century; while under the broad umbrella of nationalism, political parties supported the Indian women's movement once Independence and legislative equality were achieved, their interest and support waned. The current slump in the women's movement has resulted from the lack of evolutionary change, whereby social legislation became an end in itself, a public symbol, rather than the result of closely fought and debated social, political and economic issues between different socio-economic groups of women. Simultaneously, political changes have increased the importance of ethnic groups, while economic changes have made the participation of women more difficult. These dual realities resulting from political and economic changes (discussed in Ch.6) have made the participation of the women more difficult in the new structures. Under the circumstances, Muslim women, like women of all communities, have found progress more difficult than has been envisaged by such changes. Without an organization with a clearly articulated ideology, Indian women in general have little understanding of the problems and issues that confront them as a group. For Muslim women, members of a small minority community, it has been doubly difficult to consolidate their gains or to regroup to meet current or future challenges.

The analytical tools used to assess the status of women need to be further refined if they are to be used to evaluate the status of women in a minority commmunity. In many situations, the status and role of women in a minority community can be misrepresented when just one factor or other is taken into account; a fuller consideration of all factors might well reveal an altogether different picture. This study, by considering all three determinants of status—that Muslim women are Indian, Muslim and women—has gone beyond the stereotype which was based primarily on two determinants, religion and gender. Historical research has tended to confirm the validity of this approach, since it demonstrated the relevance of all three factors leading to the present status and role of Muslim women. Such a perspective strengthens and deepens an understanding of the interaction of various factors which, over time, can alter the perceptions and situation of a community and can affect the status and role of women in it. Such an analysis also juxtaposes self-interest and rationale as the ultimate determinants of community behaviour, as indeed has Maxine Robinson when he noted that

> ... social consciousness may assume many different forms. It can exercise in most ideal form a powerful influence over decisions taken by whole societies and by groups. It can give a specific orientation to their attitudes towards the problems that confront them. On the one hand, one cannot deny its roots in social reality, while on the other, among the decisions that must be taken, figure in the front rank those that concern the survival of the group or society, through its activity or passivity in relation to other groups or other societies outside, and in relation to its essential internal ... activity. The decisions taken may be judicious or stupid, pregnant with consequences, either good or bad, sometimes even self-destructive. In any case they cannot be understood except in relation first of all to those essentials of any and every human society.
>
> Robinson, 1973:210

Despite these difficulties Muslim women have the potential of restructuring the ideology  and organization of the community, inducing changes by organizing as a group. But this can only come about when such goals and potential which have remained elusive for all other communities of Indian women, come closer to realization.

# Shah Bano:
# Evaluating the Impact

The Shah Bano controversy, leading to the enactment of the
Muslim Women's (Protection of Rights in Divorce) Act 1986, is
one more indication that events have outstripped the ability of
the Muslim community to deal with its social problems, just as
political problems had done in an earlier period. Even as Muslim
women, emerging from a long eclipse, were seeking solutions to
their very real social and economic predicament, their efforts to
redress it through the judicial system have been severely curtailed by the government succumbing to the pressure from the
conservative Muslim lobby. With no real effort to address the
problems that have forced women to legal action, the well organized conservative Muslim lobby was able to exercise enough
pressure on the government to nullify the ruling by the Supreme
Court of India awarding Shah Bano maintenance after divorce.

Shah Bano, 62, of Indore, already separated from her husband
of 46 years, was paid her Rs 200 per month for two years as
maintenance. When the payments ceased she filed suit before a
magistrate court under Section 125 of the Criminal Procedure
Code (Cr.PC) for maintenance of Rs 500 per month. Her husband,
Mohammad Ahmed  Khan, a lawyer, thereupon divorced her,
paid her Rs 3,000, claiming that that was her mehr, and refused
her any further payments,citing Muslim Personal Law in his
defence. The lower court awarded her Rs  25 per month; Shah
Bano appealed to the Madhya Pradesh High Court which raised
her maintenance to Rs 179.20. Ahmad Khan then appealed to the
Supreme Court arguing against any further payments, and on
April  25, 1985 a five-member Constitutional bench of the Sup-

reme Court headed by the Chief Justice of India, Y.V. Chandrachud, upheld the right of Muslim women to maintenance under
Section 125 (CrPC 1973), which makes it obligatory for a man to
maintain his wife, even if divorced, if she is destitute and has
not remarried. Maintenance comes under criminal law and is,
therefore, applicable uniformly to all citizens. The bench went
on to consider Surahs 241 and 242, Chapter 11, of the Quran
and concluded that this ruling in no way infringed religious
provisions. In his concluding remarks Chief Justice Chandrachud
referred to Article 44 of the Constitution that called for a common civil code and noted that ". . . a common civil code will help
the cause of national integration by removing disparate loyalties
to laws which have conflicting ideologies."

The importance of this decision was evident as representatives
of the All India Muslim Personal Law Board, the Jamiat-ul
Ullema-Hind and the Jamiat-ul Islami were present to hear the
verdict, along with the parties concerned. The Supreme Court
had earlier settled two cases using Article 25 in favour of Muslim
women seeking maintenance but these had made no reference
to either the Quran or the need for a common civil code and had
passed without opposition from the conservative Muslim lobby,
as had a 1983 petition to the Supreme Court by Ms Shahnaz
Hussain, pleading that her divorce violated Articles 13, 14 and
15 of the Constitution and that Muslim Personal Law violates
the Fundamental Rights of Indian Muslim women which guaran-
tee equality before the law and no discrimination on grounds of
religion, race or sex.

The proponents and opponents both within and outside the
community used the Supreme Court ruling to air, promote,
preach and prescribe their favourite theories, prejudices and
self- serving opinions on this crucial issue that concerned Muslim
women. In the course of the highly publicised and tendentious
debates the central issue of the social and economic problems
that beset Muslim women were all but set aside as groups and
political parties tried to use the issue for their own political
purposes.

Muslim conservatives with no real regard for the social or
economic position of Muslim women, for the implementation of
their existing rights or for adopting changes made in other Muslim societies, were immediate in their condemnation of the
Supreme Court judgement, using their control over existing organizations and much of the Urdu press to flex their muscles

and take political advantage of the situation. They were able to use the attempted Quranic interpretation by the Supreme Court and the mention of a common civil code to play on the traditional fears of a minority, fears relating to freedom of religion (in this particular case reinterpreting a religious text without referring it to the proper authority) and the danger of assimilation. Liberal Muslim opinion which lacks the institutional infrastructure of the conservatives responded through newspaper articles, letters to the editor and through the setting up of a few organizations to counter conservative propaganda. That many of these organizations were set up by Muslim women coming together signalled their return, after 40 years, to active participation in the struggle of Indian women to secure their rights.

Despite many representations to government and many rational arguments that were advanced in favour of the Supreme Court judgement, to prove that it in no way violated the spirit or the injunctions of the Quran and that precedence for such action already existed in a number of Muslim societies, the conservatives remained adamant and intensified their campaign to nullify the Supreme Court judgement in favour of maintenance. Government decided to yield to conservative pressure without, as had been promised by them, the benefit of a comprehensive background paper which could analyse the economic and political position of the Indian Muslim community and to try and determine their socio-religious requirements and their willingness or otherwise to bring about change. In February 1986 the Muslim Women's (Protection of Rights in Divorce) Act was introduced in Parliament. Under the provisions of the bill Muslim women would be entitled to maintenance during the period of *iddat* or three lunar months, after a divorce. If she maintains the children, conceived before divorce, reasonable provision and maintenance would be extended for a period of two years from the birth of those children. (No provision is made, however, for those children who might remain in the mother's custody after divorce.) The divorced woman is also entitled to mehr and all properties given to her by her husband, relatives, friends and husband's relatives. She can apply to the magistrate if these are denied her. After the period of *iddat* if the woman is unable to maintain herself she should apply to the magistrate who is empowered to make an order for payment of maintenance from her relatives from whom she can inherit property as they can inherit hers. If these relatives do not have sufficient means to pay maintenance, the magistrate can direct other relatives of means to do so; and if all these fail the State waqf board would be required to support her.

These provisions for the protection of Muslim women make a mockery of protecting women and of the Quranic injunction on maintenance which states, "And for the divorced woman provision must be made in kindness. This is incumbent on those who have regard for duty." (*Al Baqrah* 241) According to a number of Hanafi jurists this provision is made in addition to the dower money due to the wife and its payment is compulsory and should be generous. (Tafsir Kalzir, vol. VI, pp. 148, 172; Rafiullah Sahab, "A Pak View of Muslim Law," *Times of India*, 8.3.1986). Further Hanafi jurists stated that if provisions made by the husband were not sufficient the wife could have a suitable amount fixed by the court. In  fact the allowance made to the wife would continue  to be paid even after divorce. (Al Bahr al Raik, vol. IV, pp. 189,190). The provisions of the Bill make it clear that government has no real interest in providing poor Muslim women with maintenance since taking relatives to court would alienate her from the very family on whom she is emotionally dependant.

Additionally, instituting a court case involves expenditure and time which many women cannot afford. The further provisions of throwing divorced women at the mercy of the waqf boards is equally unconsidered, since boards are organizations that are based on contributions made by donors for specific charitable works and their funds cannot, at will, be diverted to other purposes. Not all states have waqf boards and among those that do, in many cases their funds are modest and cannot cater to the financial needs of indigent divorced Muslim women. Moreover, if the waqf boards were indeed to provide such maintenance the State would have to fund it.  To the purists on the All India Muslim Personal Law Board to whom any government interference was anathema, it must be pointed out that with the passage of this bill the Government of India has indeed legislated on Muslim law; it has interfered in the Shariat, because there is no provision in the latter for maintaining divorced Muslim women through waqfs or charitable organizations. If in fact the government  were to provide funds to waqf boards for maintenance such interference  becomes direct and institutionalized. Again, the conservative insistence on precluding Muslim women from the purview of Section 125 (which the bill does) violates

Article 14 of the Constitution which states that the "State shall not deny any person equality before the law". It also violates Article 15 which prohibits discrimination by the State on grounds of "religion, race, caste, sex or place of birth" since it excludes Muslim women on the basis of religion. This law has forced a number of Muslim women to petition the Supreme Court into declaring the law unconstitutional.

The sequence of events that led to the enactment reveals some of the pressures that government and communities experience as the democratic process both works and is manipulated by a variety of interest groups. As the debate on the Supreme Court judgement warmed up the government experimented with both supporting the judgement and denouncing it by using both proponents and opponents of the judgement within the party to air their views, hoping to ward off any political mileage other parties might gain from the controversy. The defeat of the ruling party in a Bihar by-election in November 1985 appeared to many in the party to clinch the internal debate on need for control to staunch the haemorrhaging of Muslim votes away from the party. This, despite the lure of altogether abandoning the minority Muslim votes and concentrating on the majority Hindu votes, weaning them away from Hindu right wing parties, convincing them by deed and rhetoric that they need look no further for the propagation of their interests. Some of these debates and attitudes have been widely disseminated and discussed in the press, and no doubt affected both the government's actions and those of the Muslim community, both conservative and liberal, even as both government and Muslim conservatives evoked secularism as the basis for demanding and getting communal legislation passed. Appeasing conservative Muslim opinion in the Shah Bano controversy could be easily and cheaply achieved by restricting the rights of Muslim women who were anyway without institutional support, thus removing one irritant for government. It would improve their credentials with the organized Muslim conservatives who could deliver the Muslim vote, without pressing for a resolution of the really important Muslim issues, such as widening economic and educational opportunities, actively preventing communal riots and meting out justice to those responsible for the killings and the lootings, and so on, on all of which the government could not or did not want to deliver. In the debate on the pros and cons of rescinding the use of Section 125 (Cr.PC) for Muslim women, no consideration of the rights of women as Muslims or Indians animated the discussions of the Muslim conservatives, whose main concern remained that of politically uniting the community. Doing so on grounds of religious endangerment would create a unity which could be translated into votes, to be used to advantage later. Because of controversy over the Ram Janmabhoomi/Babri Masjid issue it was easier to play the politics of fear, particularly since the government's conduct of and intervention in minority issues had never been considered objective enough to inspire confidence within the community. Women and their problems played almost no part in the finely tuned calculations made by both sides; why else would no consideration have been given to the manner in which many Muslim societies had dealt with family legislation, or any attempts be made to solicit the opinion of Muslim women in dealing with their problems? Then again, the readiness with which Muslim conservatives and their supporters were able to accept the government's version of the Shariat, especially foisting the maintenance of destitute divorced Muslim women on the waqfs for which there is no precedence either in the Shariat or in other Muslim societies, points to the desire of both sides to brush aside the real problem. The ease with which the rights of women were subverted, extended not only to their claims on their husbands' earnings to which they had contributed, but to their claims on the community or government for redress.

The Shah Bano case in many ways exemplifies the manner in which the Indian, Muslim and women factors are reactive, and can create and sustain a schism between political and private religion, particularly in minority communities. Political religion defines the parameters of the community and provides a cohesion which enables the community to act in unison on certain key issues, demonstrating a unity that can be politically important. Private religion is more adaptive to social and economic changes and enables family units and communities to move forward, doing what needs to be done to keep in step with the rest of society. While the Muslim community has so far used political religion by way of definition and for political cohesion, this survival strategy, formulated in the 19th century and born out of the imperatives of the time, has never been re-evaluated in the post-independence period for its continuing effectiveness. Despite past precedents women must be included in this process, since it is on them that the burden of maintaining family laws, used to define the community's identity, has fallen. The case is also pivotal in that it marks a departure from the alliance that seemed to exist between Muslim men and women, indeed within the community, on the best way to unify and strengthen the community, to perpetuate it as a cultural and social entity and provide it with the economic and political muscle necessary to survive in India. The differences created by the Shah Bano case between the sexes and between the liberals and conservatives within the Muslim community have implications for political religion in its traditional form, i.e., using the pre-1947 interpretations of Shariat law to weld the community together. There needs must be some questioning within the community on the need for a debate on reforming Muslim law in an attempt to better unify the community and question whether depriving women of their legitimate rights would not ultimately prove to be more divisive.

## Reactive Indian and Muslim factors in play

Communal politics continues to be the greatest scourge of mass mobilization in India. As each group (religious, caste, linguistic) has sought to represent itself through ideologically disparate political parties, the latter, while absorbing them have juxtaposed the interests of competing groups, weighting them on their ability to commandeer votes or to create a crisis if ignored.

Secularism as a constitutional concept has often been used to justify the manner in which a group's interests (particularly religious or caste) can be dealt with, sometimes facilitating progress, at other times blocking it. The latter is particularly evident in the arguments used to justify the enactment of the Muslim Women's Bill, whereby both government and Muslim conservatives forwarded the argument that secularism demanded the enactment of this communal legislation while rescinding the secular, uniform 125 CrPC. Government further cited the support of the majority of Muslims for the Bill (without making an effort to quantify this support) and, while decrying the lack of a uniform civil code, noted that it could not be imposed on a country with such vast diversities. (*Indian Express*, March 4, 1986) Muslim conservatives too cited secularism as the basis of their demands for the withdrawal of 125 CrPC and the enactment of the Muslim Women's Bill, while Hindu right wing parties used secularism to insist on the removal of Muslim privileges and the enactment of a uniform civil code. The hastily convened opposition to the

Bill also cited secularism to justify its stand. Secularism, it appears, is all things to all Indians. The dynamics of the judgement and the passing of the Bill should force a debate on the parameters of secularism and its various constituent parts in the Indian context; in clarifying these isses a discussion on whether the passage of an enabling uniform civil code constitutes a threat to minorities who would still be free to use their laws, is necessary. There are other aspects of secularism that need to be examined and institutionalized, such as objectivity on the part of government and refraining from using, encouraging or exploiting religious symbolism in national life to promote the interests of one community at the expense of another. In many ways this lack of objectivity has created a cynicism regarding the conduct and prejudices of the government and has fuelled the conservative Muslim lobby characterization of government as incapable of providing a just solution to Muslim problems; this of course helps the Muslim conservatives who are reluctant to give their constituents any choice since it may free them from the fear of cultural absorption and loosen the conservative grip. It has been adequately demonstrated by many societies that secularism or the complete abolition of Shariat laws (as in Turkey) or reform (as in a number of Muslim countries) does not impair either religious belief or dilute cultural strength. In examining its own motives government shoud acknowledge the extent to which its own policies, both economic and political, have not served the interests of minorities; on the contrary, they have lowered government's credibility to such an extent that it continuously enables Muslim conservatives to use "fear" of exploitation, injustice and "absorption", to their advantage. Then again none of the political parties appear to encourage grassroots liberal Muslim leadership, one that can tap their constituents' hopes rather than play on their primeval fears.

## Woman factor

Few examples could have demonstrated with such immediacy the paucity of Muslim woman power in India, or the marginalization of their concerns both by government and by the Muslim conservatives, as the Shah Bano case. It was indicative of the lack of political and economic power of Indian women in general that there was no attempt at consulting either Muslim women or other women by either the government or Muslim conservatives on the issue of the Supreme Court judgement or the Muslim

Women's Bill. Government could possibly justify this on the grounds that women within the legislature expressed support for the Act, though this cannot be independently confirmed since a three line whip was exercised to enforce compliance among ruling party Members of Parliament. But among Muslim conservatives and the community in general not even a token attempt was made to treat women as partners to be either consulted or helped. There was no acknowledgement of the support provided to the community by women, and therefore no acknowledgement of the need to reach an accommodation with them on this or any other issue. This is in sharp contrast to the manner in which political deals with other parties or politicians are struck, when discussions and accommodation on all issues are open and continuously undertaken, irrespective of ideology, by Muslim conservatives.

While some women's groups expressed their support for Muslim women in their struggle for maintenance, the lack of involvement with the general problems of Muslim women on the part of many of those groups tended to make this support seem opportunistic. Also the inevitable discussion of the backwardness of the Muslim community and its laws did not always sit well with Muslim women, and even tended to throw up some justification of both. Even Shah Bano was opportuned by the community to repudiate the public denunciation of the community and its laws. Muslim men, lawyers and journalists had already succumbed to these pressures and had found enough aggravation in the wording of the Supreme Court judgement to unequivocally condemn it (Dr. Tahir Mahmood, *Sunday Observer*, March 9, 1986; "P.M. and Shahbano's Case," A.G. Noorani, *Indian Express*, December 28, 1985) and while supporting and justifying the Act, called for certain modifications. ("Glaring Flaws in the New Bill," A.G. Noorani, *Indian Express*, March 3, 1986.)   Just as the lack of a social institutional infrastructure has hampered the development of an alternative voice to that of Muslim conservatives, so it hampers the progress of Muslim women. Without a forum from which to function, their concerns and problems cannot be communicated to the community or to society at large. They indeed become faceless and voiceless. They cannot fall back upon the existing women's groups because the structure of Indian politics and society tends to be divisive even among a group as generally disposessed as Indian women. Muslim women seem to face the double jeopardy of being a minority within a minority.

The current situation could still be turned to the advantage of
Muslim women if the heightened awareness among Muslim
women and liberal Muslims can be used to forge lasting institutions which can counter the arguments advanced by Muslim
conservatives on a variety of social and political issues. The
government could undercut Muslim conservatives trading on
"fear" by dealing with Muslim problems with some degree of
objectivity. Given a Supreme Court reversal of the Muslim
Women's Bill Muslim women will be better prepared and the
next fight may not be so one-sided. Then again, there is the
recourse still open to the community of using existing secular
laws to protect women. Political religion, never dispensible for
minorities for reasons of political survival, can be reforged by
the community to be a positive force to move it towards the
future rather than hark back to the past. A number of social issues
involving Muslims are indicative of the unresolved problems
carried over from the 19th century, and the solutions appear to
be complicated now, as then, by the communal attitudes of both
the majority and minority communities; communal prejudice has
tended to imprison both. Indian democracy and secularism, and
the imperatives of the twentieth century demand creative solutions by both communities so that important political and
economic problems can be dealt with through a recognition of
the fact that there is no alternative to coexisting.

# Field Trip Notes

## Introduction

The field trip was undertaken well after the survey and the initial analysis of the data. It became a means of verifying the results of the survey, which tended to refute the long held belief that Muslim women remained apart, insulated from the many changes that had taken place in the status and role of women in India. From the survey results it was clear that while the behaviour and attitudes of Muslim women were based mainly on their socio-economic stratum and were comparable to those of women in similar circumstances in other communities, they also reflected the community's need to maintain its identity and to survive as a distinct group. Though this need for identity did not appear to have interfered with the respondents' capacity to comprehend and adapt changes to their particular requirements in their daily lives, it tended to subjugate the interests of women to those of the group. The question, however, remained why, if the traditional image of Muslim women both in practice and certainly in attitudes, had undergone considerable change, were there no overt mainfestations of this change, either through the pronouncements of Muslim leaders or in the emergence of women leaders or institutions which would reflect these changes. It was hoped that the field trip through the nine cities already surveyed would provide some of the answers. The field trip focussed on Muslim women and men leaders who were actively involved either in social projects or politics or both. Few leaders interviewed were nationally known and certainly none of the women leaders were. Their involvement, however, in the community and in society gave them a special perspective on the problems and prospects of the community in the region. Some leaders of other communities were also interviewed for their assessment of the Muslim community. Community institutions were visited to evaluate their role and effectiveness.

The results of the field trip are presented for each region so that specific regional problems and concerns are readily identifiable as are their concerns, nationally. The examination of institutions provides an insight into the concerns and difficulties confronted by different Muslim communities and by women.

As in the survey, the questions posed to interviewees pertained to legal changes in the status of Muslim women, their economic participation, the economic conditions of the community, the incidence of polygamy and unilateral divorce, the advantages of using a standard Nikahnama or marriage contract form to overcome any difficulties that might exist in marriage practices, education and literacy in the community, institutions and their role in promoting economic and social change. Different regions had dealt differently with many of these social and economic problems, due to lack of a national social organization in the community or because economic opportunities varied between regional communities and depended to some extent on existing occupational structures. Politically, of course, there is no unity between regional communities, each being intent on securing their particular economic and social positions in their particular regional context. The twin underlying concerns of regional and national survival are evident in the responses of leaders in all nine cities.

## Delhi and Lucknow

These two cities are considered together because they represent the Urdu-speaking north Indian Muslim community and because the region traditionally sought to lead and represent Indian Muslims. The people interviewed at Delhi were social workers and politicians, some from different regions, but aspiring to speak for and identify with the general aims and preoccupations of the Indian Muslim community. The women leaders had all been educated and brought up in families which had supported their desire to play public roles. Most agreed that Muslim women's education in the region had initially been confined to the upper middle class and had only very gradually spread to other socio-economic strata. Purdah, which was widely practised by Muslim and non-Muslim communities, had been an important factor in holding back women's education. The lives of women in the early part of the century tended to be domestic, with social interaction limited to the family. The pattern varied between the pace at which families had adapted to change, particularly for women. Even within the same family, depending on the views of the immediate family concerned, differences existed in the education of women and rigidity of observance. (M.R.S. Shervani, Allahabad, 15.09.1977.) Regional differences also affected the observance of purdah; in Hyderabad and Bhopal women were less subject to rigid purdah than they were in the north (Begum H.H., MP, Delhi, 14.09.1977). In Bhopal, the ruling Begums of Bhopal had laid great emphasis on women's education and emancipation, and though there were no women cabinet members there were women advisors to the ruler. In Hyderabad the influence of elite families was progressive (Begum M.S., MP, Delhi, 13.09.1977).

Most women leaders actively involved in social and political work described the problems they had faced in their work not as a struggle against individual or even family resistance to education or family planning, but as reflecting a reluctance to transgress traditional norms in the neighbourhood in which they lived. The maintenance of purdah and other customs was observed in deference to the neighbourhood but discarded beyond its confines. Women leaders often couched their message of change subtly so as to redefine tradition rather than break it, thus making it more easily acceptable. There was an attempt by Muslim clerics to counteract change, but they were increasingly ineffectual in urban areas against the tide of education and social and economic change.

The adult centres for women and other institutions set up in the two cities were well attended by women once they became aware of their usefulness. Women in purdah too, appeared to be mobile and well aware of trends in society. Purdah was much less prevalent among the younger generation, except in the lower middle class; the problem was being solved in "bits and dribbles". (Begum M.S.)

Most women were not aware of their property rights under the existing law and, due to the zamindari system, Muslim women rarely inherited their share of the family property. Tradition and culture too conspired to keep women from exercising their right either to parental property or to mehr, and the husband's property. (Begum H.H.)

Before 1947, Muslim women in the region had participated

with women from other communities in group activities that focussed on women's issues such as purdah, education, child marriage, polygamy—issues that affected all women. (A. Habibullah, writer, Delhi, 10.11.1975). After 1947, the north Indian Muslim community was hard hit, losing both leadership and its economic base as property was seized when some members of a family migrated; this task was completed by the Abolition of Zamindari Act. In Maharashtra, however, because they were neither landed gentry nor dependent on government employment, Muslims were much less affected by Partition. (Badruddin Tyabji, civil servant, Delhi, 14.09.1977.)

Most communal riots were specifically aimed at the economic base of the community, and generally added to the existing prejudices against the community, making it more difficult for community members to find employment and forcing them to be self-employed. (H. Ahmad, MLA, Allahabad, 9.9.1977)

Women leaders were particularly concerned at the difficulties Muslim women faced in getting their share of property rights, mehr, maintenance, or custody of children. There was a widespread realization of the need for such laws as existed to be implemented to give women a fair chance. Education was certainly regarded as a means by which women could become more assertive and independent (H. Kidwai, social worker, Delhi, 15.12.1975.) The feeling was that the community was a "beleaguered garrison" (Attia Habibullah) and had fundamental problems of employment and security to contend with; making legislative changes would split the community and detract from the symbolic importance of the Shariat as central to the community's identity. (H. Habibullah.)

Several leaders noted that circumstances made the formulation of social, semi-political Muslim organizations inevitable in the region, for better representation of political and economic grievances even though such organizations still tended to stir old fears and could in fact prove counter-productive. (Niaz Hasan, politician, Lucknow, 12.9.1977.) Even organizations such as Basm-e-Urdu, formed in 1971 to promote an interest in Urdu were not entirely free of suspicion. (Begum G. Hussain, social worker, Lucknow, 9.12.1977.)

Muslim theological institutions of Deoband and Firangi Mahal situated in this area continuously seek to guide and direct constituents on religious and social matters. However, most leaders felt that the training imparted to clerics was inadequate and their continuous pronouncements tended to confuse rather than clarify issues. (H. Habibullah) These religious leaders were unable to provide guidance for a community passing through difficult times; the Urdu press in the region was better able to reflect the problems and the mood of the community. Most leaders felt that their traditional culture and customs had been eroded beyond recall and there was uncertainty about what was going to replace it. (Begum G. Hussain.)

Leaders in the educational field noted that fundamental changes had occurred in the student body in the last 30 years. (I.U. Khan, Principal, Karamat Hussain Intermediate College, Lucknow, 12.9.1977.) Earlier, the student body was predominantly from the upper socio-economic strata, now they were from lower socio-economic groups. There was no resistance, other than economic, to the higher education of girls. While, at an earlier time, the institution had to make elaborate arrangements for purdah, now only 10-15 per cent of the girls were in purdah. In the inner city branch of the college, situated in a predominantly Muslim area, girls did still observe purdah. Their parents were either employed in government or were self-employed. Most fathers were educated but mothers were either illiterate or informally educated in Urdu.

Urdu was and continues to be important for Muslims of the region. Several interviewees were actively working towards its wider acceptance so that it could still provide economic returns. Most felt that the language should be linked to its literature and not to its religious associations since this created unjustifiable resistance to it. (H. Habibullah)

Muslim women were involved in various economic activities ranging from embroidery and carpet weaving to bidi making. At other levels of education the most likely occupations were still medicine and teaching. (I.Khan)

Certain Muslim leaders were sharply critical of the community's inability to deal with its social, political or economic problems (Basheer, writer, retired librarian, Aligarh University, 19.9.1977), while others felt that people had come to terms with their situation and were determined to carve out their place in India. "Even though they face prejudices they are going to fight to live here." (H. Habibullah)

### Srinagar

Jammu & Kashmir is the only state in India with a majority

Muslim population, though this is confined to Kashmir. Muslims in Kashmir were mainly peasants ruled over by a Hindu monarch (Bazaz, P.N., 1959:204). It was only after 1930 that education and social change brought about mobility in the kingdom (Begum Sheikh Abdullah, MP, Srinagar, 9.26.1977). Both men and women leaders interviewed were conscious of the importance of their majority position for the Indian Muslim community (A. Ali, civil servant, Srinagar, 27.9.1977); they were also aware of the limitations of their majority position, "... we have to consider the sentiments of the minority community in any decision we take."

Muslim women in the region worked alongside men in the fields; purdah was only used to emphasize class distinctions and was more in evidence in urban areas. The middle class attitude towards women working outside the home continues to focus on teaching and medicine. Social workers were of necessity able to function only if they projected a conservative image. (S. Mufti, social worker, Srinagar, 27.9.1977.) Muslim women in the region, as elsewhere, seldom obtained their economic rights due to the indifference of the community and the quality and incompetence of clerics. (S. Mufti) Most formal education among women was limited to urban areas, though the extent of informal education among women could not be adequately gauged. Joint families were considered more repressive of women's rights than nuclear families. Women's labour was exploited without adequate recompense either by the family or by the employer, because women were not organized. (Begum Sheikh Abdullah)

The work of women's organizations in promoting and marketing women's handicrafts was cited many times as promoting social and economic change. However, there was disappointment at the performance of women politicians who seldom addressed themselves to women's issues. (S. Mufti.)

Both women and men leaders interviewed appeared conscious of the role they could play in the Indian Muslim community given their majority status, but the late development of the state and political pressures keep them uncertain of their goals and therefore unable to provide the bold, innovative leadership they are uniquely capable of.

## Calcutta

Bengal was one of the two Muslim majority states that was partitioned in 1947. Muslims in Calcutta are only a small percentage of the city's population, and consist of Bengali Muslims and migrants from Bihar and other neighbouring states who have come to seek employment. (M. Ghulam, Calcutta, 31.9.1977.) Bengali Muslim women shared many customs and practices with their Hindu counterparts, including seclusion, applying red sindur in the hair as a sign of marriage, and so on (Ward, 1963:304); they do not wear an outer garment for purdah but a shawl, like other Bengalis. (A. Nayeem, treasurer, The Calcutta Muslim Orphanage, 3.9.1977.) Women running the Calcutta Muslim Orphanage had conducted a survey on the needs of the community in a predominantly Muslim area. They found that Muslim women despite poverty and illiteracy were conscious of the need to educate their children and to limit the size of the family. (A. Nayeem.) The Orphanage provided girls with education and vocational training and it also arranged their marriages, using a standard Nikahnama which rules out the possibility of unilateral divorce or polygamy. Such contracts, according to those in charge, were in use even before 1947. (M. Tahir, secretary, The Calcutta Muslim Orphanage, 30.9.1977.)

Due to the partition of the province at the turn of the century and in 1947, communal politics has always been a factor in Bengal politics. After 1947 communal harmony was seriously disrupted in 1963 and 1969, apart from the smaller and less serious skirmishes that form a regular feature of urban life. Despite the great need for contact between the Muslim elite and the masses to address social problems facing the community, there was no notable Muslim leadership in Calcutta. (A. Nayeem, U.Tahir.) Several Muslim organizations were operating, including the Khilafat Committee established in the 1920s and attached to the main mosque. The Committee was active in promoting women's education and in mediating marital disputes. The Anjuman Mufidul-Islam was similarly involved and had both men and women members. (Sakina Nawaz, social worker, Calcutta, 31.9.1977.)

Like women of other communities, Muslim women in Calcutta face hardships due to lack of employment opportunities. Those able to get contractual work are mainly in bidi and paper-bag making. The Islamia Hospital is run on donations and caters to the medical needs of the Muslim and other communities. Muslim women active in different social welfare forums have organized meetings to try and identify problems that confront women in the community. (A. Nayeem.)

Lack of effective Muslim representation in the city has often meant that Muslim areas were neglected, seldom picked up for social welfare schemes. At the political level few Muslim leaders articulated their concerns for fear of being labelled 'communal' or only interested in their own community. There is not enough representation in private industry or government to ensure the safeguarding of Muslim employment or interest. It was generally felt that the community and Muslim women had not benefited over the years through government efforts but only through education and their own will to survive. (M. Ghulam.)

## Hyderabad

Before Independence Hyderabad was under Muslim rule, though Muslims were a minority; the state was taken over by the Indian government in 1948. There were some communal tensions at the time (Cormack, 1961:48) resulting in some migration to Pakistan (Imam, 1975:81), and some dispersal of the elite ruling class. Then there were several decades of communal quiet, giving way to tension and strife almost as endemic as it is in the north. Economic changes in the region, relative Muslim prosperity resulting from employment opportunities in West Asia and the intensifying of communal activities by both Hindu and Muslim political parties can generally be assumed to have caused ethnic tensions.

The disappearance of the Muslim aristocracy resulted in a loss of patronage and the impoverishment of those dependent on it. (Dr. Manan, Hyderabad, 15.9.1977.) Therefore, the opening up of employment in West Asia had lured many men to work abroad and to repatriate funds to families in Hyderabad.

Traditionally, aristocratic Muslim women in Hyderabad had taken to western education and to the formation of clubs and organizations. This trend was strengthened by the induction of two westernized Turkish princesses into the royal household. (M. Begum, politician and social worker, Hyderabad, 16.9.1977.) At the lower socio-economic level women were and still are subject to purdah, although this does not stop them from seeking employment, it often comes in the way of their marketing their goods and getting the money directly; this is often kept by male members of the family. (A.W. Ahmad, hon. secretary, Bharatiya Grameen Mahila Sangh, Hyderabad, 19.9.1977.) Class interaction through organizations or forums, so necessary for formulating and transmitting change, remains limited. But the importance of such organizations was demonstrated at the Conference organized by the Muslim Educational Society's meeting in 1976 which was attended by 6,000 women, all eager to air their problems and participate in discussions. (A. Khan, Principal, Nasr School, Hyderabad, 16.9.1977.) Great concern was voiced at the lack of employment opportunities and considerable interest was expressed at the setting up of an employment advisory service. The entire gamut of Muslim problems was discussed, and while no solutions were forthcoming, the interest generated was sought to be maintained by holding regular meetings in south Indian cities.

The community in Hyderabad was mainly interested in social and economic progress and not in politics. Several women's organizations had been set up. The Bazm-e-Khawateen which sought to contact women in mohallas and organize economic and informative activities for them, the Khawateen-i-Deccan, a social work group, Mehfil-e-Khawateen, a women's literary group (Bilquis Alladin, writer, Hyderabad, 16.9.1977), and so on. The Bharatiya Grameen Mahila Sangh ran adult literacy, vocational and other informative programmes for women in Muslim areas. (A.W. Ahmad.)

The Baitul Mal, an organization set up to channel obligatory Muslim charity into productive uses, gives outright loans for personal crises and provides seed money, to be repaid, for the setting up of small enterprises (Dr Manan). A Muslim maternity hospital and the Princess Essra hospital and charitable dispensary are run through contributions and provide free medical facilities to the poor.

Urdu is still important in the city since it was the traditional language for education and business, though Telugu has now taken its place. There is a Muslim Education Board which provides scholarships to both men and women of the community.

## Bombay

The Muslim community in Bombay tends to reflect the dynamism of other communities in the region and the economy. It also reflects the independence and activism associated with a trading community. Historically the community has been able to define its interests and to collaborate with other communities to achieve its ends. (Badruddin Tyabji, Delhi, 14.9.1977.) There have, however, been frequent outbreaks of communal violence that have heightened the community's sense of vulnerability. (F. Ismail, social worker, Bombay, 23.9.1977.) The regional character of the community had been strengthened after independence as the domination of north Indian Muslim politics has declined. The current emphasis of the community was more reflective of regional issues and pressures. (Rafiq Zakaria, politician and writer, Bombay, 23.9.1977.)

The region has Khoja and Bohra sects that are well organized to deal with their membership's social and theological requirements; this, however, has not improved the prospects of women who are not represented in its councils and often find the sect's rules and regulations more constricting than the elasticity prevalent in the community. (Kamilla Tyabji.) The Khoja and Bohra sects have committees that regulate Muslim law, arbitrate marital disputes and provide guidance in family matters; though such rulings are not legally binding, social pressures to comply can be overwhelming. Muslim women leaders in Bombay were firm in their belief that the rights given to women under the Quran specified the minimum acceptable rather than the limit. They felt that since Muslim women did not have an organization or a platform from which they could press for their rights these had been successively eroded. Identity, they felt, was important, but people were mistaken in assuming that Shariat rights defined it entirely. (Kamilla Tyabji.)

Purdah is no longer considered an impediment to girls' education (Kamilla Tyabji); the Anjuman-i-Islam schools run in Bombay cannot cope with the demand for admission. (H. Moinuddin, president, Anjuman-i-Islam, Bombay, 22.9.1977.) Great emphasis was placed on the desirability of employment for women but, as in other cities, the emphasis was on the suitable rather than the innovative. (Z. Currimbhoy, social worker, Bombay, 22.9.1977.) Women in the lower socio-economic strata, it was emphasized, should be trained so that they can gain access to the organized sector. This problem is of course universal for all communities in the city. Most Muslims were thought to be small businessmen, mainly self-employed (H. Moinuddin); though there were Muslims represented in business and government, this was not sufficient to ensure Muslim representation at all levels. Some discrimination against Muslim businesses in securing loans had resulted in small banks being set up by the community.

There was a strong feeling that communal violence was specifically directed at destroying the economic base of the community, tenuous though it was (H. Moinuddin), and the low level of Muslim representation in government and industry meant that Muslim interests, whether social, economic or political, would be inadequately defended. Muslim areas were usually neglected by social welfare authorities. (A.G. Noorani, political commentator and writer, Bombay, 24.9.1977.)

Urdu had been adopted as the language of the community in the 19th century as a mark of differentiation. (Badruddin Tyabji.) At the present time Anjuman schools taught in the Urdu medium up to middle level, then shifted to English; most Muslim children however, went to local Marathi medium schools. No provisions had been made by the community for religious instruction for children.

Bombay has a long history of the involvement of men and women of all communities in politics and social reform; this is so for the Muslim community as well. One of the social welfare organizations created and run by a Muslim woman was the Basm-e-Niswan. This organization was established in 1956 under the guidance of Mrs. Khatija Khatib and in 1977 it had ten rural centres and a centre in Bombay. Started in the aftermath of a communal riot, its aim was to inculcate self-help and self-direction in the community by inducting women into the process. Mrs. Khatib has been a genuine mediator between tradition and change. (Mrs Khatib, President, Basm-e-Niswan, Bombay, 23.9.1977.)

The Anjuman-e-Islamia, set up in 1876, has evolved into an important institution in Maharashtra seeking to educate and employ, and to protect and project Muslim tradition and culture. It runs many schools, colleges, vocational training centres, orphanages and homes for destitute Muslim women. The Anjuman- ul-Islam is smaller, but with similar aims.

### Madras

Muslim women in Madras had been particularly well integrated in the early women's movement; they participated actively in the Women's Indian Association as well as in the Muslim Women's Association. The latter continues to function, though its membership and aims are less well defined. It runs a co-operative shop and orphanages and gives scholarships to deserving girls. Both the Muslim Girls' Orphanage and the Anjuman Himayatul Islam Orphanage for boys is run by the Association. (Rehmatunissa Begum, President, Muslim Women's Association and

Matriculation School, Madras, 17.9.1977.)

Most leaders interviewed regarded the Muslim community as well established and integrated with other communities, with few tensions of the sort that plague north Indian communities. The communities' traditional trading activities continue. It has been pointed out for Tamil society generally that despite educational advances women continue to play rather traditional roles. (Cormack, 1961.) Muslim society reflected both social and economic conservatism, but in attitudes towards the education of girls and the employment of women, the community was far ahead of its north Indian counterpart. One interesting feature was that while girls were educated, in the upper socio-economic strata they were less educated than their poorer counterparts because the latter needed to compete for employment. (S. Farhat, Lecturer, South India Education Trust College, Madras, 18.9.1977.) Muslim women were working in a variety of occupations, but there were the educated unemployed as well. Due to education and employment the general perception was that Muslim women were able to secure their marital and economic rights more successfully. (S. Farhat.) The stress on girls' education was encouraged by parents and by husbands who wanted their wives to work.

Tamil speaking Muslims were better integrated and faced less discrimination than Urdu speakers. Urdu had been used as the court language by the Nawabs of Arcot who sought to identify with the north Indian Muslim community before 1947. With the resurgence of Tamil nationalism, based on a power struggle between the Brahmins and lower caste groups, language had become particularly symbolic. (A. Qadir, lecturer, Madras, 17.9.1977.) Most Muslim children were being sent to government or non-sectarian private schools and co-education was not considered an impediment to the education of girls. Only financial difficulties could keep children away from school. (Rehmatunissa Begum.) The community was, however, interested in preserving its social and religious identity and the combination of secular education with cultural and religious socialization has been incorporated into the college run by the South India Educational Trust. Justice Basheer Ahmad Sayed, the founder of the Trust, felt that a blend of western secular education with religious and social instruction served to strengthen the sense of identity, essential preparation for living and succeeding in a secular world. (Justice Basheer Ahmad Sayed, President, SIET,

Madras, 18.9.1977.) Religious instruction and Friday prayers were compulsory for Muslim women who formed 48 per cent of the student body and 57 per cent of the staff. Some students came to school in purdah, according to the Principal; the medium of instruction was English, while Urdu and Arabic were offered as special subjects. Justice Basheer Sayed, a strong advocate for the preservation of Muslim culture and identity, felt that ". . . the government should be more concerned with ameliorating the economic conditions of the community before they tried to change their laws; changes in law and the emphasis against their language and culture threaten the community". The '51 Club was formed in an attempt to preserve the community's cultural identity and gain recognition for it in a public forum, through holding talks and sharing Muslim functions by inviting members of other communities to participate. Justice Sayed was also a member of The Muslim Personal Law Board set up to advise government and to protect the Shariat laws from encroachment. Muslim law and identity were, to him, indivisible. Despite this, the Muslim community in Madras did not identify with north Indian Muslim politics; it has been and continues to retain its regional moorings as it seeks to preserve its regional social, political and economic interests.

## Trivandrum

The same regional identification and cohesion characterizes the Muslim community in Kerala, despite recent attempts to undermine this unity. As one Hyderabad woman leader remarked with some envy, "Our situation is not like that of the Kerala Muslim community; they are able to support other communities' causes and get support for their causes from other communities routinely." (B. Alladdin.) Historically, the Muslims in Kerala were partly located in Madras Presidency and were largely peasants. The former Travancore State which was noted for its liberal attitude towards communities living in its fold and for its enlightened social, political and economic policies, dominates the present state. Travancore encouraged women's education, nutrition and health, and tended to set an example for the rest of the country. Arabs, before and after the advent of Islam, came to this coastal state as traders and were welcomed. The Muslim community in the state is Malayalam-speaking and certain sects even follow the matrilineal system prevalent in the state.

There has been very little purdah in the state and no outer

garment is worn by Muslim women. Mehr or dower has always
been nominal and, typically, promptly paid by the husband, and
the age of marriage among Muslim girls has always been high.
There is a Malayalam translation of the Quran, and women were
familiar with it and followed many religious customs. Kerala
Muslims wore the same garments as other communities, only the
colours are different. (Mrs. H. Marikar, social worker, member,
Muslim Women's Association, Trivandrum, 20.9.1977.)

The Palayam mosque in Trivandrum is involved in the effort
to improve an understanding of Islam among its constituents.
To facilitate this a committee of 24 members, two each from
different Muslim sects, meets regularly to mediate on marital and
religious problems; while these are in no way binding they do
provide some guidance. There are, however, no women on the
Committee.

The judiciary in Kerala has been instrumental in helping Muslim women by interpreting Quranic injunctions directly rather
than following the traditional interpretation. (A. Abdullah, social
worker, member, Muslim Women's Association, Trivandrum,
20.9.1977.) Divorce was rare, but when it occurred women found
it difficult to get either maintenance or custody of children.
(Fatima Bibi, District Judge, Trivandrum, 20.9.1977.)

Muslim women, particularly those active in the professions
and in social work, have formed the Muslim Women's Association because of a keenly felt need to think and act constructively
on the economic and social issues faced by Muslim women in
the lower socio-economic strata. Through this association they
hope to keep in touch with each other and to undertake projects
aimed at such women. (Mrs. H. Marikar.) The Muslim Educational Society was organized by Dr. Ghafoor and Mrs Fatima
Ghafoor in 1970. This society is specifically directed towards
improving the quality of Muslim education and providing counselling for Muslim youth on employment.

The most refreshing aspect of interviewing Muslim leaders in
Kerala was their vehement denial of any discrimination suffered
by the community in the state; they also denied that the Muslim
League formed before 1947 and which continues in Kerala, is in
any way contrary to communal harmony. (A. Abdullah, Mrs. H.
Marikar.) Even the infamous Moplah Riot of 1925 is put down
to economic rather than communal reasons. (Mohammad Koya,
politician, Muslim League, Trivandrum, 19.9.1977.)

The region's robust attitude towards the Muslim community

in Kerala seems to suggest that an institutional infrastructure, both political and social, can help the community deal with change without proving threatening to other communities.

## Ahmedabad

The Muslim community in Ahmedabad is divided between Gujarati and Urdu speakers. The Urdu speaking migrant labour community from U.P. is part of the labour force in the region, and constitutes the lower socio-economic strata of the community. Cultural cohesion is evident in the retention of caste names and certain regional and cultural customs relating to marriage or birth, that are shared between communities. Gujarati speakers are naturally better integrated. (Ela Bhatt, General Secretary, Self-Employed Women's Association, Ahmedabad, 24.9.1977.) The city suffered a major communal riot in 1969, the memory of which lingers and is reinforced by subsequent riots, from which they have not yet recovered socially or economically. Many of the leaders interviewed intensified their social and economic activities on behalf of the community as a result of the riot. (Mrs. A. Mirza, Mrs. Qureshi, Members, Basm-e-Khuloos, Ahmedabad, 24.9.1977.)

Muslims were either industrial labour or ran small businesses. Upward mobility among groups in the state involves a closer identification with Urdu and purdah. Muslim weavers in the region are a traditionally conservative group uninterested in upward mobility but interested in preserving the group's social and economic interest. There was no migration from this group to Pakistan in 1947 and they have a strong stake in the stability of the state. (Mr Qureshi, President, All-India Jamaat ul Quraish, Ahmedabad, 24.9.1977.) The trading community consists of Khojas, Bohras and Memons who are in the wholesale and retail trade. There are both professionals and government employees in the community. Communal tensions were often sparked off by poor industrial labour relations between management and Muslim workers. (Mrs. Waliullah, member, All India Women's Conference, Mrs Indu Patel, President, AIWC, Ahmedabad, 24.9.1977.) The usual polarisation existed between Muslim classes with few bridging institutions between them. Communal tensions served to intensify the community's concern with religious observances and less with women's rights or place, as would be symbolized by changes in personal law. Muslim women had not been able to organize themselves or join with other women to take a stand on obtaining their rights in the Shariat, despite the fact that there were several Muslim women's organizations. The Basm-e-Khuloos established in 1956 and the Basm-e-Khawateen in 1966, are both involved in social work. There is very little purdah observance and no outer garment is worn. About 25 per cent of the SEWA membership is Muslim women who eagerly participate in its activities. The organization helps its members obtain credit and secures other benefits for them. Most of its Muslim members are the sole supporters of their families, and those who were married were encouraged by their husbands to join the organization and participate in its activities. While other women members were vegetable vendors and head-loaders, Muslim women were in garment making and embroidery. Ela Bhatt had not come across any incidence of polygamy or unilateral divorce among the membership, but felt that the community lacked political and social leadership, which created problems of communication and transition.

The Sunni Waqf Board, a rich trust organization in the region, made no effort to disburse its funds judiciously to benefit the community or to provide any leadership. (Dr Z. Desai, practising physician and social worker, Ahmedabad, 25.9.1977.) But for Ela Bhatt's organization there seemed little mobilisation among the Muslim groups in the region.

## Conclusion

The field trip focussed on the widespread concern among Muslim communities about their future symbolized by their economic and cultural insecurities. The preservation and survival of Muslim culture was clearly identified with the community's ability to become economically viable and politically effective. Education was regarded as being important in achieving this, but discrimination in the job market and the threat of communal riots directed at the economic base of the community tended to undermine the push to higher education. Muslim leaders in all cities mentioned the need for and the desirability of Muslim social institutions which could fulfil the community's need for institutionalizing change and representing the social and cultural concerns of the community. Political representation, too, was considered important to ensure that the economic and social concerns of the community were not overlooked.

There was great concern at the psychological, economic and

political damage caused by the increasing frequency of communal conflicts. A number of institutions had sprung up to help the community after such occurrences, and it was clear that people were better off in regions where there was greater communal harmony, due to financial security and confidence. In Hyderabad, Trivandrum, Madras and Bombay, there were a number of women's and community organizations that have improved social conditions and communication in the community. Muslim communities and women in other regions tended to reflect in part the economic conditions of the region, and the lack of inter-community co-operation which stultifies social progress.

Changes in social, political and economic structures have tended to affect Muslim women much as they do other women in a particular region, particularly with regard to attitudes towards women's roles and employment. The concept of "appropriate" employment for women was mentioned by women of both the Hindu and Muslim communities. In fact, with the exception of Bombay and Delhi attitudes towards women's employment remained traditional and conservative. Better trained Muslim clerics and standardization of the marriage contract were mentioned in all regions as a way around the need for legislative changes in marital laws. There are many anomalies in the overall interpretation of Muslim marital rights and duties between regions, and whether this helps or hinders Muslim women depends on particular regional attitudes and practices that affect all women, though the incidence of polygamy or of unilateral divorce has become increasingly uncommon. Another noteworthy feature was that women's organizations, despite the prevalence of the All India Women's Conference, did not have an enthusiastic following. The articulation of feminist ideology or goals was completely lacking and leadership, such as it was, reflected the social conservatism of the region. Innovative leadership was apparent only in newer economically specific organizations such as SEWA in Ahmedabad and the Basm-e-Niswan in Bombay; participation of Muslim women in these was enthusiastic.

The leadership of the Muslim community and women in the north still tended to rest with the old political families, rather than reflecting the new middle class. Politically, and even culturally, while all Muslim communities identified with the interests and problems of their regional community, the preservation of their religious entity was linked to that of other Muslim communities. The concern, therefore, with Urdu and Muslim Personal Law was seen as linking disparate communities together. However, while both remain important pragmatism clearly marks the approach of many communities which have set up community committees to deal with marital disputes and in attitudes towards Urdu which, though a Muslim *cause celebre* is not being allowed to mar the economic future of the community. Children are being educated in government schools in the regional language rather than in community schools.

The Muslim institutions visited were not all concerned with women's issues. Some were educational, others economic, not all were well established or well run, but it was clear that community leaders were interested in building an institutional infrastructure which would simultaneously help community members internally and represent the community by forging institutional links with other communities. All respondents were enthusiastic and interested in this research project and hoped that its findings would accurately represent their problems, dilemmas and hopes for the future.

The Shah Bano controversy, leading to the enactment of the Muslim Women's (Protection of Rights in Divorce)Act, indicates that once more events have tended to outstrip the Muslim community's ability to deal with its social problems, just as political events had done in an earlier period. Even as Muslim women were tentatively beginning to assert themselves, endeavouring to find some legal protection for the very real issues, both economic and social, that confronted them, their prospects were dealt a blow by the ever vigilant conservatives, to whom Islam represents not a system of overall justice, of carefully crafted women's rights, but merely an opportunity to assert minority differentiation at the expense of women. With no real effort to address the problems which have forced women to legal action, the well organized Muslim conservative lobby was able to exercise enough pressure on the government to nullify the ruling by the Supreme Court of India awarding Shah Bano her maintenance. Despite the fact that the Muslim community was split between those upholding and those denouncing the decision, the government introduced the Muslim Women's Protection Act (1986), which effectively removed the flexibility which Muslim women may have had under the Indian judicial system. The inescapable fact is that "Shariat laws" are generally not observed with any fidelity when it comes to economic justice for women; any attempt by Muslim women to secure those or any other rights are regarded as peripheral, and their interests are always made subservient to the misperceived interests of the community. There can be no change in this situation until Muslim women organize themselves sufficiently to create a platform from which they can respond to the community and the government. The conclusions, therefore, of the field trip continue to be valid and in fact gain urgency.

# References

Aaby, Peter, "Engels and Women: Critique of Anthropology," London: *Women's Issues 3*, Nos. 9–10: 25–50.

Abhenanda, Swami, "Women's Place in Hindu Religion," New York: Vedanta Society, 1901.

Act X, 1891, Paper 32; Paper 33; Paper 10; Serial 15, Paper 37; Paper 16; India Office Records and Library.

Aggarwal, P.C., "Caste, Religion and Power: An Indian Case Study," New Delhi: Shri Ram Centre for Industrial Relations, 1971.

Ahmad, Imtiaz, in Rothermund Dietmer (ed.) *Islam in South Asia*, Weisbaden: Franz Steiner Verlag, 1975.

Ali, Aruna Asaf, in Shyam Kumari Nehru (ed.), *Our Cause*, Allahabad: Kitabistan, undated.

Ali, Maulvi Muhammad, *The Status of Women in the Modern World*, Lahore: Aziz Publishers, 1975.

Almquist, Elizabeth, "Untangling the Effects of Race and Sex: The Disadvantaged Status of Black Women," *Social Science Quarterly*, Vol 56, No. 1.

Altekar, A.S., *Position of Women in Hindu Civilization from Prehistoric Times to the Present Day*, Benares: Motilal Banarsidas, 1956.

Anderson, Bernard E., "Full Employment and Equality," *The Annals of American Academy*, March 1975.

Anderson, J.N.D., (ed.) *Islamic Law in the Modern World*, New York: New York University Press, 1959.

——, "The Role of Personal Statuses in Social Development in Islamic Countries," London: *Comparative Studies in Society and History*, Vol 13, No. 1, January 1971.

Andrews, C.F., *The True India*, London: George Allen and Unwin, 1939.

Arberry, A.J., *The Koran Interpreted*, New York: Macmillan & Co., 1973.

Aziz, Ahmad, *Studies in Islamic Culture in the Indian Environment*, Oxford: Oxford University Press, 1964.

Bagchi, A.K., in Gough, K. and H.P. Sharma., (eds.), *Imperialism and Revolution in South Asia*, London: Monthly Review Press, 1973.

Bahadur, Lal, *The Muslim League: Its History, Activities and Achievements*, Agra: Agra Book Store, 1954.

Bakhle, P.S. (ed.), *Social Reform Annual*, Bombay: Servants of India Society, 1938.

Bazaz, P.N., *Daughters of the Vasista*, Delhi: Pamposh Publications, 1959.

Bell, Daniel, in Glazer, N. and D.P. Moynihan (eds.), *Ethnicity and Social Change*, Cambridge: Harvard University Press, 1975.

Beteille, Andre, *Caste, Class and Power: Changing Patterns of Stratification in a Tanjore Village*, Berkeley: University of California Press, 1965.

Bhatty, Zarina, in B.R. Nanda (ed.) *Indian Women: From Purdah to Modernity*, Delhi: Vikas, 1976.

Bill to Legalize Marriages Between Certain Natives of India not Professing the Christian Religion, 1872, Government of India Legislative Deptt. Objects, Reasons and Acts, 1872, India Office Records, Paper 6.

Blood, R.O., *The Family*, New York: The Free Press, 1972.

Bopemange, D.A. & P.V. Veeraghavan, *Status Images in Changing India*, New Delhi: UNESCO Publications, 1967.

Boserup, Ester, *Women's Role in Economic Development*, London: George Allen and Unwin, 1970.

Bottomore, T.B., *Sociology*, New York: Vintage Books, 1972.

Brass, Paul, *Language, Religion and Politics in North India*, Cambridge University Press, 1974.

Brown, Judith, *Gandhi's Rise to Power in Indian Politics, 1915-1922*, Cambridge: Cambridge University Press, 1972.

Caton, A.R., *The Key of Progress*, Oxford: Oxford University Press, 1930.

Cartwright, D. *Studies in Social Power*, Ann Arbor: University of Michigan Press, 1959.

*Census of India*, 1872, Allahabad.

*Census of NWP*, 1892, 1893, Allahabad.

*Census of India*, 1901, 1902, NWP and Oudh, Vol XVI, Part 1, Allahabad.

Chaney, Elsa, in June Nash and H.I. Safa (eds.), *Sex and Class in Latin America*, New York: Praeger, 1975.

Chapman, E.F., *Sketches of Some Distinguished Indian Women*, Calcutta: W.H. Allen and Co., 1891.

Chugtai, Muniruddin, "Post-1857 Economic and Administrative Politics of the British in India", *Pakistan Economic and Social Review*, Autumn Vol XVI, No. 3, 1974.

Cohen, Abner, *Customs and Politics in Urban Africa: A Study of Hausa Migrants in Yoruba Towns*, Berkeley: University of California Press, 1969.

Cousins, Margaret, *The Awakening of Asian Womanhood*, Madras: Ganesh and Co., 1922.

Davis, Kingsley, *The Population of India and Pakistan*, New Jersey: Princeton University Press, 1957.

Denich, Bette, in M.Z. Rosaldo & L. Lamphere (eds.), *Women, Culture and Society*, California: Stanford University Press, 1974.

Derret, Duncan, *Religion, Law and the State in India*, London: Faber and Faber, 1968.

Desai, A.R., *Social Background of Indian Nationalism*, Bombay: Popular Prakashan, 1966.

Desai, Padma, "Participation of Women in the Economies of Developing and Developed Countries", Paper prepared for the International Women's Year Conference, New York: UN, 1975.

de Stuers, Cora Vreede, *Parda: The Study of Muslim Women's Life in Northern India*, New York: Humanities Press, 1968.

D'Souza, Alfred, (ed.), *Women in Contemporary India*, Delhi: Manohar, 1975.

Dube, Leela, *Matriliny and Islam: Religion and Society in the Laccadives*, Delhi: National Publishing House, 1969.

Dumont, Louis, "Nationalism and Communalism", quoting Karl Marx "On the Question of the Jews", Delhi: *Contributions to Indian Sociology*, Vol 11 1964.

Education Commission Report, 1881-1882; Appendix to Education Commission Report, Report of the United Provinces Provincial Committee, 1884; Appendix to the Education Commission Report, Bombay, Report, Vol 1, 2; Appendix to the Education Commission Report, Madras Provincial Report.

Edib, Halide, *Inside India*, London: George Allen and Unwin, 1937.

Edwardes, Michael, *British India*, London: Sidgwick and Jackson, 1967.

Enloe, Cynthia, *Ethnic Conflict and Political Development*, Boston: Little Brown, 1971.

Five Year Plan, 1952. New Delhi: Government of India, Planning Commission.

Farquhar, J.N. *Modern Religious Movements in India*, Delhi: Munshiram Manoharlal, 1967.

Field, H.H., *After Mother India*, New York: Harcourt, Braece & Co., 1929.

Foster, Phillip, *Education and Social Change in Ghana*, Chicago: University of Chicago Press, 1968.

Fuller, Margaret B., *The Wrongs of Indian Womanhood*, New York: Fleming H. Revell Co, 1900.

Gedge, E.C., & M. Choksi, (eds.) *Women in Modern India*, Bombay: Taraporevala, 1929.

Geertz, Clifford, (ed.) *Old Societies and New States*, Glencoe: Free Press, 1963.

Geile, J.Z., & A.C. Smock, (eds.) *Women's Roles and Status in Eight Countries*, New York: John Wiley & Sons, 1977.

Ghosh, A., "Population and Planning", in A. Bose, *et al.* (eds.), *Population in India's Development, 1900-2000*, Delhi: Vikas, 1975.

Glazer, N. & D.P. Moynihan, (eds.), *Ethnicity and Social Change*, Cambridge: Harvard University Press, 1975.

Goldstein, Rhoda, *Indian Women in Transition: A Bangalore Case Study*, New Jersey: The Scarecrow Press, 1972.

Gordon, David, *Women of Algeria: An Essay on Change*, Cambridge: Harvard Middle-Eastern Monograph Series, 1968.

Gore, M.S., *Urbanization and Family Change*, Bombay: Popular Prakashan, 1968.

Gough, Kathleen, "The Origin of the Family", in R.R. Reiter, (ed.), *Anthropology of Women*, New York: Monthly Review Press, 1975.

Gough, K. & H.P. Sharma (eds.), *Imperialism and Revolution in S. Asia*, New York: Monthly Review Press, 1973.

Graham, G.F.I., *The Life and Work of Sir Syed Ahmad Khan*, London: Hodder and Stoughton, 1909.

Gray, Hester, *Indian Women and the West*, London: Zenith Press, 1944.

Haq, Mushirul, *Islam in Secular India*, Simla: Institute of Advanced Studies, 1974.

Hardy, Peter, *The Muslims of British India*, Cambridge: Cambridge University Press, 1972.

Hasan, Sakinatul Fatima Wazir, in Shyam Kumari Nehru (ed.), *Our Cause*, Allahabad: Kitabistan, undated.

Hate, C.A., *Changing Status of Women in Post - Independence India*, Bombay: Allied Publishers, 1969.

Hauswirth, Freida, *Status of Women*, New York: The Vanguard Press, 1932.

Heer, David, "The Measurement and Bases of Family Power: An Overview", *Journal of Marriage and Family Living*, May 1963.

Heimsath, C.H., *Indian Nationalism and Hindu Social Reform*, New Jersey: Princeton University Press, 1964.

Hunter, W.W., *The Indian Mussalmans: Are they Bound in Conscience to Rebel Against the Queen?* Lahore: Friends Book House, 1871, rpt. 1964.

Huston, Perdita, *Third World Women Speak Out*, New York: Praeger, 1979.

Jain, Devaki, *Indian Women*, Delhi: Government of India, Ministry of Information and Broadcasting, 1975.

Kamat, A.R., "Literacy and Education of Muslims: A Note", Bombay: *Economic and Political Weekly*, No. 23, 1981.

Kapadia, K.M., *Marriage and Family in India*, Oxford: Oxford University Press, 1956.

Kapur, Promilla, *The Changing Status of Working Women*, Delhi: Vikas, 1974.

Karandikar, M.A., *Islam in India's Transition to Modernity*, Connecticut: Greenwood Publishing Corpn., 1969.

Karim, A.K.N., "Changing Patterns of an East Pakistan Family", in Barbara Ward (ed.) *Women in New Asia*, Netherlands: UNESCO, 1963.

Karve, D.K., *Looking Back*, Poona: Hindu Widows' Association, 1936.

Kaur, Manmohan, *Role of Women in the Freedom Movement*, Delhi: Sterling Publishers Ltd., 1968.

Kazi Act 1880, Government of India, Judicial Deptt., Objects, Reasons and Acts, India Office Records, Paper 1, Paper 5, Paper 6, Appendix 11.

Khan, Mazhar ul Haq, *Purdah and Polygamy: A Study in Social Pathology of the Muslim Society*, Peshawar: Nashiran-e- ilm-Tarapiya, 1972.

Khan, Verity Saifullah, "Purdah in the British Situation" Paper, British Sociologists Association Conference, 1974.

Khan, Sir Syed Ahmed, *Causes of the Indian Revolt*, Lahore: The Book House, 1858, rpt. 1970.

Krishan, Gopal & Shyam Madhav, 1974, "Pattern of City Literacy", Bombay: *Economic and Political Weekly*, May 18, 1974.

Kothari, Rajni, *Politics in India*, Boston: Little Brown & Co., 1970.

Imam, Zafar, "Some Aspects of the Social Structure of the Muslim Community in India", in his (ed.) *Muslims in India*, Delhi: Orient Longman, 1975.

Jain, S.P., *The Social Structure of Hindu-Muslim Community*, Delhi: National, 1975.

Jeffery, Patricia, *Frogs in a Well: Indian Women in Purdah*, London: Zed Press, 1979.

Lamar, Empey, "Role Expectations of Young Women Regarding Marriage and a Career", *Journal of Marriage and Family*, May 1958.

Lateef, Shahida, "Whither the Indian Women's Movement?" Bombay: *Economic and Political Weekly*, Nov. 19, 1977.

——, "Muslim Political Leadership", *Indian Express*,1978.

——, "Indian Ethnicity Observed", Bombay, *Economic and Political Weekly*, Dec. 13, 1980.

——, in Gail Minault (ed.), *The Extended Family: Women and Political Participation in India and Pakistan*, Delhi: Chanakya Publications, 1981.

Legislative Assembly Debates, 1939, Vol I, IV, V, Simla: Government of India Press.

Levy, Reuben, *The Sociology of Islam*, Vol. I, New York: William and Norgate, 1930.

Loania, Tajamul Khan, *Women in Islam and their Non-Muslim Sisters*, Lahore: Kashmir Art Press, 1934.

Lokhandwala, S.T., *Position of Women Under Islam*, Paper, Simla: Indian Institute of Advanced Studies, 1973.

Malik, Hafeez, *Muslim Nationalism in India and Pakistan*, Washington, 1963.

Masselos, J., "Power in the Bombay Mohalla", *Journal of South Asian Studies*, No. 6, Dec. 1976.

Maududi, Maulana, *Purdah, the Status of Woman in Islam* (tr. E. Al' Ashari), Lahore: Islamic Publications Ltd., 1972.

Mazumdar, K.C., in A. Bose, et al., (eds.), *Population in India's Development 1900-2000*, Delhi: Vikas, 1975.

Meherally, Yusuf, *At the Crossroads*, Bombay: The National Information and Publications, 1947.

Mehta, Rama, *The Western Educated Hindu Woman*, Bombay: Asia Publishing House, 1970.

Memorandum on the Progress of Education in British India, 1916- 1926, Calcutta.

Menon, Lakshmi, *Position of Women*, Oxford Pamphlets on Indian Affairs, No. 2, Oxford University Press, 1944.

Minaltur, Joseph, in Alfred D' Souza (ed.), *Women in Contemporary India: Traditional Images and Changing Roles*, Delhi: Manohar, 1975.

Minault, Gail, "Muslim Women in Conflict with Purdah," Paper read at Berkshire Conference of Women Historians, Rutgers University, March 1973.

——' in Dietmar Rothermund (ed.) *Islam in South Asia*, Weisbaden: Franz Steiner Verlag, 1974.

——' *The Extended Family: Women and Political Participation in India and Pakistan*, Delhi: Chanakya Publications, 1981.

Mines, Mattison, "Islamization and Muslim Ethnicity in South India", *Man: Journal of Royal Anthropological Institute*, Vol. 10, No. 3, 1975.

Mirza, Sarfaraz Husain, *Muslim Women's Role in Pakistan Movement*, Lahore: Research Society of Pakistan, 1969.

Mitra, Ashok, *Population Aspects of Quality and Control*, Delhi: Abhinav Publishers, 1978.

*Modern Review*, January 1931; February 1924.

Morrison, Rev. J., *New Ideas in India*, Edinburgh: George A. Morton, 1906.

Mujeeb, M., *Islamic Influence of Indian Society*, New Delhi: Meenakshi Praksahan, 1972.

Nanda, B.R., *Indian Women: From Purdah to Modernity*, Delhi: Vikas, 1976.

Nash, June & Helen 1 Safa, (eds.) *Sex and Class in Latin America*, New York: Praeger, 1976.

Nehru, Shyam Kumari, (ed.), *Our Cause*, Allahabad: Kitabistan, undated.

Niazi, Kausar, *Modern Challenges in Muslim Families*, Lahore: Shaikh Mohammad Ashraf, 1976.

Nizami, T.A., *Muslim Political Thought and Activity in India*, Aligarh, 1969.

O'Barr, Jean, "Third World Women: Factors Changing their Status", Occasional Papers, Duke University Centre for International Studies, 1976.

O'Malley, L.S.S. *Modern India and the West*, Oxford: Oxford University Press, 1968.

Ortner, K., "Leisure Activity Patterns and Marital Satisfaction over the Marital Career", *Journal of Marriage and Family*, February 1975.

Papanek, Hanna, "Purdah in Pakistan", *Journal of Marriage and Family*, August 1971.

——, "Separate Worlds and Symbolic Shelter", *Comparative Studies in Society and History*, Vol. 15, No. 3, July 1973.

Pastner, C., "Access to Property and the Status of Women in Islam", Paper for Conference on the Status of Women in Contemporary Muslim Societies, Harvard University, April 19, 1975.

Prasad, Ishwari & H.K. Subedar, Hindu-Muslim Problems, Allahabad: Chugh Publications, 1974.

*Progress of Education in India, First Quinquennial Review of Education, 1881-1826*, with special reference to the Report of the Education Commission, 1888, Calcutta; *Fourth Quinquennial Review of Education, 1897-1902*, Calcutta, 1903; *Fifth Quinquennial Review of Education, 1902-1907*, Calcutta, 1909; *Seventh Quinquennial Review of*

*Education, 1912-1917* Vol. 1, Calcutta, 1918; *Eighth Quinquennial Review of Education, 1917- 1922*, Calcutta, 1923; *Ninth Quinquennial Review of Education, 1922-1927*, Calcutta, 1928; *Eleventh Quinquennial Review of Education*, Calcutta, 1939.

Rathbone, Eleanor, *Child Marriage: the Indian Minotaur*, London: George Allen & Unwin, 1934.

Reeves, Nancy, *Womanhood: Beyond the Stereotypes*, Chicago: Aldine A. Atherton, 1971.

Remy, Dorothy, "Underdevelopment and the Experience of Women", in R.R. Reiter (ed.), *Towards an Anthropology of Women*, New York: Monthly Review Press, 1975.

Report of the Age of Consent Committee, 1928-1929, Vol. 1, Vol. 11, Calcutta, 1929, Government of India.

Report of the Committee on Muhammadan Education, 1915, Calcutta: Bengal Book Secretariat Depot.

Rizvi, Janet, "Muslim Politics in India", unpublished Ph.d. thesis, 1969.

Robinson, F.C.R., *Separatism Among Indian Muslims: The Politics of the United Provinces, 1860-1923*, Cambridge: Cambridge University Press, 1974.

Robinson, Maxine, *Islam and Capitalism*, (trs. Brian Pearce), New York: Pantheon Books, 1973.

Rosaldo, M.Z., in Rosaldo & Lamphere,, (eds.), *Woman, Culture and Society*, California: Stanford University Press, 1974.

*Roshini*, publication of the All India Women's Conference; Feb 1946, No.1; May 1946, Vol.1, No. 4; Special No. 1946; Dec. 1932, Vol. XVI, No. 2; Feb. 1946, Vol.1 No. 1.

Ross, Aileen, *The Hindu Family in its Urban Setting*, Toronto: Toronto University Press, 1961

Rothermund, Dietmar, *Islam in S.Asia*. Weisbaden: Franz Steiner Verlag, 1975.

Roy, Shibani, *Status of Muslim Women in North India*, Delhi: B.R. Publications, 1979.

Rudolph, S.H. and L.I., *Education and Politics in India*, Cambridge: Harvard University Press, 1972.

Russell, R. & Khurshidul Islam, *Ghalib: Life and Letters* Vol. 1, Cambridge: Harvard University Press, 1969.

Ryder, Emily, *The Little Wives of India*, Philadelphia: Allen Lane and Scot, 1903.

Sacks, Karen, "Engels Revisited" in R.R. Reiter (ed.), *Anthropology of Women*, New York: Monthly Review Press, 1975.

Salazar, Gloria, "Participation of Women in the Mexican Labour Force", in Nash & Safa (eds.) *Sex and Class in Latin America, op. cit.*

Sanday, Peggy, "Towards a Theory of the Status of Women", *American Anthropologist,* 75, 1973.

Seal, Anil, *The Rise of Indian Nationalism,* Cambridge: Cambridge University Press, 1971.

——' "Imperialism and Nationalism in India", *Modern Asian Studies,* Vol.7, 1973.

Sen, Ela, *Testament of India,* London: George Allen and Unwin, 1939.

Shah, A.B., *Challenges to Secularism,* Bombay: Natchiketa Publications, 1969.

Shahnawaz, Begum J., *Father and Daughter,* Lahore: Nigarishat, 1971.

Shridevi, S., *A Century of Indian Womanhood,* Mysore: Rao and Raghavan, 1965.

Smelser, N.J. & S.M. Lipset, *Social Structure and Mobility in Economic Development,* Chicago: Aldine Publishing Co., 1966.

Smith, Donald Eugene, *India as a Secular State,* Princeton: Princeton University Press, 1963.

Smock, Audrey, "Bangladesh", in Geile & Smock (eds.), *Women: Roles and Status in Eight Countries,* New York: John Wiley & Sons, 1977.

Sorabjee, Cornelia, *Between the Twilight,* London: Harper Brothers, 1908.

*Status of Women in India,* a synopsis of the Report of the National Committee, New Delhi: ICSSR, 1975.

*Stridharma,* publication of the Women's India Association. May 1934, No. 7; Dec. 1935-Jan 1936, No. 1; July-Aug. 1936, No. 6; Nov. 1933, No. 1; Nov. 1934, No. 3; 1934, No. 3; July 1932, No. 19; Aug-Sept. 1935, Nos. 10, 11; Jan. 1935, No. 3; 1933, No. 3; April 1935, no. 6; June 1932, No. 8; Oct. 1934, No. 12; Nov, 1932, No. 1; Oct. 1934, No. 12; Dec. 1932, No. 2; 1933, No. 2; Dec. 1932, No. 2; 1936 No. 5; April 1934, No. 6; Dec. 1932, No. 2; March 1933, No.5

Thapar, Romila, in Barbara Ward (ed.), *Women in New Asia,* Netherlands: UNESCO, 1963.

Thomas, P., *Indian Women through the Ages,* New York: Asian Publishing House 1964.

*The Friend of India and the Statesman,* Calcutta, 9 January, 1883.

The Guardians and Wards Act 1890, Government of India, Legislative Deptt, Objects and Reasons, India Office Records.

*The Problem of Urdu Teaching in Bombay Presidency,* Government of Bombay. 1914.

Thorpe, Lloyd C., *Education and the Development of Muslim Nationalism in Pre-Partition India*, Karachi: Pakistan Historical Society, 1965.

Tinker, Irene, 1974. "The Adverse Impact of Development" in Jean O' Barr (ed.), *Third World Women*, Occasional Papers, Duke University Center for International Studies, 1974.

Tinker, Irene & Michele Bo Bramsen (eds.), *Women and World Development*, Washington: Overseas Development Council, 1976.

*Towards Equality*, Report of the Committee on the Status of Women in India, G.O.I., Delhi: Ministry of Education and Social Welfare, 1974.

Tyabji, H.B., *Badruddin Tyabji*, Bombay, 1952.

Underwood, A.C., *Contemporary Thought of India*, London: Williams and Norget Ltd., 1930.

Ward, Barbara, *Women in New Asia*, Netherlands, UNESCO, 1963.

Webster, Paula, "Matriarchy: A Vision of Power" in R.R. Reiter (ed.) *Anthropology of Women*.

*Weekly Round Table*, March 1973.

Wilkening, E.A. & D.E. Morrison, "A Comparison of Husband and Wife Responses Concerning Who Makes Family and Home Decisions," *Journal of Marriage and Family Living*, August 1963.

*Women in India*, 1975. Bombay: SNDT Women's University.

*Women in India: Who's Who*, The National Council of Women in India, Bombay: British India Press, 1935.

Wright, Theodore, "Muslim Representation in India" in D.E. Smith (ed.) *South Asian Politics and Religion*, New Jersey: Princeton University Press; 1963.

Zaidi, M.H., *The Evolution of Muslim Political Thought from Syed Ahmad Khan to the Emergence of Jinnah*, Delhi: Michiko and Panjathan, 1976.

Zaidi, S.M.H., *Muslim Womanhood in Revolution*, Calcutta, 1937.

Zakaria, R., *The Rise of Muslims in Indian Politics*, Bombay: Somaiya Publications, 1970.

Zwemmer, A.E. and M.M., *Moslem Women*, Massachusetts: The Central Committee on the United Study of Foreign Missions, 1926.

# Index